North Carolina

Sheila Turnage
Photography by Jim Hargan

COMPASS AMERICAN GUIDES
An Imprint of Fodor's Travel Publications, Inc.

North Carolina

LIBRARY OF CONGRESS CATALOGING-IN-PUBLICATION DATA
Turnage, Sheila.
North Carolina/Sheila Turnage; photography by Jim Hargan
p.   cm. —(Compass American Guides)
Includes bibliographical references and index.
ISBN 0-679-03390-4
1. North Carolina—Guidebooks. I. Title. II. Series: Compass American Guides (series)
      F252.3.T87   1998   97-38559
      917.5604'43—dc21   CIP

10 9 8 7 6 5 4 3 2 1
First published in 1998

Compass American Guides, 5332 College Ave. Suite 201, Oakland, CA 94618, USA

Editors: Kit Duane, Barry Parr   Designers: Christopher Burt, Debi Dunn
Managing Editor: Kit Duane   Map Design: Mark Stroud, Moon Street
Creative Director: Christopher Burt   Cartography
Production Editor: Debi Dunn   Printed in China
Produced by Twin Age Ltd., Hong Kong

The Publisher gratefully acknowledges the the following individuals and institutions: Anne S. K. Brown Military Collection, Brown University Library, Providence p. 194; Biltmore Estate, Asheville p. 293 (top); Darke County Historical Society p. 235; Duke University, Special Collections Library p. 139; East Carolina Manuscript Collection, East Carolina Univ., Greenville p.76; Thomas Gilcrease Institute of American History and Art, Tulsa, OK p. 41 (bottom), 248; *Greensboro News & Record* Photo Archives, Jack Moebes p.37, 43 (middle); Grove Park Inn, Asheville p. 294; Guilford College, Greensboro, Friends Historical Collection p.25; Library of Congress pp. 19, 40 (top), 42 (bottom), 43 (top), 59, 203, 251, 259, 293 (bottom); New-York Historical Society, NYC pp. 42, (middle), 165; National Museum of American History, Smithsonian Institution p.28; North Carolina Collection, Wilson Library, Univ. of North Carolina, Chapel Hill pp. 29, 33, 40 (bottom), 41(top), 48, 82, 84, 98, 99 (both), 156, 187, 282, 286; North Carolina Maritime Museum, Beaufort p. 134; North Carolina Museum of Art, Raleigh pp. 21, 108-109; North Carolina State Dept. of Archives and History pp. 128, 178, 206; Pack Memorial Public Library, Asheville p. 289; R J Reynolds Tobacco Co., Winston-Salem p. 199; Ruth Haislip Roberson pp. 230-231 (all); St. John's Museum of Art, Wilmington pp. 72, 87, 93, 143, 225; Southern Historical Collection, Univ. of North Carolina Library, Chapel Hill pp. 32, 34, 50, 58; Univ. of Maryland Baltimore County, Edward L. Bafford Photographic Collection p 207; Virginia State Library and Archives p. 27; William S. Powell, pp. 30, 42 (top). We also wish to thank Tom Ross for acting as professional reader and for contributing to our restaurant section; Ellen Klages for proofreading; Kelly Duane for photo research and fact checking; and Julie Searle for editorial contributions and for indexing, and Neal Lineback, Chair of the Geography and Planning Department at Appalachian State University.

To Rodney, whose joy and respect lighten my step.

C O N T E N T S

Topical Essays & Sidebars

A pastoral scene in Lickskillit Community, Yancey County.

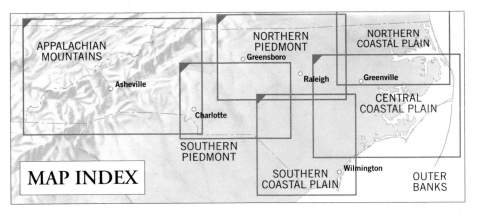

APPALACHIAN
MOUNTAINS

Asheville

Charlotte

NORTHERN
PIEDMONT
Greensboro

Raleigh

SOUTHERN
PIEDMONT

NORTHERN
COASTAL PLAIN

Greenville

CENTRAL
COASTAL PLAIN

MAP INDEX

SOUTHERN
COASTAL PLAIN

Wilmington

OUTER
BANKS

Maps

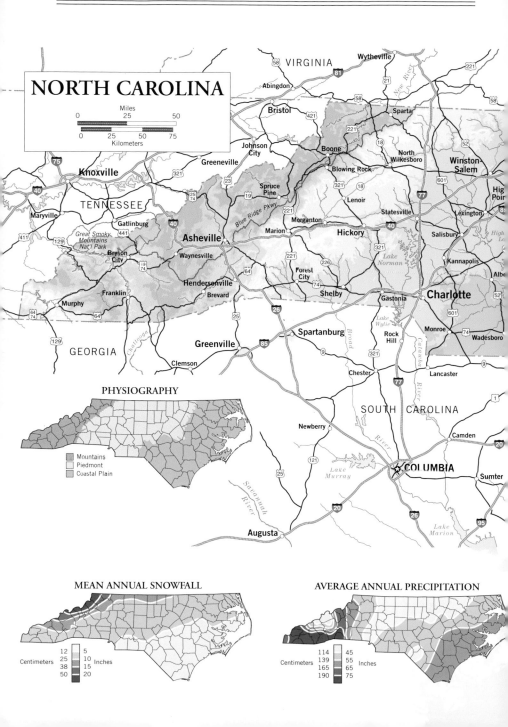

NORTH CAROLINA

Miles
0   25   50

0   25   50   75
Kilometers

VIRGINIA

Wytheville

Abingdon

Bristol

Sparta

Johnson City

Boone

North Wilkesboro

Greeneville

Blowing Rock

Winston-Salem

Knoxville

Spruce Pine

Lenoir

Hig Poir

TENNESSEE

Morganton

Statesville

Lexington

Maryville

Gatlinburg

Marion

Hickory

Salisbury

High Le

Great Smoky Mountains Nat'l Park

Asheville

Lake Norman

Kannapolis

Bryson City

Waynesville

Forest City

Albe

Franklin

Hendersonville

Shelby

Charlotte

Murphy

Brevard

Gastonia

Lake Wylie

Monroe

Wadesboro

GEORGIA

Greenville

Spartanburg

Rock Hill

Clemson

Chester

Lancaster

PHYSIOGRAPHY

SOUTH CAROLINA

Newberry

Camden

COLUMBIA

Sumter

Mountains
Piedmont
Coastal Plain

Lake Murray

Savannah River

Augusta

Lake Marion

MEAN ANNUAL SNOWFALL

Centimeters
12   5
25   10   Inches
38   15
50   20

AVERAGE ANNUAL PRECIPITATION

Centimeters
114   45
139   55   Inches
165   65
190   75

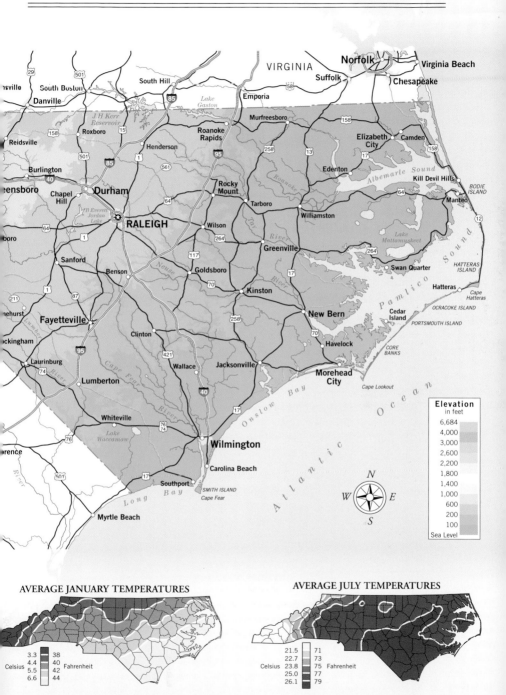

VIRGINIA

Norfolk — Virginia Beach

Suffolk — **Chesapeake**

nsville — South Boston — South Hill — Emporia
Danville — Lake Gaston

J H Kerr Reservoir — Murfreesboro — 158
Reidsville — 158 — Roxboro — 15 — Roanoke Rapids — Elizabeth City — Camden
Henderson — 258 — 13 — 158
Burlington — 501 — 85 — 1 — 95 — Edenton — Albemarle Sound — Kill Devil Hills
eensboro — Chapel Hill — Durham — 64 — 561 — Rocky Mount — Roanoke — BODIE ISLAND
B Everett Jordan Lake — Tarboro — Williamston — 64 — Manteo
RALEIGH — Wilson — 12
64 — 1 — Tar River — Lake Mattamuskeet
boro — Sanford — 117 — Greenville — 264 — 264
Benson — Neuse — Goldsboro — 17 — Swan Quarter — HATTERAS ISLAND
1 — 87 — 70 — River — Kinston — Hatteras — Cape Hatteras
nehurst — Fayetteville — New Bern — Cedar Island — OCRACOKE ISLAND
ockingham — 211 — Clinton — 258 — PORTSMOUTH ISLAND
95 — 70 — Havelock — CORE BANKS
Laurinburg — 74 — 421 — Wallace — Jacksonville — Morehead City
Lumberton — Cape Fear River — 40 — Cape Lookout
rence — 76 — Whiteville — 76 / 74 — Onslow Bay
Lake Waccamaw — 17 — Atlantic Ocean
River — 501 — 17 — **Wilmington**
Southport — Carolina Beach
SMITH ISLAND — Cape Fear
Long Bay — Myrtle Beach

Pamlico Sound

N
W — E
S

Elevation in feet	
6,684	
4,000	
3,000	
2,600	
2,200	
1,800	
1,400	
1,000	
600	
200	
100	
Sea Level	

AVERAGE JANUARY TEMPERATURES

Celsius	Fahrenheit
3.3	38
4.4	40
5.5	42
6.6	44

AVERAGE JULY TEMPERATURES

Celsius	Fahrenheit
21.5	71
22.7	73
23.8	75
25.0	77
26.1	79

ACKNOWLEDGMENTS

MANY PEOPLE HAVE SHARED THEIR TIME and expertise with me as I've written this book.

First, I thank R. L. Beasley, my fellow traveler and first reader, for his good-hearted support.

Although I visited several libraries as I researched this book, I'd especially like to thank Julie Hicks of Sheppard Memorial Library in Greenville, NC, who could always find the answers.

Southern hospitality is alive and well in North Carolina. Among the many people in Piedmont and western NC who assisted this flatlander in her research, I especially thank: Mikie Wall, Susan Moran, and Lynn Minges, of NC's Department of Commerce, Travel, and Tourism Division, in Raleigh; Michael Rouse of Smoky Mountain Host in Franklin; Millie Barbee of High Country Host in Blowing Rock; Ranger Frank Finley of the US Forest Service; Beth Sander of the Boone Convention & Visitors Bureau (CVB); Alice Alexander Aumen of the Maggie Valley Chamber of Commerce; Marla Tambellini of the Asheville Area Chamber of Commerce; David Redman of Cherokee Tribal Travel and Promotion; Claudette Landwehrmann of the Greensboro Area CVB; Margaret Pike of the Winston-Salem CVB; Jim Sanders at Old Salem; Vickie Riddle, spokesperson for Gaston County; and Gina King of the Charlotte CVB.

To the Tar Heels who spoke with me for this book or other projects over the years, and whom I've quoted here: thanks again.

Last but certainly not least, I thank: Kit Duane, Managing Editor of Compass American Guides, for her patience, guidance and encouragement; Executive Editor Chris Burt, for his clear perspective; editor Barry Parr, who appreciates the mystery of words; designer Dèbi Dunn for the balance she's given these pages; and expert reader Tom Ross, who caught my gaffs and righted my wrongs.

O V E R V I E W

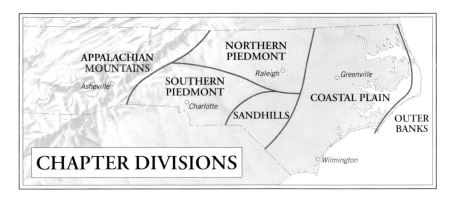

APPALACHIAN
MOUNTAINS

Asheville○

NORTHERN
PIEDMONT

Raleigh○

SOUTHERN
PIEDMONT

○*Charlotte*

SANDHILLS

○*Greenville*

COASTAL PLAIN

OUTER
BANKS

CHAPTER DIVISIONS

○*Wilmington*

■ OUTER BANKS

A long strip of barrier islands running from the Virginia border to Cape Fear, the Outer Banks are known for their miles of pristine beaches, fishing villages, lighthouses and vacation homes. It was here that English colonists settled under the sponsorship of Sir Walter Raleigh in 1585. Reminders of their "Lost Colony" can be visited on Roanoke Island today.

■ COASTAL PLAIN

The Coastal Plain is home to the state's colonial era towns, including Edenton, New Bern, Bath, and Beaufort; and to hundreds of tobacco farms. The port of Wilmington, the region's largest city, is surrounded by beaches, resorts, and sights of interest. Inland, farms and small towns dot the flat, often swampy landscape.

■ NORTHERN PIEDMONT

This region includes Winston-Salem, the marketplace for North Carolina tobacco road farms. The prosperous cities of Durham, Chapel Hill, and Greensboro are located here, as is the state's capital, Raleigh. Such famous universities as Duke and the University of North Carolina also call this area home.

■ SOUTHERN PIEDMONT

Charlotte, the center of America's third fastest-growing metropolitan area and the state's largest city, is located here. The region is also famous for NASCAR racing, Seagrove pottery, Asheboro's zoo, the reservoirs of the Pee Dee River, and the large Uwharrie National Forest.

■ SANDHILLS
Geographically part of
the Coastal Plain, the
Sandhills are defined
by their sandy soils and
sharp-smelling long-
leaf pine forests. The
towns of Pinehurst and
Southern Pines are
home to some of the
world's finest golf
courses and country
clubs. The region has
long been a vacation destination and second home to some of America's rich and
famous.

■ APPALACHIAN MOUNTAINS
The highest mountains east of the Mississippi, the heavily forested Appalachians
stretch across the western eighth of North Carolina and are preserved in America's
most visited national park, The Great Smoky Mountains National Park. Skiing
centers around Boone and Banner Elk. Asheville, the region's largest city, has long
been a favorite with
vacationers escap-
ing the summer
heat of the low
lands. One of those
vacationers from
"up north," George
Vanderbilt, built
America's grandest
mansion, Biltmore,
just outside of
Asheville.

FROM THEN TO NOW

By HISTORY'S WHIM, NORTH CAROLINA lies roughly between 34 degrees and 36.5 degrees N latitude, sharing borders with Virginia, to the north, and South Carolina and Georgia to the south. East-to-west, the state stretches 503 miles, from the Atlantic Ocean to Tennessee, which lies just beyond the crooked backbone of the Great Smoky Mountains.

By nature's more enduring design, four distinct North Carolinas co-exist within the state's boundaries, running in wide bands parallel to the coast. Geologic tides of stone, ice, water, and time sculpted the four North Carolinas: the rugged Appalachians, a piedmont plateau, a sandy coastal plain, and the Outer Banks, with their shallow sounds and treacherous shoals.

European settlers began pushing into the state in the 1600s, staking out land farmed and hunted by Algonquin, Sioux, and Iroquois people. When the wagon dust settled a century later, North Carolina's four geographic zones had become home to four new, distinct cultures, each rising from a unique history, each facing a unique future.

■ THE LAY OF THE LAND

North Carolina's geologic beginnings lie to the west, in North America's oldest mountains.

The mineral-rich Appalachians, which rose up like granite giants about 450 million years ago, cover only an eighth of North Carolina's 52,712 square miles. But their rushing waters have helped shape all that lies to the east: the Piedmont, plains, sounds, Outer Banks, and even the Atlantic shelf, which extends 60 miles into the ocean.

The Appalachians are a braid of ancient mountain chains—the Great Smoky Mountains to the west and Blue Ridge to the east—crisscrossed by smaller chains. They include the highest peak east of the Mississippi (Mt. Mitchell, at 6,684 feet), thundering waterfalls, mountaintop meadows, and rugged gorges. As you'd expect, they've mellowed over the past half billion years, trading stark granite planes for weathered faces and gentler curves.

Mist fills the valleys in the heart of the Smoky Mountains,
at one time the tallest mountains in North America.

Many rivers tumble to life in the Appalachian region and arc southeast to the ocean, but they haven't always traveled great distances to do so. The Atlantic has wandered inland at least seven times over millions of years, sculpting a series of gentle terraces that underlie today's coastal plain. As recently as 25,000 years ago, melting polar ice caps sent the Atlantic far inland. The ocean eventually receded, leaving its thick sea bed behind—today's coastal plain. As rivers flowed down from the mountains, dropping their sediments, they created a massive system of sounds, barrier islands, and the Atlantic shelf.

North Carolina's seven broad, shallow sounds make up the largest system of inland sounds in the United States. Beyond lie the Outer Banks, a narrow chain of sandy barrier islands that reach from Virginia toward the South Carolina line.

■ INDIAN SETTLEMENT

Geology's tides moved from west to east, but most of the early Native American migrations flowed from north to south.

Archaeologists believe the Algonquins swept into the area around 10,000 years ago, settling small villages on the coastal plain. Centuries later the first wave of Iroquois immigrants, the Cherokee, moved south. Many settled along the streams of the Piedmont plateau and in the Appalachian foothills. Others spread as far south as Alabama.

Later, the Sioux—notably the Catawba and Cheraw—pushed into the those same hills and rich valleys, elbowing the Cherokee deep into the Appalachians. Finally, in a second Iroquois migration around A.D. 1100, the Tuscarora wedged into the coastal plain, shoving the Algonquins east into tidewater marshlands and onto the barrier islands.

By the 16th century, North Carolina's four major native nations lived roughly within the four geographic zones. Contrary to myth, they were not peaceful. The Sioux warred endlessly with their hereditary enemies, the Iroquois—the Cherokee in the mountains, and the Tuscarora on the plain. The Algonquin tribes, including the Secotan, warred against the fierce Tuscarora. Yet within their own communities they led settled lives, built houses, grew crops, and made clothing and jewelry. Early European explorers recorded meeting hospitable people who lived orderly and materially comfortable lives.

This engraving by Theodore de Bry was based on a watercolor made by John White in 1585 during Ralph Lane's expedition. The drawing depicts the Indian village of Secoton, believed to be located on the central coastal plain near the modern-day town of Aurora.

■ EUROPEANS ARRIVE

In the early 1500s, a new tide lapped against North Carolina's barrier islands, and then against a mainland charted by French, Spanish, and English adventurers hungry for land, souls, glory, and gold.

Giovanni da Verrazano, a Florentine sailing under a French flag, explored the Cape Fear area in 1524 and eagerly promoted the land's "faire fields and plains," trees, plentiful game, and easily charmed natives. The land, he wrote, was "as pleasant and delectable to behold, as is possible to imagine." Although the Cape Fear Coast Convention and Visitor's Bureau wouldn't think so, Verrazano may have exaggerated slightly. Royal interest translated into funding—the 16th-century equivalent of grant money.

Spain visited next in the person of Lucas Vásquez de Allyón, who tried in 1526 to plant a colony on the Cape Fear River. Natives, furious at having their children enslaved, contributed to the colony's painful demise.

Hernando de Soto looped through western North Carolina around 1540 searching for "gold-bearing mountains." But the Spanish, in their quest for wealth and slaves, soon focused colonization efforts on gold-rich Central America. Enter England.

Sir Walter Raleigh, soldier, explorer, poet, investor, and alleged lover of Queen Elizabeth I, sent two English ships to the New World in 1584. On July 2, captains Philip Amadas and Arthur Barlowe anchored in Pamlico Sound, rowed ashore, and claimed all before them for Queen Elizabeth I of England—known to everyone (except perhaps the amorous Sir Walter Raleigh) as the Virgin Queen. Hence our first name, Virginia.

Days later, a Secotan warrior paddled his dugout over to greet the English, who came bearing gifts: a hat, a shirt, wine, and meat. He reciprocated with a boatload of fish. The next day, he returned with 40 or 50 friends, including Granganimeo, brother of the Secotan chief, Wingina.

The English found the natives "very handsome, goodly people, and in their behavior as mannerly and civil as any in Europe." Granganimeo "made all signs of joy and welcome," they wrote, "striking on his head and his breast, and afterwards on ours, to show we were all one, smiling and making show the best he could of all love, and familiarity."

They set up a lively trade, the Secotan swapping furs for tin plates (used as breastplates), copper kettles, hatchets, axes, and knives. Granganimeo's generosity fed the English, literally: "He sent us every day a brace or two of fat bucks, conies, hares, fish, the best in the world," they wrote. He also sent root crops, fruit, and corn.

Encouraged, the English pressed on, discovering on Roanoke Island a palisaded Secotan village fortified for war against enemy Indian nations. The Englishmen, however, received only kind treatment. After a two-month stay they

Sir Walter Raleigh provided funds and ships for the first English settlement in America, on Roanoke Island in 1585. Raleigh himself never crossed the Atlantic. (NC Museum of Art, Chapel Hill)

headed for London. "We brought home also two of the savages, lusty men, whose names were Wanchese and Manteo," they wrote.

History doesn't say what Wanchese and Manteo thought of London's cobblestone streets and lace-collared poets, or of Queen Elizabeth I and her court. But we do know this: Manteo came home a year later as the colonists' friend and ally. Wanchese came home the same day, a deadly enemy.

■ THE LOST COLONY

Sir Walter Raleigh's first colony, led by a military officer named Ralph Lane, landed at Roanoke Island in July 1585. They quickly built an earth fort, dubbed Fort Raleigh.

Lane's colony included artist John White, whose drawings open a rare window into the world of the Secotan and their neighbors, but most of Lane's 108 colonists were soldiers of fortune, more interested in wealth than in culture.

Lane explored northeast Carolina, trading brutality for hospitality as he moved from village to village. He torched one village and its corn crop in reprisal for the alleged theft of a silver cup. At a Chowan village, he kidnapped the chief's son.

His deteriorating reputation preceded him up the Roanoke River. He found villages he counted on for food deserted, their corn cribs empty. His army straggled back to Fort Raleigh half-starved from their exploration of a river teeming with fish.

Wanchese and the Secotan chief Wingina united the mainland tribes, planning to ambush Lane's men. But Lane struck first, ambushing and beheading several men, including Wingina.

A few weeks later, Lane and company hitched a ride home with Sir Francis Drake, leaving 15 luckless souls to guard Fort Raleigh.

Raleigh intended his next settlement to be England's first permanent New World colony. Led this time by Gov. John White, a diplomat, the colony's hundred-odd members included women, children, tradesmen, and farmers. Sailing from England in 1587, they planned to settle in Chesapeake Bay to the north, but stopped first at Roanoke Island to pick up Lane's men, who had been left behind at Fort Raleigh.

The stunned colonists found Fort Raleigh razed, its houses occupied by a skeleton, the only sign of Lane's men. When they attempted to reboard their ship and continue northward, they learned that their captain had no intention of taking them any further. Only Governor White was able to gain passage back to England with the captain. There White began to gather supplies for the stranded colony—which included his daughter, son-in-law, and new granddaughter, Virginia Dare, the first English child born in America.

When he returned three years later, he found the colonists' houses destroyed. The word "Croatoan" carved into a doorpost—with no Maltese cross, the colonists' distress signal—let him hope his colony had joined Manteo and the friendly Croatan people, on Ocracoke Island.

Searches turned up rumors, but no colonists. They simply walked into history, never to be heard from again.

■ ENGLAND'S INROADS

With the Lost Colony's demise, England shifted colonization efforts north, to Virginia and the Chesapeake. How, then, was North Carolina settled? Most North Carolinians, like their aboriginal counterparts, drifted south.

Because of the navigational hazards of the Outer Banks, cross-Atlantic ships usually avoided North Carolina's harbors, landing instead to the south in Charleston. It wasn't until English naturalist John Lawson chronicled his 1701 journey from Charleston to the North Carolina Piedmont, and to Bath on the Pamlico Sound, that Europeans eyed North Carolina's promising—and relatively unsettled—lands.

Coastal Virginia and South Carolina were settled in the early 1600s by wealthy Europeans with massive land grants—the basis of their plantation system. Not so North Carolina, sometimes described as "an oasis of humility between two mounts of conceit."

North Carolina's earliest settlers went first to Virginia. Some worked their way over as indentured servants, others booked passage as free men and women. Most were yeomen farmers who came for the modest land grant given to anyone willing to claim the New World for England. Eventually, they drifted south.

The natives could not stem this seeping tide. Settlers trickled steadily into the Albemarle region beginning in the mid-1600s, buying or taking land and driving the natives inland toward hostile tribes. Smallpox and other Old World diseases wiped out native villages, opening even more land.

In 1663, when England's Charles II deeded the Carolina coast to the eight Lords Proprietor to pay off political debts, settlement quickened. One pamphlet invited craftsmen and laborers to Carolina (named, now, for Charles II), offering indentured servants land, tools, clothes, and a rare chance to "raise their fortunes." They recruited women, too: "If any Maid or single Woman have a desire to go over, they will think themselves in the Golden Age, when Men paid a Dowry for their Wives; for if they be but Civil, and under 50 years of Age, some honest Man or other, will purchase them for their wives."

In 1710, Baron Christoph von Graffenried bought 17,500 acres on the Neuse River, and established a colony of 400 Swiss settlers at New Bern. In response, the Tuscarora formed an alliance with their neighbors and in September 1711, they attacked white settlers across the plain, butchering families and burning homes.

The Tuscarora War raged for two years until, in March 1713, the last of the Tuscarora retreated to a palisade fort at Nooherooka, near Grifton. An army of colonials and Indians bombed and burned the fort, taking 392 prisoners into slavery, scalping 192, killing 200 in the fort, and 166 more as they fled.

With the destruction of the region's strongest tribe, settlers surged south to the Cape Fear River, establishing Brunswick Town—colonial North Carolina's most important port—and grabbing rich plantation lands along the river. Wealthy South Carolinians, too, established massive rice plantations along Cape Fear.

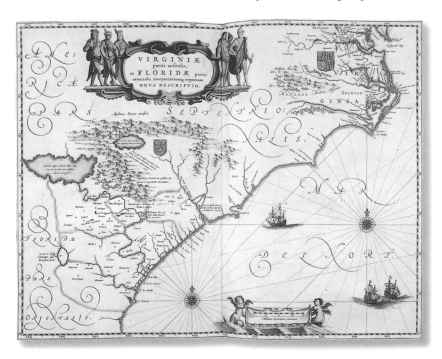

An early map of the Carolina coastline compiled by W. Blaeu and his son, circa 1638. The map contains one of the first mentions of the Appalachians.

The New Garden Moravian Mission in the late 18th century.
(Courtesy, Friends Historical Collection, Guilford College)

North Carolina's settlement began in earnest. When North Carolina's royal governor, Gabriel Johnston—a Scot—invited his countrymen over, they came in kilted droves. Settling along the Upper Cape Fear, they established Cross Creek, known today as Fayetteville.

The greatest migration began in the 1730s when German, Quaker, and Ulster Scot immigrants headed south from Pennsylvania. Traveling first singly and then in fleets of Conestoga wagons, they followed the Great Wagon Road through the Shenandoah Valley into North Carolina. In 1752, the Moravians bought a 100,000-acre tract of land and established several mission towns including Old Salem—an oasis of civilization on the American frontier, and the seed of present-day Winston-Salem. Two years later Gov. Arthur Dobbs, an Ulster Scot, encouraged a second wave of "Scotch-Irish" immigrants.

As for the native people, those who had not been killed by war and new diseases either fled before the approaching tides, or bowed their heads. Only the Cherokee survived intact, clinging to the peaks of the Appalachians. And even their lands were threatened as settlers surged against the foothills.

■ REVOLUTIONARY ERA

As Britain's 13 American colonies grew more restless with British taxes and restrictions in the mid-18th century, arguments for rebellion, democracy, and independence circulated by pamphlet and by word of mouth through city taverns and New England village meeting halls, Virginia manor houses, and backwoods hollows. Many aristocrats and American yeomen were growing increasingly confident of their own abilities to fight and to govern.

North Carolina at this time was a colony divided culturally, politically, and financially, east against west. In the East, the farmers, plantation owners, timbermen, and merchants of the coastal plain led relatively comfortable lives. They had access to their royal governor, William Tryon, and controlled the parliament, which met at Tryon's Palace in New Bern. Many were English by heritage, and maintained vital financial ties with English markets.

The "backcountrymen" led different lives and told a different story—often in German, or with a thick Scottish brogue.

Many of the Piedmont's German, Quaker, and Scotch-Irish citizens had no love for an English king. More importantly, they found themselves overtaxed by their eastern neighbors, and poorly represented in a provincial parliament, which met in New Bern—a town they'd never seen, thanks to the southeastern swoop of the rivers, which sent much of their trade to Charleston.

Unfair taxes, repression, and a thieving tax collector named Edmund Fanning finally pushed the Piedmont's backcountry "Regulators" to arms. They stormed a Hillsborough courthouse in 1770, horse-whipped Fanning, beat up the attorneys, and ran the judge out of town.

The rebellion escalated until Tryon marched his militia west, routing a ragtag throng of 2,000 rebels at Alamance County Courthouse. Tryon, an astute politician, returned to his palace, packed his bags, and hightailed it to New York.

As revolutionary ideas continued to brew, eastern Carolinians grew increasingly hostile to Parliament's taxes. When war finally erupted in Lexington, Massachusetts, in April of 1776, North Carolina's loyalties were divided. By July, when representatives of the 13 colonies met in Philadelphia to sign the Declaration of

Independence, North Carolina sent three delegates—Joseph Hewes, John Penn, and William Hooper.

Ironically, it was the comfortable easterners, with commercial and family ties to England, who swayed the colony toward independence as taxes rose. The backcountrymen opposed war—the Quakers on moral grounds, others for more practical reasons—although they felt the sting of British taxes as keenly as tidewater settlers.

The Ulster Scots along the Cape Fear remained loyal to the Crown and marched to the aid of Lord Cornwallis. After Patriots sent the Scots packing, the English steered clear of North Carolina for another four years, but Cornwallis marched back in 1780, to the Battle of Guilford Courthouse near Greensboro. After losing a fourth of his army there, he staggered to Wilmington and then to Yorktown, where he surrendered.

The Revolution gave the redcoats the boot, but did little to unify North Carolina. Wrangling North Carolina politicians took so long to ratify the U.S. Constitution, we briefly earned the status of a foreign country, and the tariffs to prove it. North Carolina finally joined the Union in 1789, claiming the flag's 12th star.

Storming a Redoubt at Yorktown *by Eugene Lami shows the Revolutionary soldiers overrunning British breastworks, leading to the surrender of Cornwallis. (Virginia State Library and Archives)*

HISTORY & REVOLUTIONARY ERA

■ ANTEBELLUM ERA

Who were we in the period between the establishment of the Republic and the Civil War? With nearly 400,000 people in 1790, North Carolina ranked third among the 13 states in population, behind Virginia and Pennsylvania.

Across the state, most whites worked on small family farms where self-reliance was the rule. They grew their own food, wove their own cloth, and minded their own business.

In the East, a few planters produced labor-intensive cash crops, like tobacco, rice, indigo, and cotton, using slave labor. Slavery was less common in North Carolina than in neighboring states, but by 1790, 100,000 slaves made up nearly a quarter of the population.

In the far west, meanwhile, pioneers—including North Carolinian Daniel Boone—began pressing into the Appalachians. Land grants to Revolutionary War veterans increased settlement, and America's first gold rush—to western North Carolina—added to the push. Until 1829, all the native gold minted in the U.S. came from North Carolina; the Cherokee's shrinking homelands became increasingly valuable.

Culturally and educationally, North Carolina lagged behind her neighbors, earning the nickname The Rip Van Winkle State.

The state's small, independent-minded farmers couldn't have funded a public school system if they'd wanted one—which they didn't. They needed children with strong backs. To them, book learning was a luxury.

In 1811 in Edgecombe County, only half the white men and a third of the

This pitcher made in Liverpool in 1790 outlines the population of the United States at that time. South Carolina's population was actually 249,000. (National Museum of American History, Smithsonian Institution)

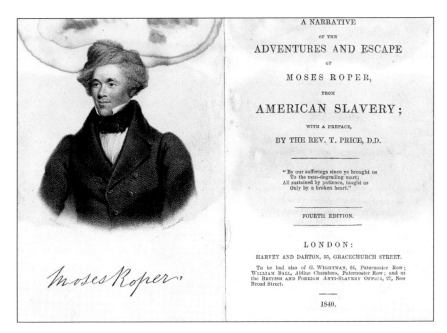

Moses Roper, a former slave from Caswell County, sold the story of his escape to a London publisher in 1838. (North Carolina Collection)

white women could write their names. Legislators controlled their unlettered population with a penal code designed to chill even 19th-century blood: 28 crimes were hanging offenses.

In the decades preceding the Civil War, The Rip Van Winkle State awakened, establishing, for white citizens at least, public schools, institutions for the mentally and physically handicapped, roads, and a railroad.

For slaves, life became more brutal. In 1831, after Nat Turner led a slave uprising in Virginia, legislators outlawed slave education, social gatherings, and black-led churches.

Native Americans also suffered. In 1835, the federal government ordered the 15,000-member Cherokee nation to abandon their homes in the Appalachian Mountains and walk to a reservation in Oklahoma. The forefathers of today's Eastern Cherokee refused to go, hiding high in the mountains. A fourth of those who walked what became known as the "Trail of Tears" died on the way, and the Cherokee homeland opened to white settlers.

Whites in the east began to fear slave uprisings, as a larger and larger percentage of the population lived in slavery. In 1860, when North Carolina's population reached 992,622, a third of that population was owned by 34,658 slaveholders. Abolitionists in Congress argued that slavery was immoral and must be outlawed, but most free North Carolinians maintained that slavery was a political rather than a moral issue. Although most didn't own slaves, they believed the federal government had no right to interfere in a state's political affairs.

■ THE CIVIL WAR: FIGHTING FOR HOME, HONOR, AND SOMEONE ELSE'S WAY OF LIFE

North Carolina's leaders, slow to join the Union in 1783, were just as hesitant to leave in 1861. The state, known for its Union sympathies, adopted a "watch and wait" attitude as seven southern states seceded. In an early 1861 election, only a third of North Carolina counties sent secessionist candidates to the General Assembly. But when Confederate "fire-eaters" fired on Fort Sumter and Abraham Lincoln ordered North Carolina troops to march against their neighbors, Governor Ellis replied, "You can get no troops from North Carolina." North Carolina was, reluctantly, at war.

The state paid dearly for its

In 1861, less than two weeks after the adoption of the Ordinance of Secession, 18-year-old Charles Powell volunteered to fight for the Confederacy. He was enlisted as first sergeant of Company E of the Fourteenth Regiment of Volunteers. (Courtesy William S. Powell)

A CIVIL WAR LETTER

Dear Burwell

Yours of the 26th reached me a few days since, and I expect you begin to want to hear from home by this time, so I will write you a few lines.

I wonder if your uncle Tom has told you about his sheep getting drowned, he may not know of it himself. Every one he had was drowned in the big fresh, and all your uncle John's with them except the house lamb. They were all found in a raft together frozen, some ten days after the water fell. There was between 30 and 40 of them, and it was the very last of the month that they thawed enough to get them out and save the wool. That is a considerable misfortune these hard times. Ours happened not to be in the low ground.

. . . All this talk of armistice and peace etc is very cheering to despondents, I don't know how we shall all feel when it blows over. . . .

Mat has been ordered into service twice and only got as far as the depo each time. I shall not commence gardening this month I guess. A great many soldiers pass here now, they generally stop at your uncle Sam's. Pat Sherrin is knitting fancy gloves for some of them, who happen to fall in love with her, or she with them, or both we tell her. . . . Your Pa gets on slowly with his plowing and other work I expect. Your Grand Ma is going to see Mrs. Cheek. She went to John Newells the other day, she says it is a sad looking place. Write soon and a little more.

As ever your
Ma
Feb 5th, 1865

—Author unknown, excerpted from
Awakenings: Writings and Recollections of Eastern North Carolina Women,
[published] 1978

role in the "War for Southern Independence." North Carolina, which was home to one-ninth of the South's population, supplied a sixth of all Southern troops, and a quarter of all Southern dead—a particularly shocking casualty rate since only one major battle was fought in North Carolina.

By the war's end, North Carolina was in shambles. The eastern part of the state, occupied throughout the war, lay in ruins. Washington, New Bern, and Wilming-

The 1861–1865 THE TAR HEELS ROLL OF HONOR

NORTH CAROLINA, With a male population (military age) of 115,000 CONFEDERATE SOLDIERS, 127,000 CONFEDERATE SOLDIERS. Lost 40,375 of her brave sons, DOUBLE the loss of any other state with 5,000 to spare. FIRST AT BETHEL FOREMOST AT GETTYSBURG FURTHEST AT CHICKAMAUGA THE LAST AT APPOMATTOX "God Bless North Carolina" R E Lee

When 125,000 North Carolinians joined the Confederate Army they earned the nickname "Tar Heels," for their willingness to stand their ground. (Southern Historical Collection, Julius Leinbach Papers)

ton were torched by exiting Union soldiers. As William T. Sherman's massive army rambled north to Appomattox Courthouse in Virginia, his calvary slashed through the mountains, destroying millions of dollars worth of factories, railroads, homes, churches, and schools; and stealing food and supplies. Smoke hung over Raleigh, Asheville, Salem, Greensboro, Waynesville, Salisbury, Shelby, and other western towns.

Still, some northerners thought North Carolina got off too easy. One newspaper opined, "More fire would have made more healthy spirit in the State."

In all, some 125,000 Tar Heels—more than could vote—marched to war, earning the nickname "Tar Heels," for their willingness to stand their ground. Forty thousand died—half in battle, half from disease.

Those who came home found their homes burned, their fields fallow, their businesses smoldering, and their taxes impossible to pay. Thousands of acres of land changed hands, and thousands of families plunged into poverty. The slaves—a third of the population—had been freed. But with no money, property, or education, they had nowhere to go. Many stayed put, working for ex-masters as sharecroppers.

The bitter years that followed saw the rise of the Ku Klux Klan and of a Reconstructionist government whose primary legacy would be a century of anti-Republican, anti-Yankee sentiment.

■ ECONOMIC AWAKENING

Textiles and tobacco—small industries in pre-war North Carolina—paved the way for North Carolina's emergence from economic and social chaos.

By 1880, North Carolina farmers tripled their pre-war cotton production. More importantly, 49 new mills—new elements of North Carolina economy—

cranked out $2.5 million worth of textiles. Mill towns, with all their faults, sprang to life across the Piedmont, employing entire families. By 1900, women provided 34 percent and children 24 percent of the mills' labor.

Across the east, more and more farmers were planting bright-leaf, flue-cured tobacco for the factories of the Piedmont. The invention of the cigarette rolling machine in 1881 shifted the economy into high gear as tobacco barons, including James B. Duke of the American Tobacco Company and R. J. Reynolds, grabbed control of the world tobacco market. Their factories in Greensboro, Winston-Salem, and Reidsville employed thousands.

Riding a rising economic tide, furniture factories rumbled to life around Hickory and Lenoir, while in the Pine Belt, timbermen harvested turpentine, tar, and pitch.

Asheville, in the southern Appalachians, boomed. Building on its history as a health resort, the city attracted a monied clientele. The most prominent resident was George Vanderbilt, who built his 255-room mountain hideaway there. The creation of Biltmore Estate single-handedly jump-started the local economy.

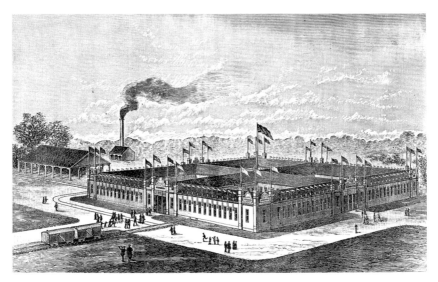

The North Carolina Agricultural Society erected this building near the present site of Raleigh's Little Theater for the North Carolina State Exposition of 1884. The four inner courts held a variety of displays of industrial products, livestock, handicrafts, and minerals. Tens of thousands of North Carolinians attended the fair. (North Carolina Collection)

TOBACCO: A 1930S PERSPECTIVE

*D*urham, (405 alt., 52,307 pop.) is a modern industrial city in the eastern piedmont. The universal demand for tobacco, coupled with the genius of the Duke family and other business leaders, is exemplified in long rows of factories where thousands work daily, filling whole trains with their products. Here was created the fortune that endowed Duke University.

Often the air is permeated by the pungent scent of tobacco from the stemmeries and the sweetish odor of tonka bean used in cigarette manufacture. From 9 to 5 o'clock Durham's streets reflect the activity of its business houses and professional offices. When the American Tobacco and the Liggett and Myers whistles blow, an army of workers pours forth—men and women, white and colored. Buses and trucks, heavily laden, rumble along the thoroughfares. For an hour or two the streets are alive with the hurry and noise of a big city. Then the bustle subsides and relative calm is resumed.

—WPA Guide to North Carolina, 1930s

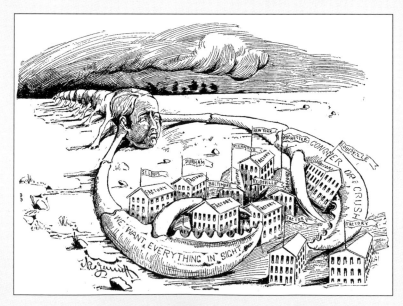

A satirical cartoon of James B. Duke grasping for control of the North Carolina tobacco industry. (Southern Historical Collection, University of North Carolina)

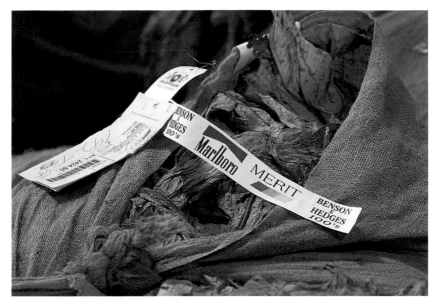

Tobacco manufacturing became a major industry in North Carolina in the 1880s, and by the turn of the 19th century the Tar Heel State had gained world dominance in the trade.

Generally affluent (and privately educated) legislators did little for public schools, but created three colleges for white students, and four for blacks—all of them in the Piedmont or eastern North Carolina. In the Appalachians, educational opportunities remained "few and far between" until private schools began accepting labor and crafts as tuition. Still, as the 20th century dawned, 19.5 percent of all North Carolina whites, and 47.6 percent of all blacks were unable to read.

■ 20TH CENTURY

The first half of the 20th century saw a 350-percent increase in the production of tobacco, whose value jumped from $8 million in 1900 to $356 million in 1945. Tobacco's impact didn't stop with paychecks for factory workers and farmers. Tobacco money helped fund universities, museums, symphonies, and medical facilities.

The Great Depression staggered the economies of the east and Piedmont, but on the isolated Outer Banks and in most of the Appalachians, Depression years looked pretty much like other years—except that the WPA came calling. WPA workers sculpted the Blue Ridge Parkway through the mountains, knocking on cabin doors that opened in on the 18th century, and laying the groundwork for preserving some of the state's most scenic wilderness areas.

World War II changed North Carolina more than any single event except, perhaps, the Civil War. Military bases, including Camp Lejeune (Jacksonville), Cherry Point (Havelock), and Fort Bragg (Fayetteville) sprang up almost overnight and entered the national consciousness. Some, like Operation Bumblebee on Topsail Island, would become closely guarded secrets.

Wartime industries pitched their tents alongside. In all, 83 North Carolina plants sold over $1 billion worth of war goods to defense agencies. Ultimately, though, war's greatest impact didn't come through the 362,000 North Carolina men and women who marched off to war, or from the $2 billion pumped into local economies by Uncle Sam. The war rode in on a tidal wave of new ideas. For the first time, Tar Heels were forced to deal as comrades-in-arms with people of different faiths, accents, skin tones, and opinions. White soldiers worked alongside African American and Native American soldiers, and together they won.

At home, Carolina women let the kitchen door slap shut behind them and found jobs that paid "cash money." They raised families alone, made decisions alone, and succeeded alone.

When North Carolina came marching home, it was to another season of change.

Military men flocked to North Carolina's colleges and universities to take advantage of the G.I. Bill and a revised workplace. For the first time, an across-the-board mix of white Tar Heels had access to education.

For African Americans, however, frustrations grew. North Carolina's "separate but equal" school system ran heavy on separate, short on equal, and education wasn't the only inequity. Jim Crow laws segregated hospitals, restaurants, businesses, even water fountains. The laws were hard to change: Until 1965, African Americans had to pass a literacy test before they could vote, and few were willing to risk stepping forward to try.

Integration came slowly, but for the most part peacefully, to North Carolina. Although The University of North Carolina at Chapel Hill began admitting

Ezell Blair, Franklin McCain, David Richmond, and Joseph McNeil, refused service at a lunch counter at a Woolworth's in Greensboro in 1960, staging the first "sit-in" of the Civil Rights movement. (Courtesy Jack Moebes, Greensboro News & Record *Photo Archives)*

African Americans to its law, medicine, and graduate schools in 1951, the public school system as a whole wouldn't be fully integrated for another 20 years.

It was in Greensboro, where Quakers had opposed slavery and spirited slaves north in false-bottomed wagons, that North Carolina's most noted Civil Rights leaders took their first public stand—or seat, actually—for equality.

On February 1, 1960, four black students from North Carolina Agricultural and Technical College walked into Woolworth's, on Elm Street, and quietly sat at the lunch counter, asking to be served. Their months-long sit-in worked, and the technique spread across the South.

One by one, the Jim Crow laws toppled.

■ So, Here We Are

Today, 6,633,000 people live in North Carolina, the 10th most populous state in the Union.

African Americans make up 22 percent of our number, Native Americans and Hispanics a little over one percent each. With a 12-percent growth rate, we're the 16th fastest-growing state in the nation, with the white population growing slightly faster than the black.

We began as a state of farmers and still rank 10th among the 50 states in the number of farms. But 57 percent of us live in the metropolitan areas of the Piedmont: Charlotte, Raleigh, Durham, Winston-Salem, and Greensboro.

How do we pay the bills? About 28 percent of all Tar Heels work in manufacturing—in the textile mills, tobacco factories, and hundreds of other industries located primarily in the Piedmont. We wear far more blue collars than white. While we rank No. 1 in the number of manufacturing employees, we rank 47th in union members. Fewer than five percent of those manufacturing workers carry union cards.

According to census takers, 54 percent of us are church members, with Baptists filling the lion's share of the church pews (23 percent). Methodists and Presbyterians come in a distant second and third. We have little faith in matters of the heart, however. Among the 50 states, we rank 46th in marriages per capita, and ninth in divorce.

Our education system, historically a glaring weakness, still needs work. Only nine states produce fewer college graduates than we do, and our SAT scores are 48th in the nation.

North Carolina remains a state of very modest means. We rank 44th in per-capita income (around $11,000), and about 12 percent of us live in poverty.

Crime doesn't pay very well, either. Only two states lock up more criminals per capita than we do, and only four execute more.

Will Rogers once quipped that North Carolina would remain dry as long as we could stagger to the poles to vote. We may not have changed much. According to census statistics, we rank 42nd in alcohol consumption—and fifth in alcohol-related deaths.

As a group, about 75 percent of us stay put: "Tar Heel born and Tar Heel bred, and when I die I'll be a Tar Heel dead," as the saying goes. North Carolinians still eat barbecue, collards, and grits (not in the same meal), and scarf more soft drinks than anyone else in the country: 55.4 gallons each, every year.

We say "hey" instead of "hi," and most of us say "y'all," meaning two or more of you all.

Some of us golf at Pinehurst, but more of us prefer NASCAR racing, a sport founded by North Carolina moonshine runners who once sped bootleg liquor up and down the Eastern Seaboard. (We rank third among the states in moonshine seized, by the way.)

But if you really want to understand who we are, consider the highest of Tar Heel compliments: "*Good* people."

We often (but not always) apply the label singularly, and we draw the word out flat: "He's *good* people," we say, nodding once for emphasis. Or, even, "She's just *plain good people.*"

We won't say it very often, but when you hear it, take note. It tells you who we are, what we value, and that we trust you to value those things, too.

It's not an assessment of wealth or social standing; it's an evaluation of the heart.

Participants in the Easter Bonnet festival of Dillsboro watch
the annual parade from the town hall.

HISTORY & 20TH CENTURY

HISTORY TIMELINE

1500s
Algonquin people flourish in eastern North Carolina, living in organized villages, hunting, and planting pumpkins, tobacco, and sunflowers.

1585-1590
Settlers build a fort on Roanoke Island and attempt to establish an English colony. Two years later a second group of settlers find no trace of them. Virginia Dare, the granddaughter of the governor of the colony, is the first English child born in America. When resupply ships arrive they find the second group has also disappeared, and they become known as the Lost Colony.

The Indian village of Secoton.

1600s
During the 1600s small groups of English settlers from the Virginia colony establish farms in North Carolina. Some whites try to enslave Indian children, earning tribal enmity, and farming proves difficult.

Naturalist John Lawson and Baron Christoph von Graffenried are taken captive by Indians in 1709.

1709
John Lawson, English naturalist, writer, and traveler, publishes a book describing his travels among Indians, whom he admires. Two years later, Indians capture him along with Baron von Graffenried and a black companion, and execute Lawson with fire.

1711
Tuscaroras attack settlements along the Neuse and Pamlico Rivers, killing settlers and burning farms and villages. Two years later they are crushed.

1718

Blackbeard, most infamous of the pirates that prey on coastal shipping and small communities, is captured and killed.

Blackbeard

1774

Women of Edenton refuse to drink English tea as a patriotic gesture and are satirized in the English press.

Edenton Tea Party caricature

1776

Three North Carolinians, Joseph Hewes, John Penn, and William Hooper, sign the Declaration of Independence.

1789   North Carolina becomes the 12th state to join the Union. During the Revolution, Patriot soldiers rout Lord Cornwallis.

Sequoyah, a Cherokee silversmith and warrior, invented the Cherokee alphabet in 1821.

1798-1840

Samuel Price Carson kills his opponent in Congress in a duel, and in 1827 goes on to help establish the Republic of Texas along with fellow North Carolinian Robert Potter, a legislator and Texas naval officer. Early in Potter's career he castrated a North Carolina minister, but his career did not suffer because of this.

1838

Failing to reverse the 1835 federal government mandate, Cherokee Indians of the Appalachians are driven to Oklahoma on "The Trail of Tears."

HISTORY & TIMELINE

1847
President James Polk visits his alma mater at Chapel Hill.

1861
North Carolina joins the Confederacy after some hesitation. Volunteers line up to fight for the Southern way of life and defend states' rights.

1862
New Bern is captured and occupied by Union troops.

1865
The Battle of Bentonville, fought between C.S.A. General Johnston and U. S. General Sherman, results in 4,000 casualties. Johnston surrenders to Sherman 17 days after Lee surrenders at Appomattox.

1868
Parker D. Robbins, a free black carpenter who joined the Union army and served as a sergeant-major, is elected to the State House of Representatives.

1884
North Carolina, a primary tobacco state, leads the world in cigarette production.

1903
Wright brothers fly the first plane near Kitty Hawk and Kill Devil Hills on the Outer Banks. Flight lasts 12 seconds and goes 120 feet.

1926
John Coltrane is born in Hamlet and later moves to High Point. He goes on to become one of the country's most famous tenor saxophonists.

1929
Novelist Thomas Wolfe publishes *Look Homeward, Angel*, based on life in his hometown of Asheville.

1930s
Construction begins on the Blue Ridge Parkway, a WPA project designed to help lift the country out of the Depression. Working on the Parkway brings economic relief to laborers in nearby counties and unwanted commotion to highland farmers.

1960
The state's Civil Rights movement begins with a sit-in at the lunch counter in Greensboro by four students from North Carolina Agricultural and Technical College.

1972
Jesse Helms is the first Republican senator elected in North Carolina in the 20th century. Over the next two decades he becomes a powerful conservative force in Washington, fighting against restrictions on tobacco and guns.

Jesse Helms

O U T E R B A N K S

A PHOTOGRAPH SNAPPED IN SPACE shows North Carolina's Outer Banks as a thin arm of sand elbowing its way into the Atlantic. Time-lapse photography would create a more fluid image.

For centuries, these barrier islands have shielded North Carolina's low, mainland coast from pounding surf, ravenous currents, and the storm surge of hurricanes. How do the islands stand against such force? They don't.

They dance.

The banks' survivability is founded not on resistance, but on their ability to change. Geologically, the islands are a three-way dance. The partners are the sand, the wind, and the sea.

■ THE ISLANDS' DANCE

When Tar Heels say they're going to the Outer Banks, they're usually heading for the sandy spits of land that stretch from Virginia to Ocracoke's southern inlet. But barrier islands protect the length of the North Carolina coast.

Two strong, underwater rivers continually shape the barrier islands. The Labrador Stream's chill fingers slide south to Cape Hatteras, while the warmer, inkyblue Gulf Stream flows north. The collision of these two currents creates some of the world's most consistently turbulent waters and winds, and the shiftiest real estate on the East Coast.

Inlets and land change place like magic among the islands. The "inlets," named by sailors looking for a way "in" to the mainland, are actually "outlets" carved by sound waters pushing to the sea. Inlets typically wander slowly, spewing everchanging fans of sand into the ocean, but hurricanes, which can swallow towns and pitch ships into mainland peanut fields, can send the ocean crashing over the islands, bulldozing new inlets in a very short time. The hurricanes of 1848 and 1899 created the Oregon and Hatteras inlets overnight.

Despite fierce storms and strolling inlets, some islands are so heavily developed that the honk of cars drowns out the honk of wild geese. Fortunately, Cape Hatteras and Cape Lookout National Seashores alone include over half the barrier islands' 300-mile oceanfront. The U.S. Fish and Wildlife Service maintains several

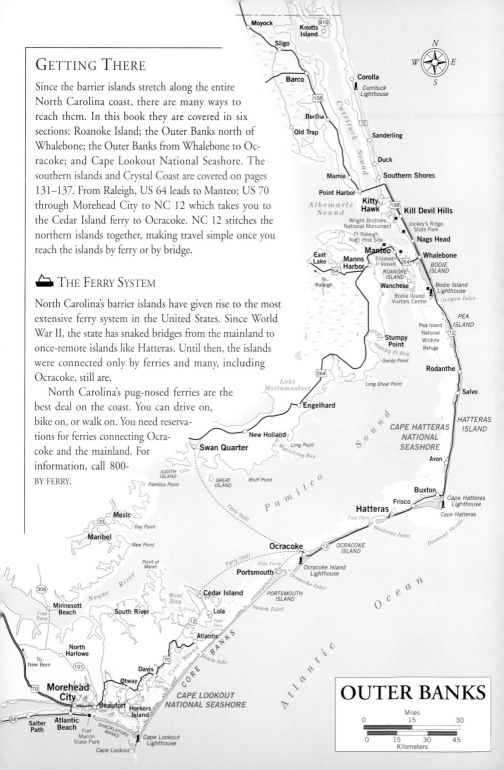

GETTING THERE

Since the barrier islands stretch along the entire North Carolina coast, there are many ways to reach them. In this book they are covered in six sections: Roanoke Island; the Outer Banks north of Whalebone; the Outer Banks from Whalebone to Ocracoke; and Cape Lookout National Seashore. The southern islands and Crystal Coast are covered on pages 131–137. From Raleigh, US 64 leads to Manteo; US 70 through Morehead City to NC 12 which takes you to the Cedar Island ferry to Ocracoke. NC 12 stitches the northern islands together, making travel simple once you reach the islands by ferry or by bridge.

THE FERRY SYSTEM

North Carolina's barrier islands have given rise to the most extensive ferry system in the United States. Since World War II, the state has snaked bridges from the mainland to once-remote islands like Hatteras. Until then, the islands were connected only by ferries and many, including Ocracoke, still are.

North Carolina's pug-nosed ferries are the best deal on the coast. You can drive on, bike on, or walk on. You need reservations for ferries connecting Ocracoke and the mainland. For information, call 800-BY FERRY.

Map labels

Moyock, Knotts Island, Sligo, Barco, Corolla, Currituck Lighthouse, Bertha, Old Trap, Sanderling, Duck, Mamie, Southern Shores, Point Harbor, Kitty Hawk, Albemarle Sound, Kill Devil Hills, Wright Brothers National Monument, Jockey's Ridge State Park, Ft Raleigh Nat'l Hist Site, Nags Head, East Lake, Manns Harbor, Manteo, Elizabeth II Vessel, Whalebone, BODIE ISLAND, ROANOKE ISLAND, Wanchese, Bodie Island Lighthouse, To Raleigh, Bodie Island Visitors Center, Oregon Inlet, PEA ISLAND, Pea Island National Wildlife Refuge, Stumpy Point, Stumpy Pt Bay, Sandy Point, Rodanthe, Salvo, HATTERAS ISLAND, Long Shoal Point, Lake Mattamuskeet, Engelhard, New Holland, CAPE HATTERAS NATIONAL SEASHORE, Avon, Long Point, Swan Quarter, Wysocking Bay, Bluff Point, Pamlico Sound, JUDITH ISLAND, Pamlico Point, GREAT ISLAND, Buxton, Frisco, Hatteras, Cape Hatteras Lighthouse, Cape Hatteras, Mesic, Bay Point, Maribel, Maw Point, Hatteras Inlet, Diamond Shoals, Ocracoke, OCRACOKE ISLAND, Point of Marsh, Ferry (toll), Portsmouth, Ocracoke Island Lighthouse, Cedar Island, West Bay, PORTSMOUTH ISLAND, Ocracoke Inlet, Minnesott Beach, Neuse River, South River, Lola, Atlantic, Swash Inlet, North Harlowe, Davis, Core Sound, Drum Inlet, To New Bern, Otway, Beaufort, CORE BANKS, Morehead City, Atlantic Beach, Harkers Island, SHACKLEFORD BANKS, Fort Macon State Park, CAPE LOOKOUT NATIONAL SEASHORE, Salter Path, Cape Lookout Lighthouse, Cape Lookout, Atlantic Ocean

OUTER BANKS

Miles
0   15   30

0   15   30   45
Kilometers

wildlife refuges. The state owns several natural areas, historic sites, and estuarine reserves. In these protected areas, sea turtles trudge ashore to nest on moonlit beaches, wild ponies gallop along the sound, and migrating snow geese fuss and flap beneath wintry skies. Like us, they come in response to the undiminished call of the sea.

■ OUTER BANKS HISTORY

English explorers Philip Amadas and Arthur Barlowe visited North Carolina's Outer Banks in 1584, landing on a low, sandy island about 20 miles long—probably Hatteras. Along the sound, they wrote, flocks of white cranes rose with a cry like a rising army. The sound-side forest contained the "highest and reddest Cedars of the world," pines, cypress, sassafras, deer, rabbits, hare, fowl, and a "profusion of grapes."

■ ALGONQUIN HOSPITALITY

Algonquins, who lived in small villages, soon came to trade with the explorers, paddling fire-hollowed canoes shaped with metal from "Christian ships." They brought coral, leather, and "divers[e] kinds of dies very excellent." Among the traders was a Secotan leader, Granganimeo, who brought his family along.

The Englishmen did not record Granganimeo's wife's name (we can only wonder what Queen Elizabeth thought of that), but noted she was a pretty, bashful woman. Like her husband, she wore a leather cloak and shift, and a headband decorated with white coral. Her pearl earrings hung to her waist and, the metal-hungry English noted, Granganimeo wore a gold or copper headpiece.

Soon, the Englishmen became bold enough to visit Granganimeo's village, whose nine cedar houses sat in a palisade on Roanoke Island. Being English, they arrived unannounced.

Southern hospitality began here.

Granganimeo's wife "came running out to meet us very cheerfully and friendly," they wrote. Her husband was absent, but she ordered her people to pull their boat ashore, and carry the men to land. Then she invited them home for lunch.

In the outer room of her five-room house, by a great fire, she washed and dried their clothes. In an inner room, she laid out a feast: wheat porridge, venison, fish, melons, vegetables, fruits, wine, and teas. During the visit, armed hunters entered, setting the Englishmen's nerves on edge. Noting her guests' discomfort, their hostess broke the hunters' arrows, and had the hunters run from the village.

Artist John White visited the following year with Sir Walter Raleigh's disastrous first colony. His watercolors capture the details of life among a people rapidly approaching extinction.

Today, place names of the northern islands echo Algonquin voices: Hatteras, Roanoke, Manteo, Wanchese. In rare cases, Algonquin words have crept into everyday language. If you camp in Cape Hatteras National Seashore, and if your trash is raided by a masked bandit, and if you mutter, "Raccoon," you are using an Algonquin word.

■ LOST COLONY ON ROANOKE ISLAND

In 1585 Sir Walter Raleigh's first colony plundered this land and its people, changing a climate of peace to one of rage. In 1587 he sent a second colony of around 116 men, women, and children. The colonists planned to settle on Virginia's

Reconstruction of Elizabeth II, *the British ship which brought around 116 colonists to Roanoke Island in 1587. Three years later, the colony had disappeared.*

WHEN PISTOL RHYMED WITH BRISTOL

The "Ned Teach" in this 1718 ditty is Blackbeard the pirate. The songwriter may have been a young printer's apprentice named Ben Franklin.

NORTH CAROLINA COLLECTION

Then each man to his gun
For the work must be done
With cutlass, sword, and pistol.
And when we no longer can strike a blow
Then fire the magazine, boys, up we go.
It is better to swim in the sea below
Than to hang in the air and feel the crow,
Sang jolly Ned Teach of Bristol.

Chesapeake Bay, but their ill-tempered pilot, Simon Fernandes, refused to take them farther than Roanoke Island. He allowed their leader, Gov. John White, to return to England with him for supplies, but left the colonists in a fragile skeleton-occupied fort, surrounded by murderous natives. When Governor White returned with supplies three long years later, the colony had disappeared.

Some say the colonists merged with friendly tribes. Some say they were lost at sea, or massacred. The Lost Colony's demise and the treacheries of the North Carolina shoals stymied colonization attempts for generations. And that suited the pirates just fine.

■ PIRATES

Blackbeard, Gentleman Stede Bonnet, Calico Jack Rackham, Ann Bonney, Mary Reed, Charles Vane, and Israel Hands all plied their trades along the North Carolina coast in the early 1700s. In fact, more than one island village claims among its founders pirates who washed ashore, retired ashore, or fled ashore.

Many pirates—including Blackbeard, who lost his head at Ocracoke—began as privateers. At first, colonial politicians welcomed pirates for the same reasons today's politicians might welcome outlet malls: in the short-run they were good for the economy. Pirates sold pilfered, cut-rate cargoes to grateful merchants in Charleston, New York, Norfolk, Philadelphia, and Boston.

But by 1718, 2,000 pirates were working the Eastern Seaboard. Piracy begat more pirates as legitimate sailors chose to become buccaneers rather than walk the plank themselves. Carolina shipping lanes made easy pickings, and the North Carolina coast became a haven for pirates, whose light sloops waltzed across the shallow sounds.

As the pirates became bolder, ports closed, business suffered, and the colonial navies stepped in. Maritime history's most colorful chapter died with a blast of gunpowder, a glint of steel, and the snap of a hangman's noose.

■ GRAVEYARD OF THE ATLANTIC

Off the barrier islands, the Atlantic has swallowed over 2,300 ships since colonial days, but the loss of life would have been much greater without lighthouses, life-saving stations, and islanders willing to risk their lives to snatch strangers from the sea.

The Baywatch *of Nags Head, circa 1890s, is this Life Saving Patrol.*
(Southern Historical Collection, University of North Carolina Library)

Every inch of island beachfront can recall some kind of shipwreck. But some shipwrecks are anchored so firmly in history, people talk about them as if they happened last Tuesday. Stop by a country store some February night, when the wind's so cold the marsh grass wears ice shackles, and someone's likely to say, "It's as cold as the night the *Crissie Wright* came ashore."

The *Crissie Wright* ran aground on Shackleford Banks one screaming, icy day over 100 years ago. As horrified islanders watched, the three-masted schooner rolled onto her side, and the storm's waves poured over her. The islanders tried twice to launch a rescue boat, but the storm slammed them back to shore.

In desperation, they sang hymns to comfort the trapped sailors. As night fell, the temperature dropped into the single digits, and the freezing crewmen slipped into the sea. When a whaling crew finally fought their way to the *Crissie Wright,* they found every man on board frozen stiff except the overweight cook, Cookie Johnson, who was saved by the warmth of his own fat.

Lighthouses began guiding ships around treacherous waters in the late 1700s. Today, six lighthouses help mariners get their bearings at sea. Each flashes a distinct light pattern and each sports a different painted design, clearly visible by day.

The Graveyard of the Atlantic is dangerous to swimmers, too. The Outer Banks are noted for deadly riptides, which can snatch swimmers out to sea.

Valiantly Saving the Shipwrecked

The steamer Metropolis *was wrecked off Currituck Beach on January 1878 with the loss of 85 lives. The account of the incident was later reported in* Harper's Monthly.

Peculiar cries, like that of many human voices mingled with the shrieks of the sea, led to the discovery of the stranded vessel by persons on the shore, who could see nothing through the fog. A boy was sent running to the nearest house, a half a mile inland, the occupant of which mounted his horse and galloped to the nearest station, some four and a half miles away. . . .

❖   ❖   ❖

Three or four precious hours had already been consumed; the water was filled with floating fragments of the wreck. Efforts to throw the shot-line failed, and the despairing people, giving up all hope of rescue before the ship should break entirely in pieces, accepted their last alternative, plunging into the treacherous waves. The surf was running high, and the struggling drowning mass of human beings drifted toward the shore. The life-savers and citizens ran into the water to meet them and save them, and strove nobly in the inner breakers and undertow, dragging them ashore in great numbers. The incidents of that awful hour defy any attempts at description. The air was filled with encouraging shouts and agonizing screams. Upward of a hundred were rescued, and many were restored from apparent death.

A handsome Newfoundland dog participated in the work, incited by the example of his master, and came dripping through the surf, bringing safely ashore a half-drowned man.

Illustration from Harper's Monthly, *February 1882.*

OUTER BANKS & HISTORY

■ NATIONAL SEASHORES ESTABLISHED

Islanders have always fished, raked clams, set crab pots, and netted shrimp, but until refrigeration came ashore, most islanders took little more from the sea than their sustenance. After World War II, some villages became commercial fishing centers.

The Park Service came ashore around the same time, and the government's creation of the islands' natural areas remains a sore topic at the bait shop. Beginning in the 1950s, the government condemned thousands of island acres for the two national seashores, forcing islanders to sell land for as little as $1 an acre. Today, beachfront property easily fetches $1,500 per oceanfront foot. You see the problem.

This unhappy history explains the islands' development pattern: small villages nestled among pristine beaches and maritime forests; and beyond the preserves, tracts of privately owned land developed with a vengeance. Ironically, it's the undeveloped, endless golden beaches and vibrant estuaries that call visitors and tourism dollars to the islands.

The controversy over the serene Carolina seashore is best illustrated in these two photographs, one a subdivision on Pine Island in Currituck County . . .

■ ABOUT THAT ACCENT

Until the 1950s, the Outer Banks really were islands unto themselves.

Change bypassed the islands for centuries, preserving 17th-century traditions, like the celebration of Old Christmas on January 6th. The language didn't change much, either. Islanders speak a dialect close to the Elizabethan English spoken by the Lost Colonists.

You'll know the dialect when you hear it, though you may not immediately understand it. Islanders speak with their lips close together, and their tongues near the roofs of their mouths. "Ou" sounds like "oo," as in "aboot the hoose." (About the house.) They pronounce "i" as "oi," and short "a" and "ar" sounds as "ah," as in, "The toid's so hoigh, the shahks ahr eatin' the cahbbahge." (The tide's so high, the sharks are eating the cabbage.)

People who use this musical dialect "have high tide in their voices." Today, that high tide is being washed away by outsiders' influences. But spend time around the docks, hardware stores, or churches, and you'll still hear high tide in the island voices.

. . . the other the MacKay Island National Wildlife Refuge, also in Currituck County.

■ EXPLORING ROANOKE ISLAND

US 64, which meanders along the southern, wooded shore of the Albemarle Sound, leads from points west to Roanoke Island.

Roanoke Island is surrounded by sounds which, depending on Nature's mood, may glitter like sapphires, or glower like a grey-faced god as you drive over them. The island itself is a place of quiet neighborhoods, pine forests, and the village of Manteo, on Shallowbag Bay. Historically, the Lost Colony put Roanoke Island on the map; the modern island returns the favor. Four sites focus on Sir Walter Raleigh's Lost Colonists.

The Elizabethan Gardens at Fort Raleigh National Historic Site in Manteo.

■ FORT RALEIGH NATIONAL HISTORIC SITE

Soon after you cross the Croatan Sound on US 64, signs will point the way to Fort Raleigh National Historic Site. From its visitors center and museum, you have access to the Elizabethan Gardens, Fort Raleigh, and the Lost Colony outdoor drama. This is also a good place to pick up information on activities within Cape Hatteras National Seashore. Look for a free paper, *In The Park*.

Standing by Fort Raleigh, a tiny, star-shaped earthwork in a forest of whispering pines, it's easy to imagine the Lost Colony's men, women, and children facing an angry New World, protected only by this fragile outpost of empire. Today, families stroll these gentle walkways, passing between the museum and this re-created fort, or rambling along a nature trail that leads to the sound. Another trail leads a few yards north to *The Lost Colony's* amphitheatre.

The Lost Colony, premiered by Pulitzer prize–winner Paul Green in 1937, tells the story of the Lost Colonists, including Virginia Dare, the first English child born in America. You need reservations for this popular production, which runs during summer only. Bring industrial-strength mosquito repellent. *(800-488-5012)*

❖

The adjacent 10-acre **Elizabethan Gardens,** created by landscape artists Umberto Innocenti and Richard Webel, include a rose garden, wildflower garden, formal sunken garden, herb garden, 16th-century statues, and a great lawn laced with live oaks, hollies, dogwood, and magnolias. Colonists who built Fort Raleigh in 1585 may have rested beneath the live oak in this garden. Queen Elizabeth and Sir Walter Raleigh never set a velvet slipper on American soil, but they may have strolled through a pleasure garden like this one while planning their New World.

■ NORTH CAROLINA AQUARIUM

The North Carolina Aquarium introduces some of the area's underwater residents, both freshwater and salt, including the American alligator, sea turtles, and sharks. "The fish we display would be more typical of the fishes that we would see from Cape Hatteras north along the Atlantic Coast," says curator Rhett White. Inexpensive field programs include collecting cruises, canoe trips, beach walks, even fishing lessons. *Three miles north of Manteo on Airport Road (just past the Fort Raleigh Historic Site); 252-473-3493.*

■ *ELIZABETH II*

The *Elizabeth II* lies further along US 64 on Manteo's waterfront, near shops and restaurants. If Fort Raleigh didn't give you a sense of the vulnerability of England's early colonists, the *Elizabeth II* will. Her billowing, white sails may make her *feel* larger, but this ship, a replica of the one colonists sailed to America in 1584, is a mere 69 feet long—and she was trusted to cross the Atlantic.

Colonists traveled as cargo, crammed into a four-and-a-half-foot-tall space between decks for the 42-day voyage to the West Indies, where ships took on fresh water and supplies, and then sailed up the coast, to Carolina. Costumed interpreters give tours in summer.

STEDE BONNET: GENTLEMAN PIRATE

Major Bonnet, a wealthy planter from Barbados, came to piracy in mid-life as modern men of a certain age come to red sports cars. One day in 1718 he looked at his wife and their high-society friends, strolled down to the waterfront, bought a fast sloop, hired a seedy crew, and sailed away.

Bonnet highjacked several ships off the North Carolina and Virginia coasts, and then set his sites on a large warship, *The Queen Anne's Revenge*. He realized his error the moment Blackbeard peered over the warship's gunwale, his jet-black beard billowing in the wind. When Blackbeard invited him on board *The Queen Anne's Revenge* as his partner, Bonnet quickly agreed.

Blackbeard now captured several other ships, imprisoning passengers and crews, and blockaded Charleston Harbor. For four days he held Charleston hostage, demanding medicine for his prisoners' lives. Why? Some say he was addicted to laudanum (an opium extract). Others say wife number 12's dowry included syphilis.

Charleston came through with the drugs, but the blockade left the city in a murderous mood. Once Blackbeard set him free, Bonnet made up for lost time, sacking ten ships and then heading for the Lower Cape Fear, for repairs. It was a rookie's choice: one way in and one way out. South Carolina's navy attacked on September 27, 1718, taking Bonnet and his crew. Charleston's judges, still smarting from the blockade, welcomed Bonnet's crew to the gallows.

Bonnet spent his last days begging for a reprieve. In a letter displayed at the Southport Maritime Museum, he offered to forfeit his arms and legs if he could keep his life. Once again, he had no luck.

■ OUTER BANKS NORTH OF WHALEBONE

🚗 Leaving Roanoke Island, US 64 crosses the Roanoke Sound, heading into an overgrown maze of high-rises, shops, and malls on Bodie [pronounced BODY] Island. At Whalebone, a left takes you north through heavy development to the Wright Brothers Memorial, the Corolla Lighthouse, and Currituck Banks. A right leads south to Cape Hatteras National Seashore's undeveloped beaches and estuaries, and the village of Ocracoke. *See page 72.*

North from Whalebone, NC 12 pushes through an area of dense, uninspired development where cottages, condos, restaurants, and shops seem to stand on each others' shoulders, vying for attention. There's an ocean in there somewhere: You'll pass a beach access on your way to Nags Head, one of the islands' first resort communities.

■ NAGS HEAD

Nags Head is known for its 30 or so very relaxed, 19th-century cottages, whose wrap-around porches usually shelter rocking chairs. These old cottages stare serenely out to sea, ignoring the newer cottages, amusements, and eateries that have elbowed in alongside.

In the early days, shipwrecks helped keep Nags Head's economy afloat. The law was "finders keepers," and islanders were enthusiastic finders. Story is, they'd drop a corpse enroute to the graveyard if someone shouted "Ship Ashore!"

In fact, Nags Head may have taken its name from the practice of local land pirates, who hung a lantern around a nag's neck and walked her along a starlit beach. Sea captains, mistaking the bobbing light for a ship rocked by safe waters, headed inland and their ships foundered on the shoals. Islanders then waited for salvageable cargoes to wash ashore.

■ JOCKEY'S RIDGE STATE PARK

US 158 heads north from Nags Head to the East Coast's tallest sand dune, protected by Jockey's Ridge State Park. In 1975, developers planned to flatten and

On the East Coast's highest sand dune at Jockey's Ridge State Park, hang gliders take advantage of the same conditions that attracted the Wright brothers to the area—strong winds and soft sand.

pave Jockey's Ridge. Fortunately, the Nature Conservancy stepped in. Today, the ten-story dune is still great to climb up, and even greater to roll down. This park includes a picnic area, and a nature trail that winds through the dunes to the sound.

In the Annual Hang Gliding Spectacular, sponsored here each May by Kitty Hawk Kites, national competitors lift off in the world's oldest hang gliding competition. Spectators pitch lawn chairs in the dunes for the day-long show. Hang gliding lessons are popular year round.

■ NAGS HEAD WOODS

Continuing north, US 158 crosses West Ocean Acres Drive. Take a left to Nags Head Woods, one of the islands' last maritime forests. Parts of the islands were once thick with forests, but early shipbuilding and lumbering industries have taken their toll.

Along these quiet, dune-sheltered trails, you may see a pileated woodpecker flipping among red oaks 500 years old, and an osprey nesting on a piling in the sound. Unless you're a Nature Conservancy member, you can visit only on Tuesdays and Thursdays.

Summer visitors stroll the boardwalk at Nags Head, a popular beach resort in the 19th century.
(Southern Historical Collection, University of North Carolina)

John Daniels, a member of the Kill Devil Hills Lifesaving Station, took this famous photograph of the first moment of mechanized flight on December 17, 1903. Daniels had never operated a camera before the Wright brothers asked him to witness and record their first successful flight. Years later he recalled the historic moment, "The machine looked like some big, graceful golden bird sailing off into the wind. I think it made us feel kind o' meek and prayerful like." (Library of Congress).

■ KILL DEVIL HILLS

Kill Devil Hills is a resort community possibly named by colonist William Byrd, who said its people drank rum "so bad and unwholesome, that it is not improperly called 'Kill-Devil.'" If you grow lonely for the ocean, head a few blocks east and drive along NC 12, known locally as Beach Road.

Wright Brothers National Memorial located about three miles north on US 158, offers respite from the midday sun. Its museum houses a replica of Orville and Wilbur's 1903 airplane. Orville and Wilbur built theirs in six months for under $1,000—including round-trip tickets from Dayton. It took 50 craftsmen three years to build the half-million-dollar replica.

Outside, trails lead across the dunes to the brothers' camp, rebuilt from old photos, and to a granite memorial marking the site of their historic first flight. This memorial hosts kite flying contests and other events throughout the year. (Wear real shoes. This sand sprouts prickly pear cacti.)

THE WRIGHT STUFF

The dawn of the 20th century found mankind racing for heavens, with scientists in Europe and the Americas rushing to perfect flying contraptions. But the world paid scant attention to Orville and Wilbur Wright, amateurs who designed gliders in their Dayton, Ohio, bike shop. In 1900, the Wright Brothers wrote to the National Weather Bureau, seeking a test site for their gliders. The Kitty Hawk–Kill Devil Hills area, with its soft dunes and strong winds, looked promising. They contacted the lifesaving station.

Captain Bill Tate wrote back: "If you decide to try your machine here and come I will take pleasure in doing all I can for your convenience and success and pleasure, and I assure you you will find a hospitable people when you come among us." Wilbur arrived on September 13 after a hideous two-day schooner voyage from Elizabeth City, and pitched his tent near Tate's home.

The brothers' first visit caused a stir, not because of their cockamamie notions, but because they brought gasoline to the island. Islanders, who found the brothers amusing and their cash endearing, worried about having the explosive near their homes.

That first year, the brothers flew their glider like a giant kite, studying its wing motion. When they returned in 1901, their improved plane had a 22-foot wingspan, almost twice that of their first glider, and flew without lines. On their 1902 glider, whose tail featured a moveable rudder, the brothers made over 1,000 test flights, gliding up to 600 feet per flight.

Finally, in 1903, the brothers unveiled their masterpiece. The airplane sported a 40-foot wingspan, a rudder control, and an aileron control to adjust direction and altitude. No glider, this. A four-cylinder gasoline engine powered the propellered craft, and a launching system made flat land take-offs possible.

On December 14, they raised their signal flag, calling neighbors to witness the flight, and pull them from the wreckage if necessary. They launched the plane, but Wilbur raised the nose too high, stalled, and fell to earth.

On December 17, the brothers raised the flag again. This time Orville launched the plane into freezing 27 mph winds. As stunned islanders watched, the plane rose above the sand. Orville flew 120 feet in 12 seconds, Wilbur running alongside, flapping his arms and screeching encouragement.

The brothers made three more flights that day, the last one a distance of 852 feet. Ironically, the witnesses to this landmark feat were men so isolated from the 20th century, they told the story in a dialect similar to the Elizabethan English they're forebears spoke.

The villages to the north of Kill Devil Hills are now more in tune with summering tourists than migrating geese. The condos and quick-stop groceries disappear as you drive through Pine Island Sanctuary, but as you approach Corolla, you'll enter another thicket of shops and cottages.

■ COROLLA

Pronounced COR-AH'-LA, this village is literally the end of the road. The unpainted Currituck Lighthouse stood on this sandy shore in isolation until a few years ago, when the state paved NC 12 just beyond its door. Now people "pitch and putt" next door.

Still, for a few dollars you can climb the 1875 lighthouse for an uninterrupted view north, into the wildest Outer Bank—unpaved, uncluttered, unspoiled.

Currituck County takes its name from the Algonquin word "Coratank," which means wild geese. In the early 1900s, wealthy northerners established hunting clubs here, protecting thousands of acres of land. The clubs are gone now, but acres of undeveloped land remains.

The Currituck Lighthouse and the lightkeeper's noble house in Corolla.

OUTER BANKS & CURRITUCK ISLAND

BIRDS FLY. MEN DRINK.

*E*very December, on the anniversary of the Wright brothers' first flight, a motley fraternity of pilots, aerospace engineers and writers about aviation gathers at Kitty Hawk, North Carolina. After an all-night party, these celebrants assemble bleary-eyed on the sand dunes where Wilbur and Orville's craft of hickory sticks stuck together with Arnstein's Bicycle Cement first started forward into the wind. At the precise moment of the Wrights' lift-off in 1903, two Navy jets representing the two brothers come roaring in low from the sea, rise to clear the sand dunes, kick in their afterburners over the Wright monument, and then, in a thundering instant that rattles the earth, turn straight up into the sky and climb until they are out of sight. The day is often raw and windy, but the faithful club members are always out there for this small, moving ceremony. They style themselves the "Man Will Never Fly Society." Their motto is, "Birds fly. Men drink."

I am not a member, but when I am bouncing around up there among thunderstorms, I always recall the society's name and credo with profound appreciation.

—Charles Kuralt, *A Life on the Road,* 1990

The sand banks to the north contain some of the highest, most restless dunes on the East Coast, extensive maritime forests, and rich estuaries. For better or worse (my money's on better), the small protected areas on Currituck Banks are accessible only by four-wheel-drive, or boat.

From Corolla, you can double back to Whalebone to head south, or drive inland at Southern Shores to explore the northern Coastal Plain.

■ FROM WHALEBONE SOUTH TO OCRACOKE

From Whalebone on Bodie Island, NC 12 heads south into Cape Hatteras National Seashore, where you can look for public beach accesses every few miles. There are four camping areas within the seashore: at Oregon Inlet, Cape Point near Buxton, Frisco, and Ocracoke. **Coquina Beach,** on the southern tip of Bodie Island, is named for the millions of tiny coquina clam shells along the shore.

■ BODIE ISLAND LIGHTHOUSE

Bodie Island's black-and-white striped lighthouse is the third built to watch over the Oregon Inlet. The first, built in 1848, tipped over. Retreating Confederate soldiers blew up the second. This one first flashed its light seaward in 1872.

The lighthouse keeper's home, where children once schemed to tame wild island ponies, is now inhabited by nature exhibits and ecology films. A nature walk winds through the marshes to an observation platform overlooking yaupon, cattails, wax myrtle, bayberries, and "profusions" of wild grapes, like those Amadas and Barlowe reported in 1584.

The skeleton of the *Laura A. Barnes,* which came ashore during a 1921 nor'easter, rests near the parking lot.

■ HATTERAS ISLAND

At the south end of Bodie Island, the Herbert C. Bonner Bridge spans **Oregon Inlet** to Hatteras Island. The Oregon Inlet Campground and Oregon Inlet Fishing Center (charters, public launch) are popular with fishermen.

All inlets walk, but the Oregon Inlet strolls, moving south at around 100 feet per year. The sand you drive over before reaching the water's edge marks the distance the inlet has moved since 1964. This inlet is historically one of the most important deep-water inlets along the Outer Banks, and one of the most dangerous. Waters near inlets are deadly. Out-flowing currents will sweep you out to sea.

Hatteras Island is named for the Native Americans who once lived here. In the villages along the sound are cottages, small motels, fishing charters, piers, private campgrounds, etc.

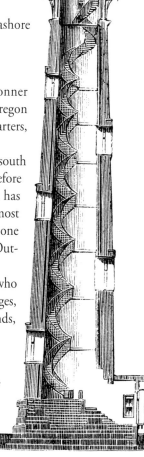

*An architectural rendering of the interior of
Bodie Island's lighthouse.*

Houses damaged by the encroaching sea at Rodanthe.

■ PEA ISLAND NATIONAL WILDLIFE REFUGE

Along the northern section of the island, NC 12 meanders beside the grass-edged sound in the Pea Island National Wildlife Refuge, which offers excellent birding year-round. Listen for the mellow bugling of whistling swans and the high-pitched hownk-hownk of snow geese, as they end their several-thousand-mile journeys and settle into the refuge.

The refuge's water habitats (ocean, brackish, and sound) attract more than 260 bird species each year. Another 50 species are accidental tourists, driven in on the wings of storms. Spring brings egrets, ibises, herons, yellow legs, plovers, and American avocets. Peregrine falcons, eagles, and osprey fish in summer and autumn. In August, awkward young brown pelicans learn to fish here. Human fishermen flock here, too, casting for spot, blues, trout, flounder, and drum.

Congress established the Pea Island Wildlife Refuge in 1938. It encompasses 5,915 island acres, plus 25,700 acres of Pamlico Sound. Its wildlife "buffet" took root during the Depression when the Civilian Conservation Corps planted the dunes with sea oats, and the ponds and marshes with winter food for migrating birds. Blinds overlooking the buffet line attract birders, photographers, and biologists.

■ CHICAMACOMICO LIFESAVING STATION

South of the refuge lies the village of Rodanthe. Follow the signs to the Chicamacomico Lifesaving Station, now a museum honoring the men who risked their lives to snatch strangers from the sea. Each Thursday during the summer, the staff re-enacts the breeches buoy drill on the beach. Open daily.

As shipping increased off these shores in the 19th century, shipwrecks increased, too. In the late 1800s, the government built Lifesaving Stations every seven miles along the coast. Surfmen patrolled the beaches, and maintained a 24-hour watch from the stations' towers. For nearly 80 years—from 1878 until 1954, when the stations were replaced by the Coast Guard—these island surfmen built a reputation for dedication, daring and skill. Their motto said it all: "You have to go out." No one said they'd come back in.

When possible, they worked from the beach. Fastening a line to a cannon shot and firing over the sinking ship, they dropped the line on deck. Then they towed passengers and crewmen ashore one-by-one in a breeches buoy—a lifesaving ring with a seat in it. But when the ship was far from shore, the surfmen honored their motto. They went out.

Today, the Chicamacomico Lifesaving Station is a museum.

KEEPER OF THE LIGHT

Rany Jennett's life has come full circle.

Jennett, whose father was the Hatteras Lighthouse's last keeper, was born in the keeper's house in 1921. Today, as a summer ranger for the Cape Hatteras National Seashore, Rany Jennett welcomes visitors to his boyhood home.

Unaka Jennett, his father, joined the Lighthouse Service in 1904, serving as captain of the Hatteras Lightship at Diamond Shoals, a deadly bank of shifting sand ridges 12 miles offshore. "Lightships did the same thing, basically, as lighthouses," Rany Jennett says. "Only they were out in the water, of course."

When Unaka moved to the Hatteras Lighthouse in 1919, he brought his wife, Jenny Luanna, and their young children, who grew up in a sun-baked Eden.

The Hatteras Lighthouse employed three keepers who worked long hours. "The three keepers had duty every 72 hours," Jennett says. "They had 24-hour duty. They had to light the lamp a half-hour before sunset, and extinguish it at sunrise."

A Fresnel lens magnified and concentrated light from a kerosene mantle lamp. The lens system, made of over 1,000 glass pieces, stood about 12 feet high and six feet in diameter. "Of course, they also had to do maintenance on the houses and also on the lighthouse," he says.

That included painting the lighthouse's candy-cane stripe. Unaka used to tell children he painted vertical stripes on the tower, and then gave it a quick twist to create its famous swirl.

As a boy, Rany Jennett spent happy hours in the lighthouse, polishing the brass works, and watching ships sail the indigo Gulf Stream. Hurricanes, he adored. "You don't have sense enough to be scared at that age," he says.

Ironically a series of hurricanes, one of which sent ocean waters swirling up into the lighthouse, convinced Unaka to take his family inland. The Coast Guard decommissioned the lighthouse in 1935. When the Seashore restored it in 1992, Rany Jennett came home to a new season of guests.

Continuing south, beach accesses lead through the dunes to wide, golden beaches noted for open spaces, surf fishing, pelicans and laughing gulls. (Swim in areas supervised by lifeguards.)

Windsurfers love **Canadian Hole**, soundside a half-mile north of Buxton, for its wide expanse of shallow water. French Canadian windsurfers drift down in fall—which explains the name. You can rent windsurfing equipment at Avon or Buxton.

(preceding pages) Cape Hatteras Lighthouse, the tallest brick lighthouse in the United States at 208 feet, dominates Cape Hatteras National Seashore.

■ CAPE HATTERAS LIGHTHOUSE

Oceanside, the famous Cape Hatteras Lighthouse dominates the shoreline near Buxton, as it has since 1870. (Follow the signs.) At 208 feet, this lighthouse—with its black and white candy-cane swirl—is the tallest brick lighthouse in the U.S. Originally built 1,500 feet from the shore, it warns sailors from Diamond Shoals and overlooks a sea that has eaten its way inland to threaten the lighthouse.

The keeper's house, next door, is a museum and visitor's center. (Open 10 AM to 4 PM Memorial Day to Labor Day.) Just southeast of the lighthouse, at Cape Point, the surf fishermen cast beyond the breakers. This is the number-one fishing spot on the islands. (Between fishermen and beachgoers, the lighthouse parking lot often fills up by 10 AM. Park on the shoulder.)

■ BUXTON WOODS

NC 12 continues through Buxton Woods, a serene maritime forest that includes the graves of seven Nazi spies whose arrival on these shores was poorly timed. In 1942, when U-boats were nearly as plentiful as porpoises offshore, islanders swore German sailors came ashore for Saturday night movies. Maybe, maybe not. But one evening around dusk, seven Germans did walk into the village of Avon. Their graves, which no one recalls digging, were located decades later in Buxton Woods.

Buxton's cottages, motels, and eateries cater primarily to fishermen, although other visitors are moving in.

■ FRISCO NATIVE AMERICAN MUSEUM

Frisco lies a few miles south of Buxton Woods. The Frisco Native American Museum displays exhibits on the Algonquin people who lived on these islands, including an Algonquin canoe found on the museum grounds. Behind the museum, nature trails wind through lichen-covered oak trees to the sound.

■ VILLAGE OF HATTERAS

🚗 ⛴ A few miles down, the village of Hatteras is known for its fishing charters, pier, and the free ferry to Ocracoke Island. The free ferries pull away every 30 minutes during the day, from April 15 through October 15, and every hour otherwise. You can't make reservations; bring some good will and a book. The ride takes about a half-hour. You'll skirt the shoals as the water's tones change from grey-green, to turquoise, to deep blue. The laughing gulls who follow the ferries always appreciate a piece of bread or a cracker; a few will eat from your hand.

■ OCRACOKE ISLAND

Rumbling off the ferry, you're on Ocracoke Island. Sixteen miles long, it supports a population of 700 permanent residents. In summer, the village of Ocracoke bustles. Off-season, you'll have much of the island to yourself.

This is still Cape Hatteras National Seashore. Access roads cross the dunes to popular fishing beaches, whose relatively gentle waves and low, gradual strands create some good shelling, especially in the off-season.

Ocracoke ponies once grazed in the low dunes and grass flats to the south. These descendants of Spanish mustangs once freely roamed Ocracoke Island. Today they live in a 170-acre pasture near the village of Ocracoke, on the southern tip of the island. (Feeding times: 8:30 AM and 6 PM.)

The Seashore's Beachcomber Campground is oceanside about three miles down the road. As with all Seashore campgrounds, shade is scarce. *(Reservations: 800-365-CAMP)*

Deep-sea fishing boats such as these may be rented at various marinas along the Outer Banks.

Ruth Fountain feeds black-faced laughing gulls from the Ocracoke-Hatteras ferry.

■ FERRY FROM MAINLAND TO OCRACOKE VILLAGE

The most serene way to visit the Outer Banks is to begin on the mainland at Swan Quarter or Cedar Island, and take the ferry to Ocracoke village. This route not only bypasses the jarring development around Whalebone, it puts you in touch with the rhythm of the sea before you set foot on the islands.

At Cedar Island *(see page 130)*, the ferry loads by a rambling, white visitor's center. The 22-mile trip across the Pamlico Sound to Ocracoke takes a little over two hours. You'll need reservations; *800-856-0343*.

As the ferry glides away from shore, passengers move forward to peer over the bow. Gradually, the waters lose the earth's green-grey colors, and reach up to grab the azure tones of the sky. White-caps roll across the sound, teasing the ferry from side to side, while on the upper deck, sunburned vacationers doze as the laughing gulls wheel around the ship's broad stern, hoping for bits of bread.

As the mainland fades away, a white shrimp boat sweeps by. Plowing through its wake, the ferry kicks up a cloud of silver spray. To the starboard, a line of pelicans drift by, like a ragged brown tail on a low-flying kite.

An hour into the trip, sky meets water in every direction, and the hazy line between worlds broken only by a white ship lingering on the horizon. After threading restless shoals marked with sun-bleached posts, the ferry nears the island, then cuts a gentle arc, and moves at a stately pace toward the narrow entrance between stone jetties into Ocracoke village's salt water lake.

■ OCRACOKE VILLAGE

If you arrive at Ocracoke village in summer, you abruptly enter a bustling world of small groceries, sandwich shops, and restaurants. But as you turn south off of NC 12 and head into the old village, you'll find a community of unpretentious little houses set along shaded drives.

The Island Inn—a white, two-story hotel built in the early 1900s—was once the only place to stay in Ocracoke. Today, this serenely eccentric little inn on NC

Fishing nets and boats on Parkers Creek on Ocracoke Island are timeless emblems of island life, (above and right). The painting above, Loading Nets, Ocracoke, *is by Claude Howell and was completed in 1986. (Courtesy St. Johns Museum)*

12 is far from the only place, but it's the best. There are no wake-up calls and no alarm clocks, but the rooster a few blocks over sounds off around 7 AM.

From the inn's grassy sideyard, you can follow the faint scent of cedar away from NC 12, into an early-morning community of small, white cottages. Pale pink hydrangeas lounge by the front steps, and snaggle-toothed picket fences yawn as the joggers pass by.

Many of these old houses, which rest beneath the arms of broad shade trees, are summer houses now, rented out by local realtors. They didn't begin that way. Some have family graveyards tucked in the corner of the yards. Others still have silvery-grey fishing nets piled by driveways, ready to go.

A few blocks down from the inn, a boardwalk leads to the **Ocracoke Light-house.** Built in 1823, this is the state's oldest continually operating light. The 60-foot tower, closed to visitors, still guides ships between Ocracoke and Portsmouth Island.

The 1920 general store down the street now stocks gifts and pottery. Farther down, a sleepy-eyed gentleman sells watermelons in his yard, and around the corner, his neighbor weeds a garden, while his rooster welcomes the day.

Ocracoke is best seen by foot or bike. Rent a bicycle down on Silver Lake, the jetty-protected harbor where the ferries dock (locals call it The Creek). You can also rent a kayak , and explore the nearby estuaries with a guide, or on your own.

It's an easy paddle across Silver Lake's gentle swells. Time your exit to scoot out between ferries if you can, hook a left and paddle down along the cottage-lined waterfront to **Teach's Hole.**

In these tidal creeks, oysters spit water at terrapins, while black skimmers plummet from the sky, hunting small fish. Life here is peaceful, and slow. You'd never guess this was where Blackbeard made his last stand.

■ CAPE LOOKOUT NATIONAL SEASHORE

Cape Lookout National Seashore, a 55-mile strip of golden islands, begins at Portsmouth Island and etches south. Villages once thrived here, but the islands are wild today. No bridges, no highways, no drinking water.

⌂ The National Seashore and U.S. Coast Guard regulate small **ferry services** from Ocracoke, Beaufort, Davis, Atlantic, and Harker's Island, allowing you to

RISING WIND ON THE BANKS

*M*r. Jack's weather forecast proved accurate. In the predawn hours of Friday, the usual breeze that eddied casually from the Sound, playing about in the low-lying shrubs around the cottage, suddenly increased its intensity and changed its mood; it whipped rather than caressed the aspen, causing the leaves to set up an incessant, clattering protest; it hissed through the stunted cedars; it nosed its way importunately under the eaves of the cottage, drummed on windowpanes, and sent a small, unidentified object—plastic, from the sound of it—skittering across the cement floor of the Stricklands' screened porch. The shallows sprouted small breakers, which dashed themselves against the stones of the narrow strip of beach, making an urgent, gulping sound, like a thirsty animal drinking.

The noise woke Nell briefly. Those must be Mr. Jack's "hoigh winds," she thought, then drowsed off again, having identified the natural causes of the disturbance.

The winds did not completely wake Cate, but they infiltrated her sleep. She dreamed agitatedly of bashed ships' timbers and sailors' cries. . . .

—Gail Godwin, *A Mother and Two Daughters,* 1982

boat across to deserted beaches, peaceful marshlands, a lighthouse, and lost towns. You can reach Cape Lookout and the southern end of the seashore by ferry from Beaufort on the mainland. Some services maintain island cottages. For a current list of operators, call *252-728-2250*. To visit Portsmouth Island and its ghost town from Ocracoke, you need a private ferry. For information, call the Ocracoke visitor's center at *252-928-4531*.

■ PORTSMOUTH
Walking along the inlet's edge, across the flats, up the white-sand hills to Portsmouth, you enter a silent, sun-bleached village of homes, churches, and stores. Listed on the National Register of Historic Places, the town was inhabited until 1971. Today, of its 21 well-preserved buildings, only one house (a visitor's center), and the Methodist Church are open to visitors.

Two centuries ago, tall ships from England and the West Indies docked along this waterfront. Seamen loaded ships' cargoes into lightboats, to be "lightered" to mainland ports. In the taverns on the waterfront, bartenders improved on yarns spun by sailors a half-world from home.

After picking up its cargo from tall ships docked at Portsmouth in the Outer Banks, a lightboat is unloaded at a wharf in Washington, NC around 1910. (East Carolina Manuscript Collection, East Carolina University, Greenville)

Portsmouth boomed. Wharves and warehouses lined the deepest inlet in the islands. Stores, churches, schools, a post office, customs house, and hospital lined the streets. Green-shuttered houses sat on lush lawns, kitchens built out back to keep the fish smell out of the parlor curtains.

In 1848 a fierce hurricane partially filled the inlet, but the Civil War dealt Portsmouth her death blow. People fled as Federal forces approached. By the war's end, most had new lives on the mainland. A few came home, but with the marine traffic heading for new, deeper inlets, Portsmouth's life ebbed away.

You can ferry to Portsmouth for day trips, or overnighters. There's no camping in the historic district, though.

■ SHACKLEFORD BANKS

From the mainland, Shackleford Banks seem to hover on the horizon, a sandy mirage between water and sky. Standing on Shackleford Banks today, it's difficult to imagine this as a booming whaling town, but the stretch of sand three miles northwest of Cape Lookout was the heart of an industry.

No one knows when **Diamond City** tumbled ashore, but it must have been here when New England whalers passed through in 1726. The whalers headed north, to colder waters, but not before the islanders netted a few ideas. They substituted their island for a ship, and trees for a crow's nest.

Six crews kept 25-foot boats onshore from February to May, when old men climbed the trees and scanned the horizon. When they spotted a whale, the men rushed to sea. They beached the whale at high tide, and went to work. Men and children cut the blubber while the women melted it in vats, running the oil through reed strainers into old molasses barrels buried in the cool sand.

The oil and whalebone fetched a pretty penny in Beaufort. Diamond City's 500 citizens landed four whales a year; the $18,000 windfall sent the economy into overdrive. The town claimed three stores, a porpoise-processing plant, oyster house, and crab-packing house. They even built a school.

Then the hurricane of 1899 slammed ashore, drowning gardens, flooding forests, floating coffins, and lifting homes from foundations. Worse, ravenous currents gnawed the beach away, leaving the city vulnerable and exposed. A sad exodus began. Families dismantled homes, and floated them across the sound to Harker's Island, Marshallberg, or Morehead City's "Promised Land." By 1903, all that remained were traces of curving streets in the shifting sands.

■ CAPE LOOKOUT LIGHTHOUSE

This diamond-patterned lighthouse blinked to life in 1859, and still helps sailors skirt Cape Lookout shoals. From the lighthouse grounds, you may see small boats bobbing on the choppy waters off the island curve known as The Hook. If the reels are spinning, the blues are running. Like the other sites on the seashore, the lighthouse is reached via ferry or chartered boat.

■ RACHEL CARSON ESTUARY

Boating between Beaufort and Shackleford Banks, you pass through the Rachel Carson Component of the North Carolina National Estuarine Research Reserve —quite a mouthful, which is why most folks just say, "I'm going to Rachel Carson." Naturalist Rachel Carson researched her book, *At the Edge of the Sea,* here in the 1940s. Today the reserve is best known for the 30 or so wild ponies that live on Carrot Island, across from Beaufort's yacht-lined waterfront.

You'll find a remarkable diversity of life in this complex of salt marshes, tidal mudflats, sand flats, eelgrass beds, and upland islands. If you go over at low tide (the best time), you'll find fiddler crabs in their burrows along the creek. The short seaweed-encrusted tubes sticking out of the wet sand are escape hatches for iridescent, plumed worms. They peek out at high tide, and filter meals from the sea.

Further along, you'll cross a salt marsh covered in cord grass. The pony trail leads to the top of a sand berm overlooking Beaufort Inlet, which is crucial to the estuary. Its tides move nutrients into the reserve, and flush pollutants out.

Along the mudflat, where humans forage for clams, birds probe the mudbanks. The eelgrass in the shallow waters conceals marine life including fish, scallops, crabs, and snails. The brackish ponds host long-legged waders, while raccoons and grey fox live in the nearby thicket.

Two North Carolina organizations besides the reserve offer tours: the Maritime Museum in Beaufort, and Pine Knolls Shores Aquarium. This is one of six protected estuaries along the North Carolina coast.

Cape Lookout Lighthouse.

C O A S T A L   P L A I N

NORTH CAROLINA'S BROAD COASTAL PLAIN rises, barely, from a mainland coast inlaid with hundreds of tiny harbors, inlets, and bays. The plain stretches west—in most places flat as an ironing board—to the Piedmont's rolling hills. Where the Piedmont's lively rivers slow to a lazy crawl, a coastal plain was built with sediments eroded from western mountains.

The plain's seven broad, shallow sounds make up the largest inland shoreline in the United States—a boon to pirates, moonshine runners, and ne'er-do-wells who have hidden along shores so low that trees seem to walk on water. The 2.2 million acres of estuaries along these shores are also the nurseries for North Carolina's seafood industry.

Today's coastal plain consists of two geographic zones. The shore claims a spattering of fishing villages, a growing number of resort and retirement communities, and miles of undeveloped marshlands overlooking indigo sounds. Inland, the plain is a land of molasses-slow rivers, family farms, and towns so small a wily mayor's apt to park an unmanned police car near the lone traffic light, to create the illusion of a police force.

This is a lush land of ages-old cypress swamps, rich estuaries, and drowsy colonial river towns. It's also a land of trailer parks, ticky-tack military towns, and poverty.

■ HISTORY

In 1700, a rakish young naturalist named John Lawson became mainland North Carolina's first literate tourist. Happily, he found plenty to write home about.

Lawson set out from Charleston, South Carolina, on 28 December 1700, pressing northwest to the Indians' Occaneechi trade path, known today as I-85. He headed north through Piedmont Indian villages, and then east across the central plain, settling finally in Bath, a tiny English community on the Pamlico Sound.

During his travels, Lawson walked from Indian village to Indian village, describing homes, religious rites, and food. Shamans fascinated him. The women did, too. "Amongst Women, it seems impossible to find a Scold," he wrote. "Would some of our European Daughters of Thunder set these Indians for a Pat-

In this typical Coastal Plain scene, the trees seem to walk on water
in Jones Lake near Elizabethtown.

tern." Not that they were perfect, he added. The Wateree, were "as ingenious at picking of pockets as any, I believe, the World affords; for they will steal with their feet."

Lawson recorded the cypress, fox grapes, and vegetables; buffalo, wolves, and panthers. He described "new" creatures like the opossum, a rope-tailed, death-defying marsupial often seen scurrying beneath starlit skies. "If a Cat has nine Lives, this Creature surely has nineteen; for if you break every bone in their Skin and mash their Skull leaving them for Dead, you may come an hour after and they will be gone quite away," Lawson wrote.

He reported "insects" called alligators hibernating in the creek banks. "They roar and make a hideous Noise against bad Weather, and before they come out of their nest in the Spring." (Their offspring still roar along the Cape Fear River, and in the Croatan National Forest, on the central coast.)

As for North Carolina settlers, Lawson claimed the men had been made lazy by easy living. The women he deemed industrious and fair, with "brisk, charming eyes." They married young, wove their own cloth, and paddled their own canoes.

Lawson doesn't say where he met these brisk-eyed young women, but by 1710, settlers drifting south from Virginia had established three main ports: Edenton, Bath, and Beaufort. And they had built their one-room log cabins along the creeks and branches from the Virginia line south, almost to the Neuse River.

The southern plain remained, firmly, Indian territory.

Lawson argued for a compassionate partnership with the region's natives. "They are really better to us than we are to them," he wrote. "They always give us Victuals at their Quarters, and take care we are armed against Hunger and Thirst: We not do so by them. . . . We look upon them with Scorn and Disdain, and think them little better than Beasts in Human Shape, though if well examined, we shall find that, for all our Religion and Education, we possess more Moral Deformities and Evils than these Savages do, or are acquainted withal."

And, he warned, the Tuscarora made bitter enemies: "[T]hey strive to invent the most inhuman Butcheries for [their enemies] that the Devils themselves could invent or hammer out of Hell." The Tuscarora soon proved the truth of his words.

■ TUSCARORA WAR
In 1710, John Lawson, now Surveyor-General of North Carolina, parceled off around 18,000 acres of alligator-infested land at the fork of the Neuse and Trent

Eighteenth-century naturalist John Lawson sketched the "Beasts of Carolina" as he encountered a variety of animals during his travels through the Coastal Plain. (North Carolina Collection)

COASTAL PLAIN & HISTORY

A 19th-century drawing depicting the capture of John Lawson, his black servant, and Baron von Graffenreid by Tuscarora warriors in 1710. (North Carolina Collection)

Rivers to a Swiss playboy, Baron Christoph von Graffenreid, for a Palatine colony in the New World. It was a deadly mistake.

With invaders on their doorstep, the Tuscarora united the coastal tribes and prepared for war. When Lawson headed up the Neuse River with Baron Von Graffenreid, Tuscarora warriors marched the trespassers to Catechna, near present-day Grifton, for trial. The Baron wrote:

> *I*n the middle of this great space we sat bound side by side, sitting [upon] the ground, the Surveyor-General and I, coats off and bare headed. . . before us was a great fire and around about the fire the conjurer, that is, an old gray Indian, a priest among them, who is commonly a magician, yes even conjures up the devil himself. He made two rings either of meal or very white sand, I do not know which. Right before our feet lay a wolf skin. A little farther in front stood an Indian in the most dignified and terrible posture that can be imagined. . . . Ax in hand, he looked to be the executioner.

Von Graffenreid addressed the crowd, claiming ties to a powerful king. The

Tuscarora spared him but not Lawson, who they stuck "full of fine small splinters of torchwood, like hogs' bristles, and so set them gradually on fire."

At dawn a few days later, the Indians attacked European settlements and homesteads, killing 210 settlers during the first hours of the three-day massacre. Bodies of women were left kneeling, as in prayer. Men were scalped. Unborn babies were ripped from their mothers' bodies, and hurled into trees.

War raged for three years until, only a few miles from the place Lawson met his death, several hundred Tuscarora men, women, and children crowded into a palisade. Colonial troops and the Tuscarora's hereditary native enemies surrounded the fort, and opened fire. When the smoke cleared three bloody days later, the Tuscarora had been annihilated.

■ PLANTATION ERA

With the Tuscarora in ruins, the southern plain opened to European settlers.

Wealthy South Carolina planters quickly moved in, creating vast low-country rice plantations along the Cape Fear as affluent planters from Edenton moved in alongside. When North Carolina governor Gabriel Johnston invited his Scots countrymen to Carolina, they came lock, stock, and bagpipe.

A scan of colonial records proves early Tar Heels were average folks up to the usual misdeeds. They filed separation papers and prenuptial agreements, weaseled out of shoplifting charges, apologized when caught swimming nude in the Chowan River.

Wealth remained in a very few, very well-manicured hands. Most early settlers lived in dirt-floored log cabins, but once sawyers rolled up their sleeves, frame houses with shake roofs sprang up across the countryside. Farmers planted the land cleared by sawyers, raising tobacco, corn, and rice. Women cared for children and homes, whether those homes were rough cabins or "mansion houses"—typically two-story houses, four rooms up and four down, with free-standing kitchens. Generous porches became the sitting rooms of choice.

By the time of the Revolution, about half of North Carolina's adult slaves were "new" slaves—Guinean, Angolan, Ibo, Mandingo, or Coramentee people of West Africa. Many were rice farmers "special ordered" by plantation owners who needed their skill and expertise. The few free blacks congregated around Halifax, near the Virginia border. Small colonies of escaped slaves lived deep in the Dismal Swamp's bamboo mazes near Edenton until the end of the Civil War.

COASTAL PLAIN & HISTORY

■ CIVIL WAR

To hear Tar Heels talk, you might think white, 19th-century North Carolinians were born swaddled in Confederate grey. In reality, political sympathies were initially split. But once North Carolina cast its lot with the South, thousands of young men flooded the military training camps, bringing along violins, slaves, and bedsteads. Almost as soon as they could salute, North Carolina's soldiers were sent to Richmond, to defend the Confederacy's capital. By the time Union strategists caught their breath and invaded eastern North Carolina to cut Lee's supply lines, only green recruits remained. They were too few, and too new.

As North Carolina's barrier islands fell and federal troops closed in on the mainland, slave-owners herded thousands of slaves west. As Union soldiers marched into Elizabeth City, New Bern, Washington, and Plymouth, wealthy planters "refugeed" inland. Others took a deep breath and hoped for the best. The best was bad enough.

Even Edward Stanly, whom Lincoln had appointed military governor of North Carolina, was horrified at the destruction wreaked by occupying forces. "Thousands and thousands of dollars' worth of property was conveyed North," he wrote. "Libraries, pianos, carpets, mirrors, family portraits, everything in short, that could be removed, was stolen by men abusing slave-holders and preaching liberty, justice, and civilization."

As Union soldiers liberated slaves plantation by plantation, around 7,000 black North Carolinians enlisted in Union regiments and 10,000 moved to refugee communities. Thousands more rejoiced and stayed put.

With all ports except Wilmington blockaded and occupied, the war became a series of raids and blunders. In New Bern and Plymouth, wartime romances flourished. Near Kinston, a Confederate soldier wrote novellas between raids. Panicked Confederates near Greenville fled one dark, desperate night, terrified by a troop of cows relentlessly munching its way across the countryside.

As the war raged on and Southern ports fell, Wilmington's blockade runners became critical to the South's survival. Wilmington finally toppled in February 1865. Although the Battle of Bentonville lay dead ahead, the outcome of the war was now certain. Gen. Robert E. Lee surrendered at Appomattox Courthouse on April 8, 1865.

For North Carolina, the loss of life was staggering. Of 125,000 men who marched off to war, 40,000 died. Across the coastal plain, homes, businesses, and towns stood vacant or in ruins, and the region's economy lay in shreds.

■ FROM ASHES TO TOBACCO

A new cash crop, flue-cured tobacco, paved the way for the coastal plain's recovery. Ex-slaves became sharecroppers, splitting profits with landowners, who provided capital for their joint venture.

World War II brought massive military bases to the plain, jump-starting economies in Jacksonville, Havelock, and Goldsboro. Wilmington's shipyards sent hundreds of vessels to war, and thousands of dollars into local pockets.

Mullet Haul *by Claude Howell, 1947.*
(St. John's Museum of Art, Wilmington)

Around the same time, refrigeration helped turn quiet fishing villages into commercial fishing centers. Fleets of blunt-faced shrimp boats soon churned regularly to sea, pulling tons of shrimp and fish from the waters, and shipping them inland. Crab and oyster houses proliferated, and dockside restaurants opened, scooping fresh seafood from boat, to kitchen, to plates.

■ LIFE ON THE PLAIN

■ SMALL TALK

As you drive across the plain you'll find that small towns don't work like little cities. In small towns, people still stop when the traffic light turns yellow, inquire after everyone's well-being, and say "good morning" to strangers.

Conversation remains an art, especially among older people. Strangers may serenely ask your mother's name, where your home is, exactly why you left, and when you're going back. If you are not a lucky person, they may also explain their medical concerns.

Decoy carver Curt Salter in his workshop in the Core Sound area of Harkers Island.

If you answer politely, they'll invite you to their town festival, church supper, or community fish fry. This is their way of passing the time, fueling conversations that will take place long after you've left, and creating a history that includes you.

You can guess a small town's age by looking through its eyes. The oldest look across water —usually a river, but occasionally a sound. Most colonial-era towns have a Front Street or Water Street lined with its oldest, grandest architecture. Here sea captains' and merchants' towering old homes sport widow's walks and shady porches. Moss-gentled brick

DOWN-HOME COOKING, 1930S STYLE

*I*n the late eighteenth century a traveler, lost in the wilds of North Carolina, was hospitably received at a farmhouse. "Here," he records in his diary, "I found a large table loaded with fat roasted turkeys, geese and ducks, boiled fowls, large hams, hung-beef, barbecued pig etc. enough for five-and-twenty men."

[Even today] chicken salad, chicken pie, chicken and dumplings, chicken hash, and smothered chicken delight the Southern palate.

Every North Carolinian thinks, too, that country-cured hams are among the finest foods. They are fried and served with red gravy; or they are boiled or baked. The fat pork that is fried or used for seasoning boiled vegetables is called fat back, salt pork, side meat, middlin' meat, or sowbelly.

Dear to the heart and the health of every Southerner are the greens or "sallet," turnip, mustard, poke, and water cress, or "creases" according to the section from which one comes. A "mess of turnip sallet" boiled with hog jowl or fat meat is a common dish. It is always considered best when cooked in an iron kettle. The "pot likker," made famous in plantation days, is the juice left in the pot after the greens have been removed. Corn meal dumplings, generally called "dodgers," are some times cooked in the pot liquor. . . .

Barbecues, so popular and common throughout the State, are a relic of the old open-fire cooking. Whole pigs and often lambs, chickens, and cuts of beef are cooked over live coals. They are basted frequently with a special highly seasoned sauce, called barbecue sauce. Brunswick stew, often cooked out-of-doors to serve community groups, is a thick stew usually made of chicken, butter beans, onion, corn, and tomatoes, and seasoned with salt pork. Fish muddle, a typical eastern Carolina dish, is made by putting several kinds of fish in a kettle with layers of onions and potatoes, seasoning with fried fat meat, adding water to cover, and cooking to a stew. "Brush roasts," or oysters cooked on a wire netting over an open wood fire, are a popular out-of-doors shore meal. The oysters are served with bowls of melted butter, chow-chow, and plain corn bread.

—WPA Guide to North Carolina, 1930s.

churches wrap protective, wrought-iron arms around the cemetery and church yard, and old wharves dream of tall ships.

Away from the rivers, the small trade towns founded in the late 1700s or early 1800s face a Main Street. The older neighborhoods, the homes of tobacco families and merchants, will be a block or so off Main Street, whose business has probably slunk away to an ugly little mall at the edge of town.

Finally, towns that sat up and dusted themselves off in the mid-19th century tend to be railroad towns. Often, the railroad bisects Main Street, which may be called Railroad Street. These towns have a curious Old West feel, thanks to their low, blocky, up-in-a-heartbeat architecture. The town depot may now be a museum, or meeting hall. The town's largest houses will tell you who owned the hardware store, and who profited from the railroad.

Almost every town's main street includes a hardware store, and cafe. Cafe patrons arrive in shifts. Early risers bounce in at 7 AM to bond over ham biscuits; the Rotary Club saunters in for coffee at 8; the bridge club sachets in at 10, etc.

If you order coffee you have two choices: decaf or regular. By the standards of much of America, they are weakly brewed. (In eastern North Carolina, "espresso" means a fast train to Mexico.) Tea is syrup-sweet and iced if you don't say otherwise. If it's midday, try the lunch or dinner special. If it's dark outside, say, "what's for supper?"

These small town cafes are the most direct route to small town life. In many cases, they're also the easiest way to find out who's got the key to the local museum.

■ ALL THOSE CHURCHES

First-time visitors to eastern Carolina are always bowled over by the number of churches. It's not unusual to find towns of 5,000 souls with access to 15 or 20 area churches, all of them Protestant. This wasn't always so.

Anglican missionaries visited North Carolina in the early 1700s, hoping to save the colony's collective soul if they could find it. They couldn't.

Reverend John Blair proclaimed the colony "the most barbarous place on the Continent," and fled. Over the next few decades, Anglican ministers looked forward to a stint in Carolina like they looked forward to a season in hell. Eventually, independent-minded Tar Heels aligned themselves with "dissenting sects"—Quakers, Methodists, and Baptists. Anglican missionaries heaved a sigh of relief and sallied forth to other continents in search of cannibals.

Barbara Stephens selling tickets to a church lunch at the
First Presbyterian Church, built in 1822, in New Bern.

Today, churches dating from the 1700s onward dot the countryside. Some are imposing red brick structures, built to claim a New World. Some are light, graceful creatures with wooden steeples singing to the sky. Others are as plain-faced and determined as cinderblocks.

Churches remain the social heart of this conservative region, with Baptists filling a quarter of their pews.

Every small town has a Church Street lined with old, established churches. On it, you'll find a Baptist church (or two), a Methodist church, and perhaps a Presbyterian, Disciples of Christ, or Episcopalian church as well. (If not, they'll be on nearby sidestreets.) The newer evangelistic and Pentecostal churches, where the "amens" can go on for hours, tend to dwell on the outskirts of town.

The Baptist and the African Methodist Episcopalian Zion church (AME Zion) are particularly powerful influences within the African American community. In general, Baptist churches, which split and reform faster than the Red Sea, stretch like a string of glistening pearls across the countryside.

Regardless of denomination, folks take their church-going seriously. As a rule, children dress in their Sunday best and men wear the ties they opened on Father's Day. Women plot covered-dish suppers, Wednesday night means choir rehearsal, and everybody shakes hands with the preacher after the Sunday service is done.

The churches welcome visitors, and offer a clear sense of life on the Coastal Plain. Country churches, especially, provide wonderful music, from full-throttle gospel to tinny, shape-note harmonies first sung here centuries ago.

If your timing verges on the miraculous, you'll visit a church way out in the country, on a Sunday set aside for "dinner on the grounds." After church, the men will prop up a chicken wire table under the pines, and the women will drape tablecloths over it—white linen, red-and-white plastic, faded blue cotton.

Next come plates piled high with fried chicken, chicken stew, potato salad, corn bread, ham biscuits, corn cut off the cob just this morning, tomatoes and cucumbers, collards, turnips, and mustard greens. The Mississippi Mud cakes, sweet potato pies, and banana pudding loll at the end of the table, next to cups of iced tea so sweet, bees light on them.

It's not heaven, but if you like southern cooking, it's pretty darned close.

■ SEASONS

To see the plain at its best, visit in springtime when daytime temperatures hover in the low 70s, and a steady breeze ruffles the leaves of maples, gums, oaks, and poplars.

Spring announces its intentions in February with a wash of yellow daffodils and forsythia; white dogwoods lighten the woods' edges in March. In front of lopsided tenant houses, lavender and pink phlox spill from spare-tire parterres, flowing down ditchbanks. In April, as the wisteria twines its away across front porches and weaves itself between the arms of towering pines, the azaleas burst into bloom.

Spring's flowers slowly give way to summer's lush, jungle greens. In June the temperatures creep into the 90s and the humidity rises to greenhouse levels. When magnolias and gardenias perfume the air, summer's here. Afternoon thunderstorms make the highways and fields steam and shimmer, and the corn and tobacco grow so fast you can hear the leaves crackle.

Summer lasts forever on the plain, sending people oozing toward shade well into September. In October a reluctant autumn overwashes the land, quietly receding into a mild winter whose pale, flat landscape could have been rendered with a putty knife: a smooth gash of bone-colored earth, khaki sands tinted with streaks of faded clay. Pine forests the color of moss and pewter stand watch over sleeping fields; along chill rivers, sycamores in elegant silvery bark and oaks in thin coats of grey-white lichens turn their shoulders to the wind.

Winter also brings the rare, dizzying possibility of snow.

Tayloe House *by Francis Speight. (St. John's Museum of Art, Wilmington)*

TOURING THE COASTAL PLAIN

Check a road map of eastern North Carolina, and you'll find a network of two-lane blacktops spidering through swamps, pine forests, farmland, and small towns. They putter by pick-your-own strawberry fields and blueberry patches, breeze past regattas and old plantations, and weave their way to ancient cable ferries that haul cars two-at-a-time across sleepy rivers. They also lead to larger ferries that chug across broader rivers, and across the sounds to the Outer Banks. To really get a sense for life in the Coastal Plain, venture onto these small highways from time to time.

❖

In this chapter we've described three regions of the Coastal Plain and given you a number of suggestions for access routes, but obviously there are endless variations to these trips. A fourth region of the plain, the Sandhills, is described in a separate chapter *(see pages 232-241).*

Coastal Plain: North

Described on pages 96–110. Most visitors come to this area by driving south from Virginia, or because they are swinging west from the Outer Banks. We've described a loop, which the traveler may want to access in a number of different places, depending upon the direction being traveled. This northern section of the plain is known for its colonial-era river ports and political centers, plantations, and natural areas.

Coastal Plain: Central

Described on pages 110 to 137, this region includes the tobacco growing areas east of Interstate 95 as well as the towns and natural areas that curve around the coast of Pamlico Sound. If you visit the northern Coastal Plain first, you may wish to simply continue the S curve around the sounds. Many will take the ferry from Cedar Island on Pamlico Sound to Ocracoke Island, described in the "OUTER BANKS" chapter.

Coastal Plain: South

Described on pages 137–153, this area includes inland farm areas, Wilmington, and nearby islands. Most people traveling to Wilmington from Raleigh will take I-40 directly southeast, but there are many interesting sights and lovely drives along the way. Assuming you'll take I-40 directly to Wilmington, we begin there, then take you back to I-95 along a back-country route.

Inner Coastal Plain

For the Coastal Plain area west of I-95, including Pinehurst and Fayetteville, see "SANDHILLS" pages 232 to 241.

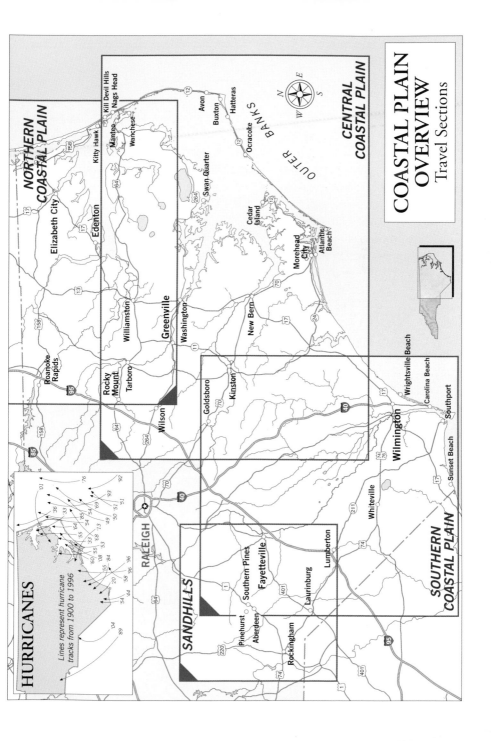

COASTAL PLAIN OVERVIEW
Travel Sections

NORTHERN COASTAL PLAIN

CENTRAL COASTAL PLAIN

SOUTHERN COASTAL PLAIN

SANDHILLS

OUTER BANKS

HURRICANES

Lines represent hurricane tracks from 1900 to 1996

Elizabeth City
Kitty Hawk
Kill Devil Hills
Nags Head
Manteo
Wanchese
Edenton
Avon
Buxton
Hatteras
Ocracoke
Swan Quarter
Cedar Island
Atlantic Beach
Morehead City
New Bern
Washington
Greenville
Williamston
Tarboro
Rocky Mount
Wilson
Roanoke Rapids
Goldsboro
Kinston
Wilmington
Wrightsville Beach
Carolina Beach
Southport
Sunset Beach
Whiteville
Lumberton
Laurinburg
Rockingham
Aberdeen
Pinehurst
Southern Pines
Fayetteville
RALEIGH

■ COASTAL PLAIN: NORTH

The northern plain gave rise to North Carolina's earliest river ports and political centers, and to massive plantations wrested from the Great Dismal Swamp's slippery grip. Today, this region is noted for river towns where 18th-century sea captains' white houses face each other across shady streets. It's also know for its natural areas, and the occasional red wolf and moonshiner.

🚗 GETTING THERE

The northern plain can be visited via a leisurely, counterclockwise loop of small highways that wind through small towns, cypress swamps, and farmlands. If you

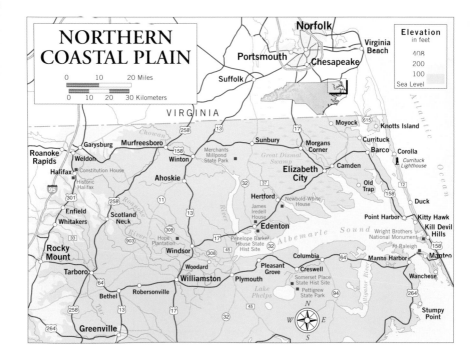

approach from the west you can access that loop at Halifax, near I-95, or by traveling US 158, which wanders east through the northern counties to Elizabeth City.

But most visitors come onto the northern plain as its first settlers did: from the Outer Banks taking NC 64 east from Roanoke Island, and then swinging north on NC 32 toward Edenton; or they travel; south from Virginia on US 17. For this reason we begin the loop in the east at Edenton, the cultural and historic heart of the region.

The Outer Banks lie east of the northern plain towns. From Elizabeth City, US 158 slips down the coast and onto the Banks, heading south to Kitty Hawk and Nags Head.

From the southern shore of the Albemarle Sound, NC 64 heads east to Roanoke Island, then on to the Outer Banks.

Edenton sits near the mouth of the Chowan River near the intersection of US 17 and NC 32.

■ EDENTON

Edenton's character reflects Tidewater Virginia's, thanks both to proximity and family ties. With its generous houses, cannon-guarded Courthouse Greens, wharves, and access to English and West Indies trade items, colonial Edenton quickly became the most graceful town in the region.

It still is.

As North Carolina's first seat of government, Edenton has been home to governors, revolutionaries, a Supreme Court Justice, and more lawyers than you could pound a gavel at.

As you drive into this small town (pop. 5,000), head south on Broad Street and park down by the water beneath the trees. Before you will be Edenton Bay at the outlet of the Chowan River into the Albemarle Sound—a broad body of water whose expression is as changeable as a three-year-old's. Here in 1774, at the white-clapboard, green-shuttered Barker House facing the water, Penelope Barker and friends drew up a petition supporting the Continental Congress and swearing off

PENELOPE'S LETTER

In the mid-1700s, as revolutionary fervor ran high in the American colonies, provincial deputies in North Carolina voiced their displeasure at British taxes. One sent the following letter to England.

*T*he Provincial Deputies of North Carolina having resolved *not* to drink any more *tea,* nor wear any more British cloth, etc. many ladies of this Province have determined to give a memorable proof of their patriotism, and have accordingly entered into the following honourable and spirited association. I send it to you, to shew your fair countrywomen, how zealously and faithfully American ladies follow the laudable example of their husbands, and what opposition your Ministers may expect to receive from a people thus firmly united against them.

(The association referred to was that formed at the home of Mrs. Penelope Barker of Edenton, when she and a group of women signed a document supporting the deputies' position.)

EDENTON, NORTH CAROLINA, OCTOBER 25, 1774
As we cannot be indifferent on any occasion that appears nearly to affect the peace and happiness of our country. . . it is a duty which we owe, not only to our near and dear connections who have concurred in them, but to ourselves who are essentially interested in their welfare, to do everything as far as lies in our power to testify our sincere adherence to the same; and we do therefore accordingly subscribe this paper, as a witness of our fixed intention and solemn determination to do so.
–[signed by Penelope Barker and her guests]

Penelope Barker

British papers—getting wind of the patriotism of Edenton ladies, satirized them. In this caricature, two women guzzle a bowl of booze, Penelope flirts shamelessly, and a mother ignores her child.

A century later patriots sanitized the illustration and published a drawing more appropriate for Victorian sensibilities. In this picture, the child sits dutifully under the table, and the women around the table appear more refined, in dress, hair, and posture.

(All illustrations courtesy of North Carolina Collection)

Penelope Barker's house in Edenton.

British tea. Around four dozen women signed the document; some, two or three times.

From Penelope's, where the mallards preen at water's edge, you can walk around the corner and along the bay, to the grassy, cannon-guarded town green. At the far end, facing down toward the water is the stately **Chowan County Courthouse**, built in 1767. Edenton, which was spared major destruction during both the Revolution and Civil War, has a graceful collection of West Indies–influenced architecture, and a number of these glistening white houses with porches and porticos face each other across the wide, sycamore-shaded green.

Old neighborhoods include numerous points of historical interest, plus an anachronistic lighthouse deposited on the waterfront by a salvager, who paid around $10 for his treasure. Many homes cluster near the waterfront and those of historic interest are clearly marked. On Broad Street a block above Penelope Barker's home is the **Cupola House**—built in 1758, and the nation's best example of Jacobean architecture. A few blocks further up Broad is **St. Paul's Episcopal Church**, chartered in 1701. Across the street at the **visitors center** (108 North Broad), pick up a self-guided walking tour.

Escaped slave Harriet Jacobs hid in an Edenton attic for seven years before finally eluding her obsessed master. Jacobs, who escaped through the Dismal Swamp, penned *Incidents in the Life of a Slave Girl, Written by Herself.* To make reservations for the privately offered Harriet Jacobs's Edenton tour, call *252-482-7981.*

Today, Edenton is a comfortable, hospitable town well situated for people who want to explore the countryside. Many old homes on Queen Street and Broad Street have become B&Bs; several offer cruises onto the Chowan River and Albemarle Sound, and beyond. The Waverly House, on Broad Street a block from the bay, is a popular dinner spot.

❖

From Edenton, NC 32 heads north toward Merchants Millpond, while US 17 crosses the broad Chowan River (where the Chowanoke Indians once scooped herring from the rivers in baskets) and heads east for Hertford and Elizabeth City.

❖

The 1685 **Newbold-White House** is about a mile south of Hertford on US 17. She may not look like much, but history has her back to you. The state's oldest dwelling faces the river. Joseph Scott, a Quaker, built this medieval hall–style house to outlast time. Its 18-inch walls contain many original bricks. Inside, the restored, furnished house wears the same cypress paneling and floorboards the colony's earliest Assembly members knew. Until 1704, this house doubled as the colony's Assembly House. Take the guided tour.

Restored kitchen in the Newbold-White House.

■ HERTFORD

Hertford is one river town you can see at its best from the highway, if you choose the right highway. Come in on NC 37 which snakes across the broad Perquimans River and over The Iron Bridge. The town's comfortable, white houses with their roses and pink azaleas stand at ease along the river.

Founded in 1758, Hertford is as placid as the river whose bank it occupies. Where trade ships once unloaded, fishermen now row flat-bottomed boats among old pilings, idly wetting a line in the Perquimans River. (The women here swear Perquimans means "land of beautiful women." It's best to agree.)

Pick up information on Hertford's walking tour at the visitors center, on Front Street (you'll see it as you drive through town). It includes 25 in-town sites, among them a pale yellow 1825 county courthouse.

Across the street is a great used-book store, the Bibliopath, whose neatly labeled shelves include the category, The Generally Ineffable. Front Street's public pier, where water lilies crowd the shore, makes a good reading spot. An even better idea for a lazy afternoon: bring along a picnic and a boat.

Hertford is home to Catfish Hunter, who pitched the Oakland As and New York Yankees to World Series titles.

🚙 Heading inland between Hertford and Elizabeth City, US 17 stretches west across vast, flat soybean and peanut fields edged in maples, gums, and pines. **Elizabeth City** is named for a settler who built her house here in the late 1600s. A small university and traffic on the Intracoastal Waterway have tugged this little town into modern life.

❖

🚙 From Elizabeth City, US 158 heads northeast to Barco. A left takes you to Currituck and the free ferry to Knotts Island; a right takes you through the small towns along the peninsula to Point Harbor, and across the Currituck Sound to Kitty Hawk and Nags Head *(see page 56)*. Heading north on US 17 towards the Virginia border, you encounter the Great Dismal Swamp.

■ GREAT DISMAL SWAMP

Today, US 17 runs along the eastern edge of the Great Dismal Swamp—a lonely stretch of road that traces a canal initiated in part by George Washington. Dug by slaves, it drained the swampland and linked North Carolina and Virginia markets.

Virginia aristocrat William Byrd II visited the Great Dismal Swamp in 1728, labeling it a "vast Body of mire and Nastiness." George Washington saw it with different eyes, describing the half-million-acre lowland as a paradise.

Since the 1600s the Great Dismal has served as a haven for runaway slaves, outlaws, and moonshiners. Now, it's a haven of another type, welcoming birders, hikers, bicyclists, fishermen, and canoeists. In summer, black bears go berrying along the old timber access roads. Deer, bobcat, mink, river otter, raccoons, and grey and red foxes frequent the park's waterways, boardwalks, and paths. Over 200 bird species frequent the refuge, but birding is most popular in April and May, when 35 species of warblers wing in from points south.

The Dismal has seen its share of human wildlife, too, thanks to the infamous Lake Drummond Hotel which once straddled the North Carolina–Virginia border.

In this canal-side "Halfway House," Virginians honeymooned on the North Carolina side of the hotel, where marriage laws were lax, while Carolinians dueled on the Virginia side of the house. "Fugitives from justice in Virginia reposed as

Dismal Swamp Canal *by Robert Salmon (1830) depicts the infamous Lake Drummond Hotel. (Private collection)*

contentedly in the North Carolina end of the building as did North Carolina fugitives on the Virginia side," one visitor wrote.

The place appealed to Edgar Allen Poe, who is said to have penned his poem, "The Raven," there. Poet Robert Frost never stayed in the hotel, but as a heartbroken young man jilted by his first love, he did visit the Dismal, determined to hurl himself into an early grave. (Fortunately, the future poet laureate got roaring drunk in Elizabeth City instead.)

The Lake Drummond Hotel is long gone, along with many of the canals which once made the swamp accessible to loggers. But the main Dismal Swamp Canal, America's oldest man-made waterway, lives on as part of the Intracoastal Waterway.

■ MERCHANTS MILLPOND STATE PARK

What did the Great Dismal look like before the canals? From US 17, if you head west on US 158 at Morgan's Corner and drive through Sunbury, you'll see the signs for Merchants Millpond State Park. Here, buoy-marked canoe trails enter a cypress swamp in its prime.

Canoes (which you can rent here) glide across this cypress-dark water into a world where troupes of tupelo-gum stand like dancers frozen in mid-pirouette, their arms trailing stoles of Spanish moss. Millions of water lilies float delicate armadas of yellow, white, and pale pink blooms across the obsidian water. As evening falls, the tree frogs and crickets spiral their serenade through the growing darkness.

Deep in this park lies a rare, virgin tupelo–bald cypress swamp. The five-mile paddle in is worth every stroke. This ancient place, where gnarled cypress knees rise from mirror-still water and owls hunt at noon beneath a canopy of deep shade, hasn't changed since the Algonquin people paddled through in fire-hollowed canoes a thousand years ago.

Come in early spring, when the water's high and the ticks and snakes are dozing. (This section is closed in summer, when the moccasins are moody and the ticks fierce.)

Canoeists, hikers, and campers usually spot deer, otter, heron, and owls in this park. Black bears, who once lived here in shaggy throngs, shy away from humans. Likewise, bobcats and mink.

Canoeing on Merchant's Millpond.

There are two interesting travel options from Merchants Millpond. For the first, head west on US 158 and take Route 13 south to Windsor and Hope Plantation. Take the Sans Souci cable ferry *(see page 106)* across the Cashie River and continue along the southern shore of the Albemarle Sound.

For a second suggestion, see page 107.

■ HOPE PLANTATION NEAR WINDSOR

This Federal-style plantation house, home of former North Carolina governor David Stone, was almost spirited away by time, neglect, and weather. Fortunately, history-minded locals rescued it, making Hope Plantation one of the finest surprises in eastern North Carolina.

Stone finished his Princeton studies in 1778, and came home to Windsor to marry Hannah Turner. Stone, who would write four books on architecture, designed their home and built it from native pine and cypress. It eventually sheltered

Mr. and Mrs. Stone, and their 11 children. Over 100 slaves worked in the plantation's corn, wheat, and cotton fields.

Stone was elected to the North Carolina House of Commons seven times, and the U.S. Congress twice. He served two terms as North Carolina Governor, two as a U.S. Senator. But Hannah's death in 1816 brought him to his knees. On a bookcase wall the grieving widower scribbled, "O for the past gone days when I could gaze at my wife."

Their home has been refurbished from a meticulous inventory made at Stone's sudden death two years later, at age 47. (Ask about furniture made by area cabinetmakers.) The grounds include a kitchen, gardens, orchard, nature trails, and picnic grounds, and the 1763 King-Bazemore House. *Take NC 308 west of Windsor four miles, and follow signs; 252-794-3140.*

THE CABLE FERRY

To reach the Sans Souci ferry (which you can, unless the river's flooded), head south on US 17, and turn east on Woodard Road, which meanders through the countryside to the ferry landing. If the ferry's on the other side of the river, honk.

Travelers must honk their car horns to get the boatman's attention at the Sans Souci ferry.

The ferry, which transports two cars at a time during rush hour, creaks across the glass-smooth water, depositing short-cut artists on the opposite shore, where a one-lane drive bordered by cypress, ferns, and wild orchids leads to NC 308. Hang a right on NC 308, turn right at the T intersection, and you'll cross the river again as you head toward Plymouth *(see page 109).*

Once small ferries transported travelers across the rivers. Today, only the San Souci and two other cable ferries remain—all in areas so remote the state doesn't want to cough up cash for a bridge. (Parker's Ferry crosses the Meherrin River in Hertford County. On the southern plain, the Elwell–Carvers Creek Ferry crosses the Cape Fear in Bladen County.)

🚐 From Merchants Millpond, an alternative route travels west on US 158 through **Murfreesboro,** a town noted for colonial charm. Continue east through a landscape of well-tended farmland and forest to US 301, then turn south toward Halifax.

■ HISTORIC HALIFAX

Today, historic Halifax is a ghost town, its growth stifled long ago when trade began to move by railroad, and the tracks went elsewhere. But this former hotbed of Revolutionary activity is worth a stop for the expectant feel that lingers in the air, and for its growing collection of restored buildings.

In 1776, when Halifax was an important political center, ships' passengers on the upper Roanoke River made their way up the long hill, past the print shop and jail, past the marketplace where free-black and white farmers sold their produce, to a hilltop tavern where they sipped a draft, and soothed the travel from their bones. At the same time, in an attorney's office on the edge of town, revolutionists worked on a draft of the "Halifax Resolves" giving North Carolina's delegates to the Continental Congress the power to declare independence from Britain, and to create a new government.

Modern Halifax's main avenue includes a few antique and crafts shops, and a plastic-tablecloth cafe. The library's genealogy room is well-used by people tracking ancestors who headed west through Halifax in the 18th and 19th centuries.

🚐 From Halifax, take US 301 south to Whitakers, and NC 33 southeast past farmland and tiny rural communities to US 64 and Tarboro.

■ TARBORO

On Tarboro's 1760 town common, the state's oldest, an art nouveau fountain salutes 18-year-old Henry Wyatt Lawson, a Tarboro carpenter who claimed the dubious honor of being the first Confederate soldier to die in battle, inspiring half of North Carolina's Civil War slogan, "First at Bethel, Last at Appomattox."

As you enter town, persevere through newer development, and turn toward the main business district. Tarboro's 45-block historic district (roughly between Battle Avenue and St. James Street) has been the beneficiary of a thriving trade economy, a post–Civil War business boom, and a few generations of complacency. The wharves are gone but restored homes from the 1700s to early 1900s line Tarboro's streets. Even Main Street has reclaimed its early-20th-century charm.

The Historic District's National Recreation Trail begins at the **Blount-Bridgers House** on the corner of St. Andrew and Bridgers Streets, which is also the visitors center. Free guided tours run every other Saturday, spring through autumn; self-

guided tours year-round. The house displays a large collection of paintings by Hobson Pittman, who spent a harrowing childhood in the area. His work also hangs in the Metropolitan Museum of Art in New York, the Corcoran Gallery in Washington D.C., and the North Carolina Museum of Art in Raleigh.

East of Tarboro on the road to Windsor lies **Robersonville** and the wonderful folk art museum, **St. James Place Museum.** It's worth a visit.

■ PLYMOUTH

The odor hanging over this town emanates from a Weyerhaeuser pulp mill, the town's largest employer, but if you breathe through your mouth, Plymouth is not without charm. On Water Street, piers and a boardwalk line the west side of the three-block business district, where on warm weekends the public parking lot looks like a showroom for boat trailers. Over on Plywood Road, old men fish from a pier, casting into the Roanoke, whose tranquil surface belies strong currents below.

Plymouth, which armies took turns burning during the Civil War, is known for its post-war buildings and Civil War history. **Port O' Plymouth Museum** resides in the old depot in a waterfront park (turn north on Washington Street, then right on Water Street). Its exhibits include artifacts from the CSS *Albemarle.* Confederates built the ironclad in an upriver

Plymouth in 1863 as painted by Merrill G. Wheelock. (North Carolina Museum of Art, Raleigh, purchased with funds from the American Legion Auxiliary, NC chapter and the State of North Carolina.)

corn field near Halifax. Gilbert Elliott, a 19-year-old from Elizabeth City, supervised the job of collecting pots, pans, rails, and bolts to melt into iron sides for his warship.

In April, 1864, General Hoke of the Confederacy called the *Albemarle* to battle, hoping to retake Plymouth from the Union. One sailor recalled that bullets hitting her sides sounded like "pebbles against an empty barrel." The *Albemarle* wreaked havoc on Federal forces for months, but was torpedoed on October 27, 1864. Today, her bullet-riddled smokestack is displayed at the North Carolina Museum of History in Raleigh. Her nemesis, the USS *Southfield*, rests on the river bottom.

🚗 From Plymouth, US 64 leads along the southern shore of Albemarle Sound, past silos and deep green pastures, fields, and historic churches, through Roper and Pleasant Grove. NC 32 cuts north, skating across the sound back to Edenton.

■ COASTAL PLAIN: CENTRAL

🚗 GETTING THERE

From Plymouth, US 64 and US 264 follow the generous curve of the Albemarle and Pamlico Sounds into the tobacco country of the central coastal plain. *(If you plan to follow this scenic route, turn to page 116.)* Approaching the central plain from Raleigh instead, you'll drive east on US 264. On this route, you'll pass by Wilson's massive tobacco market and head toward Greenville in Pitt County, the most productive flue-cured tobacco region in the world. Approaching the central plain from North Carolina's urban centers, you'll drive east through a region of small towns and blue highways—the very beginnings of Tobacco Road.

❖

The region is sprinkled with small, **tobacco related museums;** *see page 157.*

■ GREENVILLE

If you travel into the Coastal Plain from Raleigh, you'll probably drive through Greenville, the home of East Carolina University, and a regional educational and medical center. It's also the seat of Pitt County, which grows more bright-leaf tobacco than any other comparable region in the world.

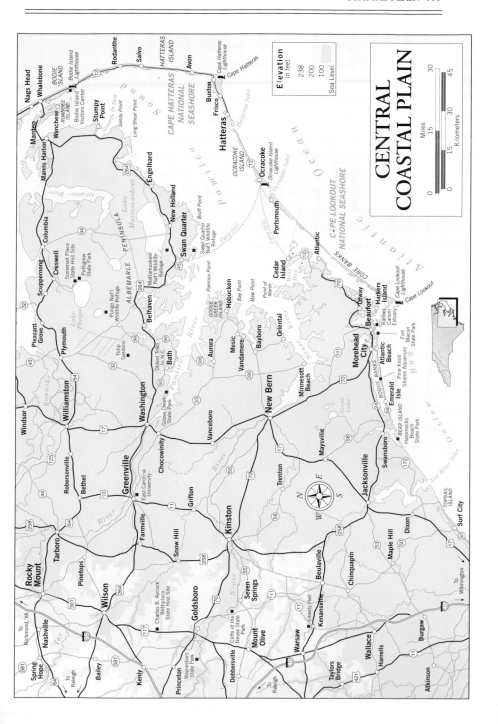

CENTRAL COASTAL PLAIN

Elevation
in feet

238
200
100

Sea Level

Miles
0   15   30

Kilometers
0   15   30   45

In late summer, tobacco's warm, rich odor still blankets parts of this small, fast-growing city. The Pitt-Greenville visitors bureau will help you locate tobacco auctions during market season, roughly July through mid-October; *252-752-8044.*

If you drift about on your own, you'll find the older warehouses downtown, and newer ones across the Tar River. (If you get lost, roll your window down and inhale, or follow the loose leaves scattered along the road.)

Inside the warehouses on market days, a procession of farmers with sun-creased faces and tobacco buyers in perma-creased slacks edge up aisles lined with mounds of tobacco, settling on a per-pound price for each pile. That staccato sound—the one that sounds like a cross between a distressed bagpipe and machine gun fire—is the auctioneer.

At midday, the market crowd heads for **Greenville's barbecue restaurants:** B's, and Parker's *(see the restaurant listings on page 336).* Purists cruise down NC 11 to Ayden's Skylight Inn—which is, depending on a visitor's mood, eastern North Carolina's most authentic/patriotic/surrealistic barbecue joint *(see page 321).*

Central Coastal Plain driving tour continues on page 116.

TOBACCO FARMS IN CENTRAL COASTAL PLAIN

As you drive through Greenville—or Farmville, Kinston, Robersonville, Smithfield, or Wilson—you'll see the massive old brick warehouses downtown, and newer ones on the outskirts of town. Between late July and early November, you'll find them filled with heady, sweet-smelling piles of tobacco.

In eastern North Carolina thousands of lives move in cadence with the tobacco seasons. In late February or early March—as soon as the fields dry from winter's grey rains—farmers shrug into heavy jackets, hitch up their discing plows, climb onto their tractors, and rumble toward slumbering fields.

If you happen to see them making their first long, patient sweeps across the earth's arched back, roll your window down. The newly broken earth fills the air with a smell as rich and full of life as December's dream of spring.

In early April, when the dogwoods bloom and the maples and sweet gums begin to hint at leaves, farmers hitch up their plows. You'll know a tobacco field when you see it, even before the plants go in. Grain fields are smooth. Corn, soybeans, and cotton like gentle rows, not too far apart. For tobacco, farmers plow the way the old Sunday School song says: Deep and Wide. They plow the furrows about a foot deep, because tobacco can't tolerate wet feet, and space the rows three feet apart to give the plants plenty of elbow room.

continues

Golden-leaf tobacco plants in flower.

Farmers transplant tobacco seedlings from greenhouses or the long tobacco beds near their homes. (Some visitors mistake these plastic-covered beds for patches of ice.)

Not long ago, "setting out 'bacca'" was backbreaking work. Workers carried baskets of seedlings up each row, bending to set each plant. Today, they ride tractor-pulled transplanters. As the tractor putters along, workers shove the plants into the earth and tamp them down, assembly-line style.

Tobacco seedlings look like young lettuce plants, and taste like bile.

They shoot skyward as the temperature rises and the rains fall in great, ragged curtains. Summer temperatures, which routinely hover in the 90s, spike to 100-plus degrees; the humidity makes the air thick enough to lean against. The coastal plain becomes a natural greenhouse. By early June, the tobacco's waist high. By late June, it tickles the chin.

continues

Once, families spent endless summer days hoeing tobacco rows, snapping suckers out of the plants, and breaking the delicate pink and white trumpet-shaped flowers that sap a plant's weight. Today, you may see a few farmers doing these chores by hand, but mostly you'll see them tooling through the fields on tractors, spraying chemicals that kill grass, reduce suckers, and stunt flowers' growth.

Around July 4, armies of local and migrant workers swarm into the fields to harvest the crop, the green leaves swishing closed behind them like living doors.

And if you stop by a country store during the grey winter months, you're sure to find a farmer who's cruised over in his new king-cab pickup truck to drink a "Co-cola" and lament the weather, crops, and luck that have brought him to the brink of ruin. These winter lamentations make "putting in a crop of tobacco" a year-round endeavor.

HOMEPLACE

You won't talk long to tobacco farmers without finding out where they're from. They might say, "down home," "up home," "over home," "home," "the homeplace," or even "yonder home." No matter how they say it, they're talking about the place their family first owned or tended land.

Some farmers own thousands of acres of land, but most tobacco farms are small—300 acres or less. A farmer may have moved his family to town, but old clapboard homeplaces still stand scattered across the countryside. Some are stately old houses, crafted by artists. Some are rambling, wisteria-draped affairs. Some are solid, no-nonsense places, remodeled generation by generation to reflect changing fortunes and needs.

All were built to withstand summers that send heat ghosts shimmying along highways and across fields. Builders designed these houses' high ceilings, tall windows, and cool plaster walls to outlast August's dense, breath-taking heat.

Most old houses sport wide front porches.

Once, the front porch was the most popular summer room in the house. Young people fell in love there; mothers rocked new babies. Children played hide-and-seek in the yard, freezing statue-still behind gardenias; men sat in stiff-backed chairs and drank glasses of sugary iced tea.

Air conditioners have made porches obsolete. But in the cool of the evening, when the oak leaves rustle like crinolines and the tree frogs break out in their wild, spiraling song, "Come up on the porch," remains the friendliest greeting along Tobacco Road.

In western North Carolina, farmers hang stalks of burley tobacco in open-air sheds (such as the one pictured right), to dry. In eastern North Carolina, where farmers raise golden-leaf tobacco, workers harvest only the tobacco leaves, placing them in tight, heated barns and baking them to a rich, golden brown.

🚐 To reach the southern shores of Albemarle Sound from Greenville, travel up US 13 to US 64 and head east toward Plymouth.

■ SOUTHERN SHORE OF ALBEMARLE SOUND

US 64 runs east from Plymouth through Scuppernong and Creswell, where brown state signs point toward a majestic, cypress-lined lane which follows an old canal to **Somerset Place.** The state now preserves this vast plantation, once tended by more than 300 slaves, as a historic site. Site manager Dorothy Redford, a descendant of Somerset slaves, deserves the credit for bringing these old brick walkways, a massive canal system, and sprawling plantation house back to life with a biannual reunion of the descendants of Somerset slaves. The reunion with its exhibits and events is also open to the public; the plantation is open year-round.

Pettigrew State Park, next door to Somerset on the southern Albemarle Peninsula, is North Carolina's largest state park, covering 17,376 acres. Lake Phelps, which lazes over most of those acres, has been popular with boatmen for millennia. Researchers have found 30 Native American canoes in Lake Phelps, one more than 4,000 years old. The park, known for gentle hiking trails, is named for CSA Gen. James Pettigrew, whose plantation embraced many of these acres.

■ SCENIC DRIVE ALONG US 264

At Mann's Harbor, US 64 leapfrogs east to Roanoke Island. (To continue onto the island and the Outer Banks, *see page 54.*) US 264 drifts south and then east along southern Albemarle Peninsula on one of the prettiest drives in eastern North Carolina.

As you walk along these shores with gulls and terns reeling overhead and fiddler crabs scurrying at your feet, the mapmaker's neat distinction between land and water fades away, blurred by the ripple of a salty breeze across fields of green bulrushes, and marshlands that breathe in and out with the tides.

Once, these sounds provided fish, oysters, and shrimp for tiny Native American communities tucked along the shores. In the late 1600s, the complexion of those scattered communities changed as English settlers moved from the islands to protected harbors.

For generations, "Down East" settlers planned their days by the mood of the sea and the sky, building modest houses in the shade of oaks, and boats that danced across the water. They worked hand-tied nets, hunted ducks and geese, and—between hurricanes and nor'easters—farmed sandy fields.

Except for a few lonely ribbons of highway and a spattering of tiny towns, the character of the area hasn't changed much. Even the most dilapidated house trailers have a boat in the yard. Occasionally, you'll see a man weaving what appears to be a tapestry of sunlight between two pines. Actually, it's a fishing net of clear filament.

Red wolves, which once freely roamed eastern North Carolina, were exterminated by government-paid bounty hunters in the 18th and 19th centuries. In this century, the government has paid big to reintroduce the wolves to the wild. You may see one of these protected animals loping along the highway as you edge along the peninsula, and heading toward Lake Mattamuskeet.

The **Lake Mattamuskeet National Wildlife Refuge** centers around North Carolina's largest natural lake. Having survived man's attempts to drain it for farmland and mine it for peat, the lake still echoes in winter with the cries of trumpeter swans. In February, huge flocks of migrating geese plummet from the grey sky to ski crazily along the water's surface, first on one orange foot, and then on the other, wings extended. Waterfowl also winter at nearby **Pungo National Wildlife Refuge** and at **Swan Quarter National Wildlife Refuge,** in Hyde County.

The low-lying coastal areas of North Carolina have a serene, wild beauty.

Eel pots, crab pots, everything for the fisherman at Belhaven Commercial Fishing Supplies.

🚐 ⛴ From Swan Quarter, you can catch a toll ferry across the Pamlico Sound, to Ocracoke Island *(See "OUTER BANKS," page 70.)* or continue along US 264 to **Belhaven,** home of the hands-down most eccentric museum in North Carolina. The **Belhaven Memorial Museum,** includes every oddity the citizens of this small town ever stumbled across, from buttons to two-headed pigs to a circus of fleas.

■ BATH

The Pamtico people abandoned their home on the tip of this peninsula in the late 1600s, bequeathing their name to the Pamlico River and Sound (a corruption of Pamtico), and stepping aside for Europeans who soon made this an English port. Naturalist John Lawson helped plat the town of Bath in 1705, making it North Carolina's oldest town.

Bath's historic structures occupy a couple of shaded blocks between US 264 and the bay. The Craven Street lot Lawson earmarked for a church is home to **St. Thomas's Church.** The brick church, which rests behind a wall made of ballast stones, was built in 1734 and is the state's oldest.

Folks still stroll down to the commons John Lawson designed, to watch the sun set on the bay. A few cottages have gone up on the creek, but Bath hasn't grown much over the centuries. The log cabins Lawson knew have been replaced by grander structures now restored, open to the public, and clearly marked: the **Palmer-Marsh House** (1744), the **Van Der Veer House** (1790), and the 1830

BLACKBEARD THE PIRATE

Blackbeard, aka Edward Teach, was one of the most infamous pirates on the East Coast. After a profitable, blood-chilling career that included taking the city of Charleston hostage, Blackbeard accepted a pardon from North Carolina Governor Eden, and retired to North Carolina.

He bought a little place in Bath, on the mainland, and wooed a local girl. Mr. and Mrs. Blackbeard settled down to the good life, visiting and occasionally robbing terrified neighbors. With help from the governor's secretary, Blackbeard soon returned to piracy, setting up camp on Ocracoke.

News travels. Blackbeard's friends dropped by: Charles Vane, Calico Jack Rackham, Ann Bonney, Mary Reed, Israel Hands, Robert Deal, and an army of lesser pirates. The buccaneers "boucaned" a few pigs, uncorked a few kegs of rum, and cranked up the band.

As the pirates cavorted, Virginia's governor developed a bad case of the jitters. On November 21, 1720—long after the party fizzled, his navy struck. Lt. Robert Maynard slipped two ships into the inlet as Blackbeard drank the night away.

Maynard approached at dawn. Blackbeard toasted his damnation, and Maynard attacked. Blackbeard crippled one ship, and blasted the other.

Before the smoke could clear, Maynard sent his crew below. As Blackbeard and his pirates swarmed the gunwales, Maynard's men burst on deck, firing. Blackbeard and Maynard met face-to-face, pistols drawn. They fired; Blackbeard staggered. They drew their swords; Maynard's snapped. As Blackbeard raised his cutlass for the final blow, he was ambushed.

The *Boston News-Letter* reported: "One of Maynard's men, being a Highlander, ingaged Teach with his broadsword, who gave Teach a cut of the Neck, Teach saying well done, Lad, the Highlander reply'd, if it be not well done, I'll do it better, and with that he gave him a second stroke, which cut off his head, laying it flat on his shoulder."

Maynard sailed home with Blackbeard's head swinging from his bowsprit.

Bonner House—which Lawson might not fully appreciate, since it sits on his lot. If he plunked himself down on its wide front porch, though, he'd enjoy the view he no doubt shared with his lover, Hannah, and their daughter.

Bath was Blackbeard the pirate's home, too. His house, which sat out on the point away from his ashen-faced neighbors, has been swallowed by storms and time. Rumors of a secret tunnel and buried treasure are timeless.

When you get to Bath, stop by the **visitors center** near the bridge, Main and Carteret Streets. Their tour includes everything worth seeing. The guides, who are townsfolk, will tell you about Lawson, Blackbeard, a bored actress who wrote a Broadway smash while stuck here on a riverboat, and the Methodist minister who hexed Bath as he was being run out of town.

🚗 ⛴ From Bath, NC 92 heads west to Goose Creek State Park and Washington. Or you can backtrack a little to NC 306 and take the free ferry south, across Pamlico Sound.

■ ALONG NC 92

The sandy beaches and marshlands of **Goose Creek State Park** provide a haven for wildlife. Broad and lazy, Goose Creek feeds into the Pamlico River at the park's western boundary, offering excellent freshwater and saltwater fishing. (Take the Dinah Landing & Goose Creek Road from 92.)

Highway 92/264 continues west to **Washington,** whose historic river-front district along the Pamlico River was occupied during the Civil War. Cecil B. De-Mille's hometown also includes several 18th-century homes, a rare prefab mail-order house (ordered from the Sears catalog), and a couple of B&Bs.

■ NC 306 TO THE FERRY

From just east of Bath, NC 306 leads to a small free ferry which putters across the tree-lined Pamlico River to the **Aurora Fossil Museum.** Since the coastal plain spent eons underwater, it's no surprise that marine creatures contributed most of this museum's fossils. The highlight of this small museum's collection include the business end of a 35-foot great white shark, and a mountain of fossils out back—

most around 22 million years old. The fossils are dredged up, literally, by a local phosphate mining company. Feel free to pocket your finds.

From Aurora, NC 33 takes on different names as it loops along the undeveloped coast, heading through tiny fishing towns which are rapidly becoming retirement communities: Hobucken, Mesic, Vandamere. At Bayboro, NC 55 heads south to **Oriental**, a village named for a ship that sank off the coast. Citizens who have taken the town's name to heart celebrate the New Year by parading a snorting, prancing dragon through town, a celebration now considered the state's best New Year's Eve party. The town also hosts the Oriental Regatta.

🚗 Heading west on NC 55 from Bayboro, you'll soon cross NC 306. Turn south to catch the free Minnesott Ferry across the Neuse River to Beaufort. Continue west to New Bern, the Revolutionary War capital of North Carolina.

■ NEW BERN'S TRYON PALACE

Walking through the double, wrought-iron gates and up the shaded, brick walkway leading to Tryon Palace, you can almost hear the hollow clap of horses' hooves and the creaking carriage that brought Royal Governor William Tryon and his family to this riverside palace in 1770. (To get there, follow the signs.)

Tryon's architect placed the 38-room brick palace on a rounded point of land overlooking the Trent and Neuse Rivers. Digging deep into the colony's coffers, Tryon supplied his new home with statuary, furniture, and paintings from Europe. His wife Margaret (the brains of the family) read in the garden while their daughter played hoops on wide lawns descending to the river's edge. On the waterfront, ships pulled into the harbor, ferrying goods in and out of the prosperous town.

Tryon and his wife—charmers, both—enjoyed the support of eastern Carolina's wealthy leaders. But Tryon faced stiff opposition and then open rebellion from irate citizens in the Piedmont, who didn't fancy putting a governor in a palace when they could barely put bread on their own tables.

After battling the "Regulators" into submission, Governor Tryon wisely moved his family to New York. Now a new governor, Governor Martin, propped his feet on the palace's brocade footstools. In the eastern part of the state, Britain's popularity plunged as taxes rose.

In August 1774, colonial leaders met a few blocks from the palace to form North Carolina's First Provincial Congress. When they called a second meeting, a furious Governor Martin tried to upstage them by calling his Assembly to order. To his horror, he found his Assembly *was* the Provincial Congress: The colony's leadership had changed sides. Martin packed his wig and fled, making surprised North Carolinians the first to give a royal ruler the boot.

After the Revolution, North Carolina's capital moved west to Raleigh, leaving behind a site that is today known for its palace (rebuilt and refurbished in the 1950s), English gardens, and the thousands of tulips that bloom here each May.

Located at *610 Pollock Street at George Street, downtown; 252-514-4900*. A palace ticket includes admission to several historic homes. The Academy Museum (next door) provides the best history overview.

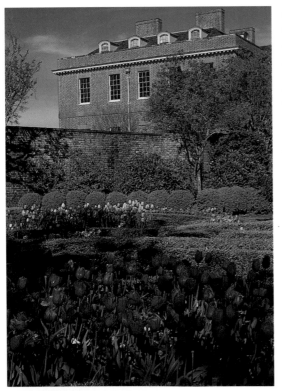

The palace's reconstruction in the 1950s set off a wave of restoration throughout this town which, along with the palace, promotes a full slate of festivals, Revolutionary War re-enactments, regattas, gardening workshops, antique shows, even a good-natured Fourth of July celebration.

Gift shops, antique shops, restaurants, and historic sites line East Front Street and neighboring avenues. River cruises are available, but be wary of activities that put you in direct contact with the polluted Neuse River.

The gardens (above) and Council Chambers (right) at Tyron Palace, which was built in 1770 for Royal Governor William Tryon and his family.

🚐 From New Bern, the most direct route to popular North Carolina beaches is US 70. It curves southeast to Morehead City, cutting through tobacco farms, pine forests edged with maples and dogwood, and roadside patches of wildflowers. As you approach Havelock, the home of Cherry Point Marine Corps Air Station, US 70 becomes a grim corridor of strip malls, pawn shops, and fast-food restaurants. Its dreariness contrasts starkly with the natural beauty of the Croatan National Forest which it bisects.

Flowering azaleas and dogwoods are a hallmark of spring throughout the South.

■ CROATAN NATIONAL FOREST

North Carolina's most famous naturalist, John Lawson, lived here in the early 1700s. Today it offers pretty much what it offered Lawson: hiking, boating, birding, and primitive camping. Several endangered species live here, including Lawson's friend, the alligator.

The Neuse River's sad condition is something Lawson would never have imagined. The water quality is very poor, thanks to pollution from upriver cities, industries, and hog farms, and run-off from coastal plains farms.

The Craven County Courthouse in New Bern.

Check with park officials before venturing onto the river; you may want to use the forest's lakes for water activities. Photographers should check out the White Oak River blind, where they'll see snowy white egrets flying with measured wing-beats through the sky, and Swansboro's fishing boats heading out to sea.

■ MOREHEAD CITY

US 70 plows straight through Morehead City, where everyone on the street may be bald. Don't let it rattle you.

Each summer, thousands of the hair-impaired from around the world flock here for the Bald is Beautiful Convention. First choice for their annual meeting site was Bald Head Island south of Wilmington, but PR people for the upscale resort nixed the notion. Morehead—more head—came in second.

From Morehead's main thoroughfare, Arendell Street, take a right on Morehead Avenue to bridge Bogue Sound and visit Atlantic Beach, Fort Macon, the Pine Knolls Shore Aquarium, etc. *(See page 131.)* The best way to find out what's going on at all of these sites is *This Week Magazine,* a free tabloid available in most restaurants and shops.

Continuing along Arendell instead of heading for the ocean, the Morehead City waterfront lies a block to your right. Here you can charter a boat for deep sea fishing or a party cruise, or catch a meal at a very casual waterfront restaurant. Sanitary Fish Market, founded in 1938, is one of the oldest, best known waterfront restaurants. The decor is 1940s chic: Formica tabletops, pine chairs, sun-darkened pine paneling, mounted barracudas and marlins on the walls. Beyond the plate glass windows, the view is softer: a sailboat glides by on sparkling water, its white sails unfurled. An egret settles on the dining room's sun-bleached pier.

North Carolina's seafood restaurants originally served everything fried: fried seafood, fried potatoes, fried bread, and slaw. Anyone who asked for a baked potato was suspect. Today, the same restaurants may specialize in fried seafood, but in deference to an influx of new tastes, most also serve seafood broiled, steamed, grilled, blackened, or gumboed. The humble hushpuppy—a golden, deep-fat-fried cornbread often flavored with onions—still occupies a lofty position on most menus.

John Capps, head of the Bald Headed Men of America Association.

🚗 Continuing east from Morehead's waterfront, you'll cross the Intracoastal Waterway. The tremendous ocean-going ships to your right have docked at the State's Port Authority.

■ BEAUFORT

After crossing the bridge, you enter the old fishing village of Beaufort, pronounced Bo'-fert. (Bu'-fert is in *South* Carolina.)

Taking an immediate right, you'll meander through a quiet neighborhood of 18th-century cottages and antique shops. Park on Front Street, which faces Bogue Sound, and walk awhile through this town of white, New England–style cottages with broad, West Indies–inspired front porches.

In the 19th century, windmills provided power at many locations along the coast including Beaufort, where this one was photographed in 1890. (NC State Dept. of Archives & History)

The main display hall at the North Carolina Maritime Museum.

The sea smells warm and close here, but as you walk down the waterfront past touristy shops and restaurants, the sharp, sweet smell of cedar slices the air. It drifts from the **Maritime Museum's Watercraft Center**, a cypress-sided barn where the museum boat-builder restores old sailing craft, and builds new ones as visitors watch from the balcony. *300 block of Front Street.*

For generations, shipbuilding has been a critical skill on the coast. Not long ago, it wasn't unusual to find ships-in-progress tucked away in backyards, their massive ribcages and sides materializing piece by piece as time permitted. (You may still see them on Harker's Island.)

Shipwrights, who traditionally scorn levels and squares, also turned their creative hands to home construction, a fact confirmed by the seaworthy angles inside many of Beaufort's old homes. (The Beaufort Historic Association's tour includes 18th- and 19th-century homes, the 1796 courthouse, an herb garden and herb cottage, and a 1858 apothecary shop and doctor's office.)

The **North Carolina Maritime Museum,** located across from the shipwright's shop, displays small boats, shells, and a spine-tingling exhibit of old-timey equip-

The Life-Car on exhibit at the North Carolina Maritime Museum was an enclosed boat formed of copper or iron in which passengers would be conveyed to the shore. When the passengers were put in, the door was bolted shut and the car was then drawn to the land, suspended by rings from a hawser which had previously been stretched from the ship to the shore.

ment used to rescue passengers from sinking ships. The museum's best activities take place outdoors: field trips to estuaries and barrier islands, wildflower hunts, seining expeditions, workshops on woodcarving, boat-building, oarmaking, etc. All require reservations. *315 Front Street; 252-728-7317.*

In the early 1700s, pirates prowled Beaufort's waters, coming ashore to take on supplies and create bedlam. Blackbeard is rumored to have arranged the murder of one of his young wives here. Divers think they've found his flagship, *The Queen Anne's Revenge,* in 20 feet of water, three miles off Beaufort Inlet.

Although Blackbeard stranded hundreds of his crewmen here, stealing their share of the loot, no known pirates rest in The Old Burying Ground, in the heart of town. Ancient live oaks veiled in Spanish moss watch over the graves of privateers, sea captains, naval heroes, and shipwrecked sailors.

Today Beaufort is a popular stop on the Intracoastal Waterway. Sailboats bob on the harbor or dock at the marinas. Anne Street's old homes include several B&Bs.

One of the most pleasant ways to view the area, including Carrot Island with its wild ponies, is to take to the sea. Tour boats depart the waterfront several times daily; other boats cater to fisherfolks, dolphin lovers, birders, and divers. You can also rent a kayak on the waterfront and explore the estuaries on your own. But if you're thinking of boarding Blackbeard's ship, forget it. It's off-limits and well patrolled.

🚗 ⛴ From Beaufort, US 70 meanders north across the rivers, tidal creeks, and saltwater marshes separating tiny coastal towns—Bettie, Otway, Williston, Sealevel—and, via NC 12, to the Cedar Island Ferry. A two-and-a-half-hour toll ferry across the Pamlico Sound takes you to **Ocracoke Island**—if you have reservations.

Call 800-BY FERRY. (For travel information on the Outer Banks see page 45. For Ocracoke Island, see pages 70-71.)

A right at Otway leads to **Harker's Island** and the **Decoy Carvers Museum.** The Down East Decoy Carver's Festival, held early each December, is eastern Carolina's best winter festival; *252-728-1500. Also see page 354.*

■ FROM CRYSTAL COAST TO CAPE FEAR

Atlantic Beach, Salter Path, and Emerald Isle were once isolated villages on a sandy strip of land known as Bogue Banks. Today, they have a catchier name: The Crystal Coast. They've almost fused into a vast, overdeveloped avenue of shops, restaurants, high-rise hotels, motels, cottages, arcades, campgrounds, and piers that cater to summer visitors and seasonal fishermen. The shore of the sound and the oceanfront both are lined with cottages usually rented by the week, but piers and public accesses allow easy access for non-renters, too.

The Bogue Fishing Pier catches the rays of sunrise in Emerald City on Bogue Banks.

🚗 You can reach the Crystal Coast's developed beaches by taking US 70 south across the bridge from Beaufort to Morehead City; follow the signs to Atlantic Beach.

■ ATLANTIC BEACH
Atlantic Beach is known for arcades, amusements, restless youth, nightclubs, and its thin public beach. In its dance clubs, you'll see men in penny loafers (no socks), chinos, and neat sports shirts dancing with women in full skirts. Women repeat a set of simple but fairly slinky steps as the men whirl around them like demon-possessed Ricky Nelsons, showing off fancy footwork while nonchalantly sipping cold beers.

This is the shag. Ultra-cool beach bums of the 1940s invented this slowed-down, slinked-up version of the Lindy so they could dance to the new music being recorded by African American artists. (In a pathetic bid for attention, Myrtle Beach, South Carolina, claims to be the birthplace of the shag. People here and at Carolina Beach, near Wilmington, can set you straight.)

If you like to dance, this is the place to learn. Sadly, you must shag to Beach Music—monotonous, depthless tunes that inspire shagging and nothing more.

Atlantic Beach likes fast food. The best seafood dwells across the bridge, in Morehead City. *(See page 126).*

🚗 From Atlantic Beach, NC 58 heads north to Fort Macon State Park, on the northern tip of Bogue Banks.

■ FORT MACON STATE PARK
This is the most visited park in the state, partly because of its public beach. But don't overlook the elegant old fort—the best preserved of North Carolina's Civil War forts.

Fort Macon, a pentagonal fort completed by civilian and slave laborers in 1834, was one of 37 forts built to protect the U.S. from a European invasion. Ironically, she never fired on foreign troops. Southern troops took the fort early in the Civil War, and Union forces reclaimed it a few weeks later.

Tours of this intricately restored fort take you over a moat and through cool, shaded tunnels to a parade yard. Gracefully curving stone stairs lead to walls over-looking what was once a cratered battle scene—now a peaceful beach.

An interior hallway in Fort Macon, a Civil War fort.

The fort's restorations reflect the Civil War and World War II, when African American troops served here.

Fort Macon's 389-acre preserve includes a nature trail and public beach. A jetty designed by Robert E. Lee protects the family beach. Bring a picnic.

■ AQUARIUM AT PINE KNOLL SHORES

If you double back on NC 58, you'll find the North Carolina Aquarium at Pine Knoll Shores near Salter Path. This aquarium puts you at eye level with the creatures of the central coast: morays, octopuses, pinfish, a queen triggerfish. In the 3,500-gallon tank along the front wall, you'll find game fish—red drum, grouper, carvel jack, black drum, snapper, and cobia, to name a few. Tropicals, which visit the central reefs in the summer, glow in a warmer tank. The aquarium also offers field trips and crafts classes for kids.

Three fishermen display a loggerhead turtle caught near Cape Lookout in 1908. Turtles were captured for their meat in the late 19th century, although the loggerhead was not favored for eating. Now endangered, they continue to nest in small numbers on the Outer Banks. Hatchlings may be observed in the North Carolina Aquarium at Pine Knoll Shores near Atlantic Beach. (North Carolina Maritime Museum)

Toward the southern end of Bogue Banks, NC 58 passes through several old fishing villages newly fitted up with beach cottages, condominiums, jet ski rentals, etc. A regional beach access near Indian Beach leads through tall oat-covered dunes to a shell-strewn beach where fiddler crabs and sandpipers dance along the shore. These are family beaches. Toddlers chase the waves out and shriek as the waves roll back in. Young people parade along the beach, studiously ignoring the fishermen who roll their pants legs up to wade into the surf, cast, and back up toward listing lawn chairs.

Most of the beach access is private (and the cottages rentable), but public accesses are scattered along the shore. The piers offer good access, too. For the price of a pier pass, you can park all day, stroll the pier, see what's biting, swim on the beach, sun, or mosey up and down the beach. (All land below the high tide mark is public land.) You can also eat an inexpensive lunch at the pier's grill.

❖

South of Emerald Isle, irregularly shaped islands cluster near the shore like strewn pieces of a giant jigsaw puzzle. No island highway stitches these islands together. Some are accessible by mainland bridges, some only by boat. Many are privately owned.

■ HAMMOCKS BEACH AND BEAR ISLAND
You can reach Hammocks Beach from Swansboro, a still-quiet fishing village at the mouth of the White Oak River. White Oak Bistro is a good place for lunch. From Swansboro follow the signs to Hammocks Beach and Bear Island

One of the most peaceful, unaltered islands in the state, Bear Island, which is accessible by ferry, is a paradise for swimmers and waders, who come for the shells. Campers pitch tents on primitive sites for 14 days at a stretch. There are, by the way, no bears on Bear Island. The island took its name from the Bear River, which exits mainland Onslow County near here. Historically, bruins were plentiful in Onslow County's lowlands.

South of Bear Island, on islands owned by the Camp Lejeune Marine Base, the term "shelling" takes on a whole new meaning. Avoid these islands: Some are used for live-fire drills.

■ TOPSAIL ISLAND
Southwest from the base, 20-mile-long Topsail Island is still recovering from Hurricane Fran.

COASTAL PLAIN CENTRAL & TOPSAIL ISLAND

Sunrise over Wright Beach south of Topsail Island.

For years, this island had a past so secret, it had no history at all. All it had was rumors of a secret rocket project and unexplained buildings: squat cement towers, a blast-proof warehouse, and the Jolly Roger Motel whose linen closet looked suspiciously like a bomb shelter and whose patio could double for a launch pad. Inquiries concerning the rocket project received a curt reply from the National Archives: "There is no evidence any such rocket program ever existed."

Recently declassified documents reveal the island was part of the Navy's secret program to develop a supersonic, jet-powered missile. In 1947 and 1948, some 200 two-stage experimental rockets were built there and blasted into the sky as technicians tracked them from the island's towers. Today, the Navy's "explosion-proof assembly shop" is a museum dedicated to "Operation Bumblebee," which led to the creation of jet engines and the Navy's first guided missiles.

A couple of blocks away, the Jolly Roger's 1950s-style rooms, pier, and launch pad/patio are popular with those who appreciate a cheerfully unfashionable beach with an uncluttered beachfront and gentle waves.

■ COASTAL PLAIN: SOUTH

🚗 GETTING THERE

Most people traveling to this region from the Raleigh area take I-40 straight to Wilmington. The country roads are worth traveling if you have the time—and we take you from Wilmington back to I-95 along one such route *(page 150)*. Wilmington and the southern coast are also reached by driving south from Morehead City.

❖

This area has only one true city, Wilmington, which sits low on the banks of the Cape Fear River, about 28 miles from the river's mouth. For the most part, though, this area is not urban, but is a place of vacation beaches, tiny farming communities, swamps, and "mysterious" Carolina bays.

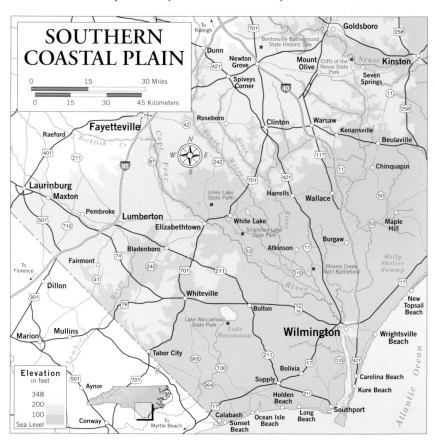

Wilmington is a latecomer, as river cities go. Europeans first sailed up the Cape Fear River in 1524, recording a fair climate, fruitful countryside, teeming waters, and friendly natives. After several settlements failed, including one by Barbadoans (who retreated to found Charleston, South Carolina), the low lands along this powerful red-brown river remained Indian territory for almost 200 years longer. The Waccamaw and other native people fled after the Tuscarora War, and rice planters moved in.

Wealthy planters founded Brunswick Town in 1725 near the mouth of the river. Hurricanes and marauding Spaniards soon sent merchants upriver to a more protected site, today's Wilmington.

From the beginning, rice cultivation suited the Cape Fear's landscape. Planters used sprawling natural lakes and lagoons to flood vast rice fields, and built docks and warehouses, turning creeping, reed-edged waterways into highways of commerce as they transported rice to Wilmington's wharves and beyond.

Rice cultivation was backbreaking work. In 100-degree temperatures and 98-percent humidity, it was probably heartbreaking as well. Slaves tilled the fields, sowed the crop by hand, harvested it with sickles, threshed it, and polished the rice with mortars and pestles. Janet Schaw, who visited in 1775, wrote, "the labor required for [rice] is only for slaves, and I think the hardest work I have seen them engaged in." As fortunes along the Cape Fear grew, so did the need for strong backs. By 1860, 60 percent of the area's population was enslaved; Wilmington's slave market was one of the state's largest.

As rice plantations prospered, Wilmington flourished. The railroad gave the city a second boost in the mid-1800s. Until the early 1900s, Wilmington was North Carolina's largest city.

During the Civil War, Wilmington became a critical Confederate port. Six forts guarded the 28-mile channel into the city, creating a deadly gauntlet for Federal ships, which blockaded the city in July of 1861. Thanks to Frying Pan Shoals, a lethal kaleidoscope of sandbars curving seaward from the Cape Fear River, Union ships were forced to patrol a 50-mile arc into the ocean, allowing blockade runners a chance to slip into the darkened port.

During the war, blockade runners snuck $65 million worth of goods into the city. Most went to the military, but in true Rhett Butler style, blockade runners also risked their lives to sneak parasols, hoopskirts, silks, and calicos past Federal ships. According to one witness, 260 blockade runners visited Wilmington between May 1863 and December 1864.

By 1864, the city was the only Southern port that hadn't been shelled into submission. Now half the food for Lee's army came through Wilmington, and Lee warned that if the forts protecting Wilmington fell, he would have to abandon Richmond.

Union forces struck on Christmas Eve, 1864. Fort Fisher fell on 15 January 1865 during the largest land-sea battle ever fought in the U.S. The tide had turned. Wilmington's protectors toppled one by one. On 22 February 1865, Mayor John Dawson surrendered the city, saving it from total destruction. Still, Union soldiers torched the 60-some-odd plantations along the river. Only Orton Plantation, which the Union used as a hospital, survived.

After the war, the rise of the textile and tobacco cities in the Piedmont signaled Wilmington's fall from the ranks of North Carolina's most populous cities. The city is still an important international port. Once, tall-masted sailing rigs and schooners glided up the channel to Wilmington's docks. Today, modern container ships nudge the 6,000-foot concrete wharf, and giant cranes dominate the landscape.

A ferry transports a carriage across the Cape Fear River in the port of Wilmington, probably around the turn of the 19th century. (Special Collections Library, Duke University)

◼ WILMINGTON

Modern Wilmington is noted for white sand beaches, historic sites, and a restored waterfront of restaurants, clubs, shops, and museums. The city's 200-block historic district, the state's largest, includes the Burgwin-Wright House, which was briefly Lord Cornwallis's headquarters during the last gasp of the Revolution; Bellamy Mansion; an 1858 theater called Thalian Hall; and shaded Victorian neighborhoods. (You'll find B&B's scattered throughout the historic district, too.)

The beaches are the number one attraction in Michael Jordan's hometown. New Hanover County maintains nearly 100 public access sites along the shoreline. Some have showers, restrooms, and lifeguards; others are dune crossovers. Look for the orange and blue signs.

Fishing piers, which hurricanes regularly shorten and owners regularly extend, also dot the coast, providing additional beach access. In spring and fall, when the blues, spots, and king mackerels run, fishermen cast elbow-to-elbow along these rails. Wilmington, home of the Azalea Festival, is prettiest in April, when banks of azaleas brighten shady parks and yards.

Feeding pigeons at Riverwalk during the annual Azalea Festival in Wilmington.

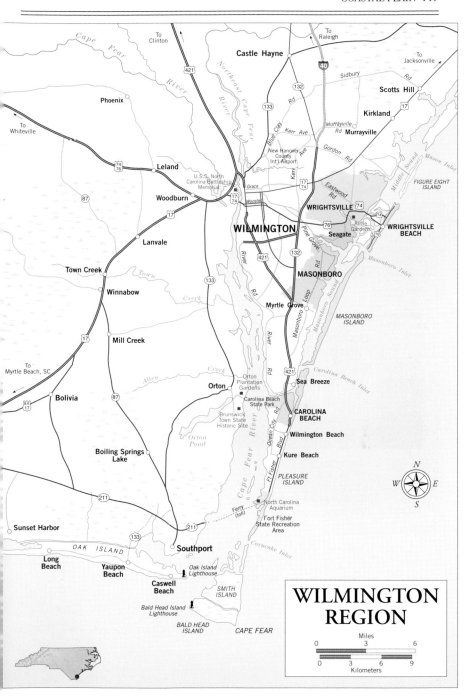

WILMINGTON
REGION

Miles
0   3   6

0   3   6   9
Kilometers

■ WILMINGTON HIGHLIGHTS ■

The eight or nine waterfront blocks between Chandler's Wharf and the Cotton Exchange are the place to go for shops, cafes, and nightlife. Seafood is the specialty at most Wilmington restaurants.

Chandler's Wharf

This two-block restored ship-chandlers' district on Water Street has shops, and restaurants serving Lower Cape Fear cuisine. *From US 17 or I-40 take the Downtown exit, and follow Market to Water Street.*

CHANDLER'S WHARF

The red-and-white tugboats you see a ways upriver are going to the North Carolina State Ports Facility, which links Wilmington with over 200 ports worldwide, exporting tobacco, textiles, and wood products. Reserve port tours at *910-343-6333.*

Riverfront Park

This is the place to catch a narrated riverboat tour up the Cape Fear, or an inexpensive taxi ride to the battleship USS *North Carolina. Located on Water Street at Market Street.*

NEW HANOVER COUNTY COURTHOUSE

Cotton Exchange

This well-preserved old exchange now houses over 30 specialty shops and restaurants. *On Water Street between Grace and Walnut.*

Cape Fear Museum

Offering the best overview of area history, the Cape Fear Museum has many lively exhibits and a tremendous collection of Civil War artifacts from the old Blockade Runner Museum. The Michael Jordan Discovery Room has exhibits designed specifically for children. *814 Market Street; 910-341-4350.*

Thalian Hall

Lillian Russell, Oscar Wilde, and Buffalo Bill Cody once performed at this gilded

WILMINGTON'S HISTORIC WATERFRONT

Victorian opera house. Today, the restored arts center books jazz artists, new plays, and dance companies. *102 N. 3rd Street at Chestnut; 910-343-3660.*

St. John's Museum

St. John's specializes in works by North Carolina artists, but also includes 13 works by Mary Cassatt and other artists from all over the world. The museum is

*CASSATT PAINTING AT
ST. JOHN'S MUSEUM*

housed in three historic buildings. *114 Orange Street at Second; 910-763-0281.*

Poplar Grove Plantation

A grand plantation home where life was lived as most North Carolina planters knew it—minus the white columns and mint juleps. Costumed guides show visitors around the 1850 manor house, tenant house, kitchen, smoke house, herb cellar, and gardens. At the Cultural Arts Center, a weaver dips a skein of wool into a vat of pea-green dye, lifts it out, and hangs it on a wooden rack, where

*FRONT PARLOR
AT POPLAR GROVE*

the wool goes from pea green, to dull blue, to brilliant indigo. Craftspeople here make traditional dyes from plants in the dye garden, while weavers keep the looms humming. (Poplar Grove's restaurant is a good place for a light lunch.) *North of Wilmington along US 17.*

■ RIVER CIRCLE TOUR

Many of the area's most dramatic historic sites and finest beaches lie along a two-hour loop around Wilmington. (That's two hours driving time. The loop, which connects plantation tours, historic sites, nature walks, beaches, and gardens, could take a day or a week.)

From US 17 in Wilmington, US 421 heads north to the **Battleship** *North Carolina,* one of the most visited historic sites in the state. The sleek, World War II dreadnought, painted in the same blue-grey ocean camouflage she wore while patrolling the Pacific, looks as fit for duty today as she did as she blasted away at Japanese ships and kamikaze pilots at Okinawa.

It's enough to give Tokyo Rose a migraine. Again.

Optimistic Japanese radio announcers heralded the USS *North Carolina's* demise six times during World War II, but despite close calls, including a direct torpedo hit, the battleship took part in every major naval offensive in the Pacific. She carried out nine shore bombardments, sank a Japanese troop ship, shot down 24 aircraft, and earned 15 battle stars.

A two-hour tour, available year-round, takes you through the restored ship and puts you behind the giant guns on deck. The battleship's sound and light show, "The Immortal Showboat," which runs in summer, includes simulated air battles off Guadalcanal, the bombardment of Iwo Jima, and kamikaze attacks near Okinawa.

USS North Carolina *was one of the largest battleships of the American Pacific fleet during the Second World War and took part in every major naval offensive in the Pacific theater.*

From the battleship, NC 133 crosses the Cape Fear and heads south to **Orton Plantation,** the only Cape Fear rice plantation that survived the Civil War. In size, it is only a faint echo of the original, but that doesn't make the white-columned Greek Revival home, manicured gardens, and grounds less appealing.

Orton's 20-acre gardens take advantage of nature's backdrop of open fields, marshlands, and Spanish moss. Indigenous trees, especially cypress and live oaks, dominate the gardens, whose brick walkways wind through wisteria, camellias, palms, and thousands of annuals.

The plantation house bears little resemblance to "King" Roger

The Luola Chapel at Orton Plantation.

Moore's original 1735 home, which has been remodeled over the years. The house itself isn't open to the public, but if you saw Sissy Spacek plug her husband in *Crimes of the Heart,* you've already visited Orton.

South on NC 133 lies **Brunswick Town,** once colonial North Carolina's busiest port. As the British fled North Carolina in 1776, Cornwallis shelled the town, reducing it to rubble. Home and shop foundations remain, while the ruins of St. Philips Church, where royal governors once married (scandalously, at times), watches over Brunswick Town in ghostly splendor. A tour trail explores the town, and crosses the earthworks of Fort Anderson, a Confederate fort.

From Brunswick Town, NC 133 continues downriver toward **Southport** and the **Southport Mariner's Museum.** Southport is the antithesis of Wilmington's bustle. If you want a quiet haven, a Southport B&B is a good bet. This town is known for old sea captains' houses set back from meandering streets, in yards where oaks drip Spanish moss. It's also known for its riverfront restaurants.

■ SOUTHPORT AREA BEACHES

■ BALD HEAD ISLAND

From the Southport marina, ferries leave on the hour for Bald Head Island. If explorer Giovanni Verrazano, who discovered Bald Head Island in 1524, could see it now, the changes would make his knees buckle. Chances are, he'd land in a golf cart.

Verrazano found a wind-swept, heavily wooded island guarded by the hazardous shoals that earned Cape Fear its name. Today, he'd find golf courses, croquet greenswards, tennis courts, restaurants, shops, cottages, B&Bs and condominiums—all designed to stay in step with the island environment.

Bald Head Island Resort, which welcomes day visitors and long-term guests, occupies the southern shore of Bald Head Island, whose jutting chin is Cape Fear. Bald Head is the largest island in the Smith Island complex, which is largely owned by the state. It teems with wildlife. Across the sound Battery Island is a breeding spot for herons, egrets, and ibises. Alligators creep through the marshlands. Loggerhead turtles and green sea turtles, both protected species, return to the island every year to lay their eggs. The turtles always have the right-of-way.

(Above) A moonrise over Flora's Bluff on South Beach.
(Left) The view from the top of Old Baldy Lighthouse looks out across Bald Head Island's sprawling salt marshes and old dock.

Old Baldy, a restored 1817 lighthouse, is the state's oldest. Shifting shoals have made Old Baldy obsolete, but you can climb the tower.

■ OAK ISLAND

Below Southport, the North Carolina coast jogs west toward Oak Island's vacation communities. The family beaches on this south-facing island are very low-key. Don't let the gentle waves fool you, though: these currents can be very dangerous. **Oak Island Lighthouse,** which replaced Old Baldy, sits on the east end of this island near Fort Caswell, a Civil War fort now owned by the North Carolina Baptist Assembly. Oak Island's best public beach access lies to the west, in Long Beach.

■ SOUTH BRUNSWICK ISLANDS

At meal time, people heading in this general direction tend to veer toward **Calabash,** a small town just on this side of the South Carolina border, on US 17. Over 30 seafood restaurants line the village streets. The local seafood, which comes in daily, is cooked Calabash style: deep-fried in a thin batter, and served with hush puppies, potatoes, slaw, and tea.

Like Oak Island, the South Brunswick Islands face south. Although arcades have slipped ashore, these are some of the least developed accessible barrier islands. The first South Brunswick Island, **Holden Beach,** has fallen prey to a cluster of amusement rides, but its beach community still smacks of Ozzie and Harriet.

The second island, **Ocean Isle,** is known for its fishing. The tackle shops still outnumber the gift shops here. To reach the cottages of **Sunset Beach,** which are tucked away behind the dunes, drive across the one-lane pontoon bridge on NC 130. A boardwalk at the end of town spans the dunes, and leads to this beach, known for gentle waves and good fishing.

■ SIDE TRIPS AND FERRY RIDES

Many people leave Southport by ferry. Some cross to **Bald Head Island,** a mix of natural beauty and manmade luxury on the southern end of Smith Island. Others catch the Southport-Fort Fisher ferry across the Cape Fear to the **The North Carolina Aquarium at Fort Fisher,** which preserves examples of life from the warm Gulf Stream, notably sharks and tropical fish. Outside, four miles of little-used public beach merge with **Zeke's Island Research Reserve.** The aquarium sponsors nature walks, canoe trips, and other activities here; most require reservations.

Gnarled live oaks shade the trail to **Fort Fisher,** whose collapse signaled the death of the Confederacy. Fort Fisher fell January 15, 1865; nature is finishing the job. Two-thirds of the earthwork fort have succumbed to erosion. Free tours.

From Fort Fisher, US 421 heads north to Kure Beach and Carolina Beach on Pleasure Island. **Carolina Beach** lies about 20 minutes south of Wilmington, be-yond the water slides, Ferris wheels, and go-cart tracks. This family beach, on the ocean side of the island, includes hotels, cottages, and several public beach accesses. It's also noted for party boats, charter boats, and dinner cruises.

Carolina Beach State Park, on the western side of the manmade Pleasure Island overlooking the Cape Fear River, is one of the most biologically diverse parks in the state. Trails wind among this park's marshes, riverbank, forests, ponds and pocosins (upland swamps). But this 1,740-acre preserve is best known for its carnivorous Venus flytraps, small, bug-eating plants that live near Wilmington, and nearly nowhere else on earth. Meat-hungry sundews and pitcher plants live here, too.

North of Carolina Beach, NC 132 intersects with US 76 which cuts east to-ward **Wrightsville Beach.** Fishing tournaments and sailing events are popular on all Wilmington's beaches, but surfing is particularly popular at Wrightsville Beach. Several Intracoastal Waterway cruise ships stop at Wrightsville Beach, too.

A small yacht basin along the Intracoastal Waterway at Wrightsville Beach.

■ WILMINGTON BACK TO I-95 ALONG A COUNTRY ROUTE

As you travel this countryside: you'll drive through sandy wooded lowlands, and past still-water swamps, creeks, and geological features known as Carolina bays, unexplained oval-shaped indentations in the earth's surface.

From Wilmington go north on US 421, to NC 210 and Moore's Creek National Battlefield.

Venus flytraps are one of the botanical oddities found throughout this coastal region of the state.

■ MOORE'S CREEK NATIONAL BATTLEFIELD

When North Carolina's royal governor Josiah Martin fled Tryon Palace on the eve of the Revolution, he called for Loyalist settlers to come to his aid. A troop of 1,600 Scots met near Fayetteville and marched toward their leader, who cowered on a ship off Wilmington's shore. As the Loyalists rumbled east, two Patriot leaders watched with interest. Richard Caswell and Alexander Lillington had only 1,020 men, but they'd enlisted cunning on their side.

Today at Moore's Creek National Battlefield, an old stagecoach trail leads to their carefully chosen battlesite: the bridge over Widow Moore's Creek. The battle fought there in the wee hours of the morning, on 27 February 1776 decided the course of the Revolution in North Carolina.

The night before the battle, Caswell's men slipped across the bridge, building campfires along the bank nearest the approaching army. Other patriots dug in on the opposite bank. The Loyalists, seeing the campfires, crept near. At dawn they charged. Nobody was home.

The Patriots had crossed the bridge, taking its planks and leaving two logs for the Loyalists to cross. Undaunted, the Loyalists sprinted for the logs, which had been greased with soap and tallow. As the Loyalists plummeted into the frigid creek 20 feet below, the Patriots opened fire.

Three minutes later, the Loyalists surrendered, giving up 850 prisoners, 2,000 weapons, and $75,000 in gold. Governor Martin and the Brits, with faces as red as their coats, headed south and stayed there until the last weeks of the war.

Today the site of their defeat includes a museum, a reconstruction of the infamously slick bridge, two trails and the Heroic Woman Monument, a tribute to Mary Slocum, who tended the wounded at this battle. *Twenty miles northwest of Wilmington. Take US 421 to NC 210, head west, following National Park Service signs.*

Getting ready for a Revolutionary War reenactment at Moore's Creek National Battlefield.

 Continue west on NC 210 until it merges with NC 53 and head up the Cape Fear River.

❖

When settlers rambled ashore on the mainland in the mid-1700s they headed inland along this route, through thick pine forests surrounding unusual, spring-fed lakes. Once geologists thought the shallow, crystal "Bay Lakes" were created by meteorite showers millions of years ago, but now most believe the lakes were created by artesian springs and by winds, and are between 5,000 and 60,000 years old.

Singletary Lake State Park, known for group camping, has cabins and mess halls. If that's too primitive, try White Lake, a few miles down the road. This privately developed white sand lake is known for motel rooms, ski shows, glass-bottomed boats, and Ferris wheels. North of White Lake on NC 242, **Jones Lake State Park** provides camping, swimming, boating, hiking, and nature studies.

Continue north on NC 242 and US 421 to **Spivey's Corner,** a peaceful little community unless it's June, in which case the noise can be deafening. With reporters coming in from as far away as Australia, the Spivey's Corner Hollerin' Contest dents eardrums around the world.

Your admission fee buys you a spot in the competition but, says spokesman Ermon Godwin, Jr., if you want to win, start practicing now. "All the people that come up here and scream and yell will not be good hollerers," he cautions. "It's not like hog-calling. It's an art. The best way to do it is take an old hymn like "Amazing Grace." Hum that tune and keep building up your voice until you can be heard a half-mile away," he advises. "You have to learn to control your voice."

Hollering was once a form of communication for rural Carolinians, whose dis-

Singletary Lake State Park.

tinctive hollers let neighbors know if they were okay, or in case of an emergency. Other contests include whistling, conch-shell blowing, and fox-horn blowing. Bring a blanket or a chair, and dress for hot weather.

■ BENTONVILLE BATTLEGROUND

Common sense suggests the Civil War in North Carolina would end with the fall of Wilmington, but her largest land battle lay ahead.

As U.S. Gen. William T. Sherman scorched South Carolina and headed north, North Carolinians despaired. "The tide of the war was rolling in upon us," wrote Chapel Hill resident Cornelia Phillips Spencer in *The Last Ninety Days of the War in North Carolina.* "The smoke of burning Columbia, and of the fair villages and countless plantations that lay in the route. . . rolled slowly up our sky; and panic-stricken refugees, homeless and penniless, brought every day fresh tales of havoc and ruin."

Sherman torched Fayetteville's arsenal, on the Cape Fear River, and turned east. Meanwhile, Confederate Gen. Joseph Johnston forged a desperate plan to block Sherman's march to Richmond.

As the two armies converged on a small farm near Bentonville, the Harper family fled their two-story farmhouse. Their home, with its neat shutters and portico, sat squarely in the sites of Sherman's 60,000-man army, and Johnston's 20,000 troops. For three days, the sky over their home rained lead. The Harpers' fields—intended for corn, soy beans, and cotton—became earthworks, killing fields, and mass graves. Their house, intended to nurture a family, became a hospital, with wounded spilling across the front yard. As Sherman's reinforcements arrived, Johnston withdrew to Smithfield. Casualties for both sides numbered over 4,000.

Gen. Robert E. Lee surrendered at Appomattox Courthouse, Virginia, on April 8, 1865. Johnston surrendered to Sherman 17 days later. The war was over.

Today, the Harper House is restored as a field hospital. (The often sighted spirit in floor-length skirts may be Mrs. Harper.) The site includes a small museum, and 100 of the 6,000 acres involved in the fray. Beyond the park, 29 historical markers along the road trace the battle. The park stages re-enactments each March.

Bentonville Battleground rests east of I-40 and NC 701 and just 15 miles south of the I-95 corridor. For visitors center call 910-594-0789.

🚌 From near Bentonville Battleground, I-40 continues north to Raleigh and the northern Piedmont.

■ SMALL TOWN MUSEUMS ALONG TOBACCO ROAD EAST ■

Kinston: An Ironclad

The CSS *Neuse,* one of three Civil War ironclads on display in the nation, is the best preserved ironclad of the lot. Not bad for a ship that went to war half-dressed.

The Confederates began the CSS *Neuse* in a tiny town now known as Seven Springs. They floated her wooden hull downstream to Kinston and outfitted her with engines and half the planned-for amount of siding, since iron was very scarce.

When ship's Commander Joseph Price received orders to sneak the ship down the Neuse to help retake New Bern, the river was so low the catfish could walk across. He shoved off, and stuck fast. By the time the ship floated free the battle was lost, and he was up the river, literally.

Price sank the ship in 1865 to keep her from enemy hands.

Today, the ship's skeleton lies in state on US 70 on the west side of town. The museum is jam-packed with ship artifacts; 252-522-2091.

Charles B. Aycock Birthplace

One of the state's most famous governors was born on this typical 19th-century "pre-tobacco" farm.

The Aycock farm nestles comfortably against a slight rise, like a sleepy child against his mother's arm. Its tiny, unpainted house rests beneath generous, wide-armed oaks, and a bucket hangs over the well. Within shouting distance, a corn crib holds corn for the livestock, and sheep crowd into a barn where the Aycocks kept horses, mules, and a cow.

Charles B. Aycock was born on this Wayne County farm in 1859 to Serina and Benjamin Aycock—relatively well-to-do planters living in circumstances that would have sent Scarlet O'Hara fumbling for the smelling salts.

Serina Aycock, who couldn't read or

A Civil War naval battle at Cape Hatteras in 1861, as depicted by Currier & Ives. (North Carolina Collection)

(Previous pages) Bald cypress trees emerge like ghosts from the swamp of Lake Waccamaw, 35 miles west of Wilmington.

write, ran the farm while her husband pursued a political career. Vegetables from the garden helped feed her family. Like their neighbors, the Aycocks made their own cloth and sewed their own clothes.

As many as 13 slaves helped keep the homestead running, but Serina's nine children pitched in, too, raising cotton, food crops and corn.

North Carolina's future "Education Governor" slept in a closet-sized room off the side porch, and could count the stars through his wall.

Charles took his love of politics and oratory from his dad, a state senator. His mother instilled in him a love of education. Charles and his brothers—but not his sisters—went to school in a schoolhouse like the one on-site: hard seats and dunce's cap included.

Charles, who earned a law degree from The University of North Carolina, was elected governor in 1900. The 1,100 public schools built during his tenure offered all North Carolina children educations, for the first time.

This North Carolina State Historic Site invites guests to pitch in with the chores Charles left behind—plowing, raking, weeding, hoeing, harvesting, canning. If your timing's good, you may even get to shear a sheep.

Bypass Goldsboro on US 70 and head north on NC 117. Follow signs to Gov. Charles B. Aycock Birthplace; 919-242-5581.

Charles B. Aycock Birthplace

Kenly: Tobacco Farm Life Museum

How much difference did a tobacco economy make? Kenly's Farm Life Museum will answer that question for you. "Our main area of emphasis is 1880, when tobacco became an important cash crop to the farmers of this area, through the Great Depression Era," says Museum Director Lynn Wagner. "A main theme of our museum is then and now," she says. "People can see what the lifestyle was like, in the areas of work, school, social life, or religious life."

In addition to the main museum, a restored farmstead includes a farmhouse, separate kitchen, smokehouse, tobacco barn, milk house, and packhouse.

continues

Tobacco Farm Life Museum

The museum stages demonstrations periodically through the year, but on the fourth weekend in June, you'll see farm history revitalized. "That weekend we always have celebration activities with demonstrations, entertainment, and vendors," Wagner says.

Visitors can try their hand at what's called "tying tobacco" in some parts of Carolina, and "looping" in others. Whatever the handle, the task is the same: two people hand bunches of green tobacco to a "looper," who has tied a long piece of tobacco twine to a long tobacco stick, which sits on a rack known as a "horse."

With a flick of the wrist, the looper ties the bundle of tobacco on alternating sides of the stick. After 20 or so bundles are in place, the looper ties the end of the stick with a rodeo-style flourish, and breaks the twine. The process is slightly faster than greased lightning, as you'll see once the tobacco starts flying and the twine starts singing.

This tiring job was once performed by women who worked 10- and 12-hour days beneath tin barn shelters, and shade trees. Men worked in sweltering fields, carefully breaking ripe leaves from the plants, packing them in mule-drawn carts, and "trucking" them to the shelter, where the women and children worked.

Today, with bulk barns, these tasks are obsolete.

US 301 North. Located inside the Kenly city limits at the north end.; 919-284-3431.

Bailey: Country Doctor Museum
The Country Doctor Museum is the only museum in the nation dedicated entirely to the country doctor.

Here you can explore a restored 1857 doctor's office and an 1887 examination room—amputation kits included. The museum also exposes the mysteries of a 19th-century apothecary shop, and features an herb garden that grows more than 60 medicinal plants used in eastern North Carolina around 1900.

Herbs played an important role in medical practices then. Few doctors' offices included herb gardens, but physicians commonly hired people to collect

Country Doctor Museum

herbs, and used them to treat everything from heart flutters to lethargy.

Most plants in this garden, which was established by the North Carolina Wildflower Preservation Society, were prescribed or were widely accepted home remedies.

6629 Vance Street. Open 10-4 Tuesday through Saturday, and Sunday 2-5 PM; 919-235-4165. (Closed Christmas to New Years.)

Smithfield: Ava Gardner Museum

In 1941 Ava Gardner—who grew up in tiny Brogden, North Carolina, near Smithfield—smoldered her way off of Tobacco Road and into an MGM limousine. But long before Hollywood took note, 12-year-old Tom Banks knew Ava was a star.

In 1939, Banks teased Ava each morning as she walked by, on her way to school. One day, the future glamour girl snapped. She chased her tormentor around the corner, collared him—and planted a kiss on his red face.

For the next 50 years, Tom Banks clipped every Ava Gardner article he laid his hands on. He collected posters from her 60 movies, saved her calendars, and hoarded her magazine covers.

His collection is now the heart of the Ava Gardner Museum in Smithfield. The museum maintains a library of Ava's movies, and a gift shop.

The Ava Gardner Museum, at 205 South Third Street in downtown Smithfield, is open 1-5 PM daily; 919-934-5830.

Ava Gardner Museum

NORTHERN PIEDMONT
AND TOBACCO ROAD

THE TERM "TOBACCO ROAD" FOUND ITS GENESIS in the soft soil of coastal Carolina as colonists rolled hogsheads of tobacco to riverports, and to ships bound for England. The trail those giant barrels pressed into the earth earned the nickname, Tobacco Road.

Almost from the beginning, tobacco received mixed reviews. In the 1580s, Queen Elizabeth's courtiers tamped it into their pipes as fast as they could lay hands on it. James I despised tobacco, calling its use a "vile and stinking" custom, "loathsome to the eye, hatefull to the nose, harmfulle to the braine, dangerous to the lungs. . ."

Modern medicine sides with King James, but that doesn't mean tobacco's hazards make great conversation in North Carolina. Old habits die hard; old economies die harder. Tobacco Road has evolved into a superhighway linking North Carolina farms, sales warehouses, and manufacturers to millions of consumers worldwide.

Tobacco, raised in 89 of 100 North Carolina counties, provides one in every 11 jobs in North Carolina, putting around $6 billion a year into its citizens' pockets. Tobacco factory workers are among the best paid in the state, out-earning textile mill workers almost two to one. The tobacco industry fills government coffers, too, paying over $700 million in state and local taxes each year.

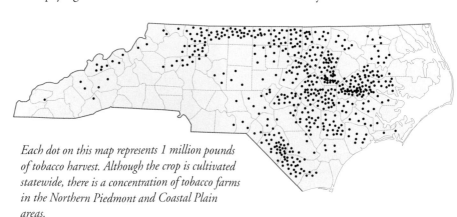

Each dot on this map represents 1 million pounds of tobacco harvest. Although the crop is cultivated statewide, there is a concentration of tobacco farms in the Northern Piedmont and Coastal Plain areas.

Workers planting black burley tobacco seedlings, a variety best suited to the Appalachian region as opposed to the golden leaf common to the lowlands.

Anytime you drive along Tobacco Road, which stretches across the central plain and through the big tobacco towns—Durham, Reidsville, and Winston-Salem—you'll witness some part of the tobacco process. Piedmont factories, of course, roll cigarettes year-round. (R. J. Reynolds in Winston-Salem offers tours.)

■ HISTORY

The bright-leaf tobacco industry came to life in Caldwell County in 1839, born of desperation and good fortune.

On this particular summer night, the story goes, an 18-year-old slave named Stephen sat up tending a barn of tobacco on the Slade Farm. Every now and then he fed the barn's fires a little wood, pushing steady, smoky heat through the tobacco-filled barn—enough heat to "cure" the tobacco; not enough to set the drying leaves on fire.

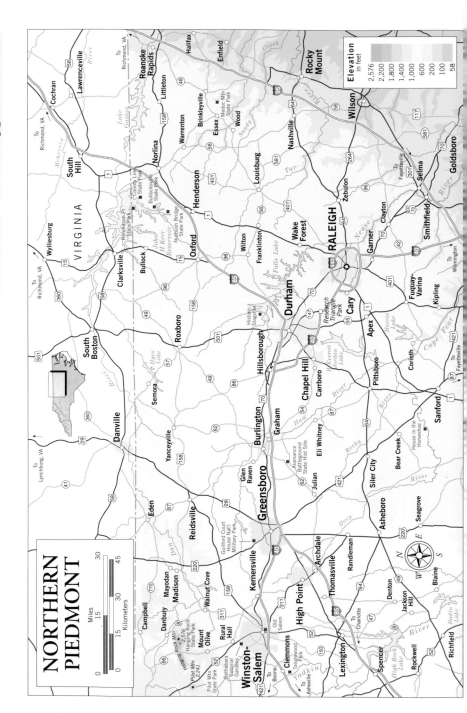

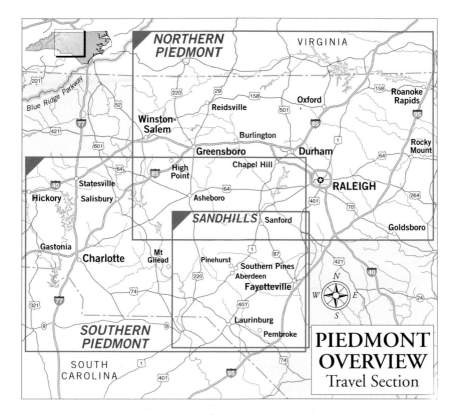

As the moon wandered in and out among the clouds, he might have talked with a girl who happened by, or hummed a tune, or shouted across the field to a friend tending another barn.

On this night, they say, he did the unthinkable: He fell asleep. When the crash of thunder jolted him awake, he found his wood soaked, his barn cool, and himself in deep trouble. He grabbed the first dry fuel he could lay hands on—charcoal, from the blacksmith's store—and built a fire hot enough to curl the Devil's toenails.

The charcoal's blast baked the cool leaves golden, and replaced their bitterness with a taste smooth as butter. Stephen's accidental bright-leaf sold for 40 cents a pound in a 10-cents-a-pound market, and an industry was born.

■ ASHES TO ASHES

In April of 1865, following the Union victory at the Battle of Bentonville, U.S. General William Sherman and CSA General Joseph Johnston met midway between their battlelines to discuss peace.

The two war-weary generals sat together at a small table in the Bennets' home, seven miles from a whistle-stop called Durham Station. A clock on the unpainted wall patiently ticked away the days as the men struggled to find terms acceptable to themselves, to a Congress outraged by the assassination of President Abraham Lincoln, and to Confederate president Jefferson Davis, who soon demanded that Johnston withdraw.

Built in the mid-1800s, this one-room barn served as Washington Duke's first tobacco factory. Today, the barn is one of several exhibits at the Duke Homestead & Tobacco Museum in Durham.

Johnston stayed put. For over a week, as the generals negotiated, their armies milled around Durham Station, joking together, shooting targets, raiding J. R. Green's two-story tobacco shop at Durham Station, and smoking something called bright-leaf tobacco.

When the generals finally shook hands, both armies went home with a little of J. R. Green's tobacco, trailing a taste for bright-leaf tobacco from one end of the country to the other.

"Within a few weeks letters scrawled by men more accustomed to the trigger than the pen came addressed to the postmaster, the station agent, or other officials," writes Joseph C. Robert, author of *The Story of Tobacco in America.* "They were out of that Durham tobacco and wanted more. From whom could they get it?

E. H. Pogue advertised "the original and only sitting bull" smoking tobacco. This popular brand spurred many imitations in the late 19th century. (New York Historical Society)

This was a day of triumph for the new Bright tobacco."

Within a decade, Bull Durham tobacco—sold in small, white cotton pouches cinched with golden threads—was the best-selling tobacco in the world, and Durham was on the map. The Durham Bull's image graced barns, businesses' walls, even the Great Pyramid, in Egypt.

Meanwhile, Washington Duke peddled packets of bright-leaf tobacco from the back of a wagon, and then from a Durham factory. "As for me," his son James B. Duke said when he took over the family business, "I'm going into the cigarette business."

North Carolina went with him.

Duke's cigarette-rolling machines—the industry's first—were ravenous, and eastern North Carolina farmers rushed to feed them. War and slavery's demise had stunned the eastern economy. Or, as country poets put it, "Five-cent cotton and ten-cent meat, How in the world can a poor man eat?"

By planting tobacco, that's how.

For the first time, eastern farmers had a major at-home market. They bought the tiny seeds—a tablespoon to plant six acres—and planted thousands of acres, some almost within earshot of the Atlantic's roar. They sawed pine planks and built tight new barns. They studied temperature charts. They went to the fields, and "put in a crop." It was, wrote the usually unflappable U.S. Census Bureau, "one of the most abnormal developments in agriculture the world has ever known."

Abnormal or not, it worked. Farmers with no bootstraps left to reach for pulled themselves up clinging to filaments of thin, blue tobacco smoke.

■ WAR BOOMS

When America marched off to the Great War, tobacco fell in alongside. "You ask me what we need to win this war. I answer tobacco as much as bullets," General John Pershing said, and he got it.

World War I entrenched cigarettes in America's lifestyle. The Great Depression concentrated the major tobacco factories in North Carolina, and World War II gave the industry another boost.

Tobacco, North Carolina's top agricultural export, still grows across the state from Onslow County on the coast, to mountainous Haywood County, where

During World War I, two 30-car freight trains were loaded every month with
Bull Durham roll-your-own tobacco and shipped off to the armed forces.
(Courtesy American Brands, New York)

rows of burley tobacco step sideways up tiny, steeple-sharp fields. The Piedmont's tobacco manufacturers—including R. J. Reynolds and the American Tobacco Company—blend those tobaccos with imported leaves, producing most of the world's cigarettes, and other tobacco products.

For over a century, it seemed like a match made in heaven.

■ VISITING THE TOBACCO-GROWING AREAS

The tobacco-growing region of North Carolina runs from the center of the Coastal Plain west across the northern Piedmont to the foot of the Appalachian Mountains. In this chapter we will take you through the region west of north-south running I-95. The tobacco area to the east of I-95—

Participants compete in a tobacco tying contest at the Golden Leaf Celebration in Wilson.

the towns and farmlands between Goldsboro, Kinston, and Greenville—are described in our "Coastal Plain" chapter, on pages 112 -114.

SONG OF AN AUCTIONEER

*T*he tobacco lies in long lines of lemon yellow piles of varying amounts in shallow baskets on the warehouse floor. The procession moves down the lines. First the warehouseman glances at a pile, cries a suggested price and the auctioneer sings it. To new ears his song, cried out of the side of a scarcely moving mouth, sounds like an idiot making a noise with his finger and his lip. There is rhythm in it but no sense. But sense begins to emerge. He is saying prices in an ascending order and begging for prices above them.

"Twenty-five, six, six, gimme six."

He seems to be talking to himself in the procession which the buyers make behind him in two rows on either side of the line of baskets. Only occasionally do they bid aloud. But the auctioneer sees the signals of their eyes, their thumbs, fingers or lips. He goes on, fancier sometimes in his song:

"Sweet as honey, honey, honey, gimme thirty, gimme thirty."

A buyer winks.

"Thirty, thirty."

No nod, no winks, no thumb lifted.

" 'merican thirty." (He says, "Sold American," only on radio programs.)

Behind the principal buyers or in lines beyond them speculators march in the procession which moves fast enough to sell 300 to 360 separate piles in an hour. "Pin hookers" they are called and most of them are little fellows who look for bargains which they may be able to resell. They throw up their arms to bid. Often the warehouse itself buys. Behind all the buying as close as they can crowd, are the farmers. If they don't like what they get they can turn their tags and sell again. Sometimes the same tobacco sold by the auctioneer will bring widely separate prices at separate sales. The average of what they pay for the grades they want is the limit on the buyers. In reaching this average they may be way up and way down on particular piles.

—Jonathan Daniels,
Tar Heels: A Portrait of North Carolina, 1941

Buyers at a tobacco auction make their bids while inspecting the merchandise in Smith's Brightleaf Tobacco warehouse in Farmville.

■ TRIANGLE AREA: RALEIGH • DURHAM • CHAPEL HILL

The Triangle Area, or the Raleigh-Durham Triangle, refers to the heavily developed urban area between and including three Piedmont cities: Raleigh to the east, Durham to the north, and Chapel Hill to the west.

A few decades ago, red farmland stretched between these small cities. Today, most farms have stepped aside to accommodate housing developments and research parks. You'll see an occasional farmhouse tended by a farmer as stubborn as the clay on his boots, but the merger of these cities' outlying development is nearly complete.

Raleigh, the state capital, is a small, progressive city known for its government employees, good museums, and many parks.

Durham, an old tobacco town, is nationally known as the home of Duke University, and a city of medical and research facilities. Duke University is the largest private employer in North Carolina.

Chapel Hill, the smallest city in the triad, is the most liberal town in a conservative state. It's home to The University of North Carolina.

In the center of The Triangle Area is another triangle. Research Triangle Park, a place of manicured lawns and buttoned-down research facilities, is one of the largest planned research parks in the world.

NOTE: **The Triangle Area** refers to the Raleigh, Durham, Chapel Hill area.
The Triangle refers to the Research Triangle Park between Durham and Raleigh.

■ RALEIGH

Legislators founded North Carolina's capital city in 1792, slicing a center for their agricultural state from plantation lands. Today, this city of 240,000 makes its living in government, education, medicine, and research. But Raleigh, a city known for its parks and oak trees, hasn't moved far from its rural roots and small town tastes.

Raleigh is known for its excellent museums, and historic government buildings. To visit from the beltway, take Edenton Street downtown to Union Square, and park beneath the North Carolina Museum of History. The most interesting stops—the capitol, North Carolina Museum of History, North Carolina State Museum of Natural Sciences, City Market, and Executive Mansion—are within walking distance. The Executive Mansion sits on the edge of a 20-block Victorian neighborhood, **Oakwood**.

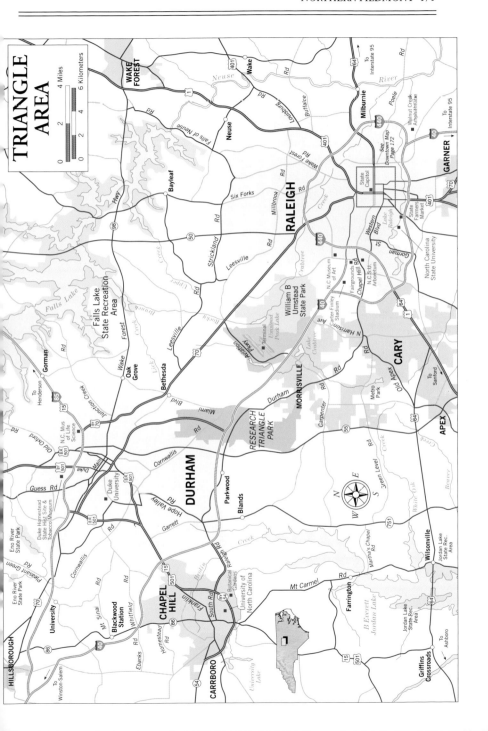

Raleigh, the City of Oaks, suits walkers—especially in spring, when choirs of azaleas and dogwoods bloom; and in autumn, when centuries-old oaks steeple golden branches overhead. Raleigh is often called "a park with a city in it," by its PR people mostly, but they have a point. Raleigh's greenways and 156 public parks keep the city well grounded. For generations, families have visited Pullen Park on Sunday afternoon, called by the 1911 carousel whose gentle stampede of carved horses, ostriches, and pigs move in rhythm with a Wurlitzer band organ.

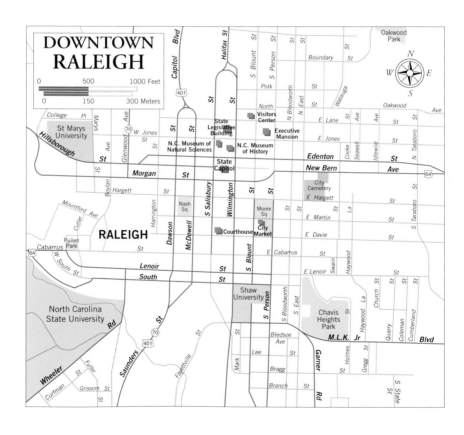

■ RALEIGH HIGHLIGHTS ■

The Capitol

North Carolina's first capitol building burned in 1831 as low-bidding workmen tried to fireproof it. Its stately Greek Revival replacement, made of local granite, overlooks walkways and broad, grassy grounds whose many statues include the three North Carolina-born U.S. Presidents—Andrew Johnson, Andrew Jackson, and James Polk.

Inside, governors, legislators, and scurrying aids have worn distinct pathways in the granite stairs and hallways leading to the legislative chambers. Antonio Canova's marble sculpture of a toga-clad George Washington dominates the four-story rotunda.

The west staircase is as chipped as a boxer's front teeth. During Reconstruction, carpetbag legislators put an open bar in an upstairs committee room. According to legend, mishandled whiskey barrels chipped the steps as they bounced downstairs.

The restored 1840 capitol is home to the governor's and lieutenant governor's offices, but the legislature meets in the State Legislative Building across the mall. Capitol: *One East Edenton Street, 919-733-4994.* Legislative Building: *16 West Jones Street; 916-733-4111.*

Executive Mansion

Walking east on Jones Street from the capitol, you'll wind up at the Executive Mansion, the state's best Victorian Queen Anne architecture. *200 North Blount Street. Tours are available through the Capitol area visitors center; 919-733-3456.*

NORTH CAROLINA MUSEUM OF HISTORY

North Carolina Museum of History

Between the capitol and Legislative Building, the North Carolina Museum of History and the North Carolina State Museum of Natural Sciences face off across the square.

Beautiful architecturally, the museum's decidedly underwhelming perma-

THE CAPITOL

nent exhibits trace state history and focus on North Carolina folklife—from shape note singing, to quilting, to wailing the blues. It also includes the North Carolina Sports Hall of Fame. More interesting changing exhibits detail specific topics—Thomas Day, for instance, a free black craftsman who created North Carolina's finest colonial furnishings. *5 East Edenton Street; 919-715-0200.*

North Carolina State Museum of Natural Sciences

Located across the square from the Museum of History, this building is molting. Its roomier, state-of-the-art skin is under construction next door, and not a moment too soon. Case in point: To accommodate a 54-foot whale skeleton, museum workers had to remove a couple of wall panels, and slip the tip of the tail into a closet. The museum's skeletons, dinosaur fossils, gemstones, and snakes will find more comfortable accommodations in the $40 million facility, slated to open in 1999. *Bicentennial Plaza, between E. Edenton and E. Jones; 919-733-7450.*

City Market

Stroll south on Salisbury Street through a run-down 19th-century business district and hook a left on Martin Street to wind up at City Market. Its renovated red-brick depot and period buildings house art galleries, artists studios, a microbrewery, restaurants, and a small farmer's market where third-generation vendors sell their produce.

Big Ed's Restaurant dangles more artifacts from its ceiling than any tasteful museum curator would ever think of displaying, and the molasses-flavored barbecue sauce isn't bad, either. *Located on Martin Street; 919-828-4555.*

State Farmer's Market

5:00 AM. Workers in jeans and rolled-up shirt sleeves stride briskly through the pre-dawn light, unloading Mack trucks and pick-ups, and stocking acres of vegetable and fruit stands.

Vendors pat North Carolina–grown tomatoes, cucumbers, cantaloupes, collards, new potatoes, watermelons, squash, and apples into place, preparing for the shoppers who will visit the state's largest farmer's market later today.

The State Farmer's Market is open every day except Christmas, and has become a weekend tradition for thousands. Farmer's Market Restaurant does a brisk Southern breakfast trade: scrambled eggs, ham and red-eye gravy, grits, and homemade biscuits. (Order the brains and eggs, and you're on your own.) *Southwest edge of town, 1201 Agriculture Street; 919-733-7417.*

North Carolina Museum of Art

The North Carolina Museum of Art is out of reach from downtown Raleigh, but worth the drive. Located on Blue

NORTH CAROLINA MUSEUM OF ART

Ridge Road, off I-40, this museum houses an outstanding collection of European art from the 13th through 19th centuries, and American art from colonial days to today. The permanent collection includes works by Raphael, Rubens, Van Dyck, Monet, Homer, and Wyeth. *2110 Blue Ridge Road; 919-839-6262.*

BELL TOWER AT NORTH CAROLINA STATE UNIVERSITY

North Carolina State University Arboretum

Of the area gardens, the best is the young North Carolina State University Arboretum, on Beryl Road. Its 5,000 trees and shrubs represent the most diverse collection in the Southeast. *4301 Beryl Road; 919-515-3132.*

Walnut Creek Amphitheatre

Walnut Creek Amphitheatre on Rock Quarry Road lures big acts to town, but Raleigh's biggest event is still the State Fair, held each October at the Fairgrounds. *3801 Rock Quarry Road; 919-831-6400.*

JORDAN LAKE STATE RECREATIONAL AREA

The Lakes

When people in the Triangle go boating or bass fishing, they're usually heading for one of three lakes: Jordan Lake State Recreational Area, west of Raleigh on US 64; Harris Lake southwest on US 1; or Falls Lake north of Raleigh on NC 50.

THE DELANY SISTERS OF RALEIGH

By the mid 1990s, the Delany sisters, natives of Raleigh then over a hundred years old, had emerged in the American consciousness as symbols of downhome humor and common sense. The quotes below were taken from their autobiography, Having Our Say, *which also inspired a popular play.*

SADIE:

Bessie and I have lived in New York for the last seventy-five years, but Raleigh will always be home. Raleigh is where Mama and Papa met, as students at Saint Augustine's School, which was a school for Negroes. Mama and Papa got married in the campus chapel back in 1886 and raised all ten of us children right there at good old "Saint Aug's." Papa became vice principal and Mama was the matron, which meant she ran things day-to-day at the school.

I don't remember my mother ever calling my father by his first name, Henry. He was always "Mr. Delany" or "Your Pa."

Jim Crow was an ugly, complicated business. Fortunately for Bessie and me, our earliest experiences with whites predated Jim Crow. North Carolina was a fairly liberal state, and Raleigh was a center of education as well as the capital. Raleigh was a good place for a Negro of the South to be living, compared to most places at that time. We remember Raleigh when there was still plenty of Confederate veterans hanging around, some lounging on the steps of the Capitol and others at the Old Soldiers' Home. Those veterans were a lonely bunch, and friendly. They always wanted to talk to anybody who walked by.

BESSIE:

Papa used to say, "You catch more flies with molasses than vinegar." He believed you could get further in life by being nice to people. Well, this is easy for Sadie to swallow. Sadie is molasses without even trying! She can sweet-talk the world, or play dumb, or whatever it takes to get by without a fuss. But even as a tiny little child, I wasn't afraid of anything. I'd meet the Devil before day and look him in the eye, no matter what the price. If Sadie is molasses, then I am vinegar!

. . . when I was young nothing could hold me back. No sir! I thought I could change the world. It took me a hundred years to figure out I *can't* change the world. I can only change Bessie. And, honey, that ain't easy, either.

NORTHERN PIEDMONT & DURHAM

■ DURHAM—BULL CITY

In 1900, Durham's young streets bustled with farmers' wagons, fast-talking auctioneers, factory workers, and the occasional tobacco tycoon. Today, only an old Lucky Strike water tower, a few warehouses and Ligget & Myers remain as direct reminders of Durham's tobacco boom.

In fact, Durham is known today as the City of Medicine USA. With a physician-to-population ratio five times higher than the national average, nearly one in three Bull City-ites work in Durham's 300 medical and health-related companies. Durham's $1-billion-a-year health industry is its top employer.

At the heart of Durham's medical and research community are five hospitals, including Duke University Medical Center, and Research Triangle Park, the largest planned research park in the United States. You can pick up a self-directed driving tour map of RTP at the Durham Visitor Information Center, 101 E. Morgan Street at the corner of Mangum; 919-687-0288.

Tobacco's influence is still visible today—from Durham's downtown historic district, to Duke University, to one of the Southeast's fastest-growing blues festivals, to the sharp crack of bat against ball as a Durham Bulls baseball player sails one high and true over the right-field wall. As for restaurants and food, Durham arguably has the most sophisticated cuisine in the state. *(See our restaurant listings, page 331.)*

The Lucky Strike water tower is one of the few visible reminders of Durham's tobacco boom.

■ MOVERS AND SHAKERS

Bull Durham tobacco put Durham on the map, but James B. Duke and the American Tobacco Company kept it there.

James B. Duke founded the American Tobacco Company in 1890. Within a decade, the company gobbled up its competitors, and dominated the world tobacco industry.

Duke tobacco money soon built electricity-guzzling textile mills across the Carolinas, and new-fangled electric power companies to keep them spinning. In Durham, Beaux Arts and Art Deco–style banks and businesses rose shoulder-to-shoulder with showy Italianate and Neoclassical Revival buildings—almost all of them built, directly or indirectly, on tobacco boom money.

Tobacco didn't overlook Uncle Sam's projects, either. Durham's Neoclassical Revival Post Office went up in 1934 at the height of the Great Depression. Taxes levied on Durham tobacco paid for it in 15 minutes the day it opened.

African American businesses thrived along Durham's "Black Wall Street," too. Activist W. E. B. DuBois said, "there is in this small city a group of 5,000 colored people, whose social and economic development is perhaps more striking than that of any similar group in the nation."

Washington Duke, James Duke's father, stands in front of his first tobacco production cabin in Durham. (NC State Dept. of Archives & History)

People's Security Insurance is one of several major insurance companies based in North Carolina.

Booker T. Washington just told people, "wait 'til you get to Durham."

The Mechanics & Farmers Bank Building, and the North Carolina Mutual Life Insurance Company symbolize Black Wall Street today. Founded in 1898 by African American businessmen, North Carolina Mutual remains one of the world's largest black-owned and managed businesses. Tours of its photo gallery are available.

■ DUKE UNIVERSITY

Tobacco money meant more than good jobs and good times. North Carolina's tobacco barons tended to be generous with their home state. In Winston-Salem, that generosity came to life in the arts. In Durham, James B. Duke established an endowment for a new school—Duke University.

Duke University's grand **West Campus**, with buildings and walkways constructed entirely of blue-grey stone, is one of the nation's most beautiful. Its two most arresting features? Duke Chapel and the Sarah B. Duke Gardens.

James B. Duke picked the location of **Duke Chapel** in 1925 as he walked along a wooded plateau. "Here's where it oughta be," the tycoon told the president of the new school. And that's where the Gothic chapel stands today, every line of its being straining toward heaven.

With a 210-foot tower and 77 stained-glass windows, the chapel dominates West Campus. The chapel, which features a 5,200-pipe organ, is open most days; non-denominational services are held Sundays at 11 AM.

Another near-religious rite—Duke basketball games—takes place on West Campus at **Cameron Indoor Stadium.** The Duke Blue Devils are consistently ranked among the nation's top teams.

The **Sarah P. Duke Gardens** spread over 55 landscaped and wooded acres on West Campus. (There's free parking at the Anderson Street entrance.) Italianate terraces designed by Ellen B. Shipman form the gardens' historic core. In April, the wisteria-draped pergola at the entryway wraps the upper terraces in perfume. The narrow paths of the Blomquist Garden of Native Plants wind through more than 900 varieties of wildflowers. The slate-roofed garden pavilion by the pond may be the garden's most serene spot. The 20-acre Asiatic Arboretum illustrates the close ties between the plants of eastern Asia and the eastern U.S. Its 550 Asian species and cultivars include collections of deciduous magnolias and Japanese maples; *919-684-3698.*

Duke Chapel (above and right) dominates Duke University's West Campus.

■ BULL CITY BLUES

Durham's tobacco markets drew more than farmers and auctioneers. Blues musicians ambled out of sharecroppers' shacks and small town juke-joints, kicked the red clay off their boots and headed for Durham—guitars slung over their shoulders and harmonicas stuck in the pockets of sun-faded, cotton shirts.

Their chameleonic art soon blended with Durham's soul. The harsh, inevitable, full-handed strokes of the Delta blues didn't match Durham's tobacco market bustle. It didn't catch the lilt in the step of a farmer with a year's pay in his pocket, the joy of a farm girl shopping for her first store-bought dress, the hope of a sharecropper starting a new life.

These African American musicians sent Durham's young energy flowing through their hands. Playing on street corners and in clubs, they finger-picked an energetic shade of blues, one that made people want to get up and dance.

Ragtime skipped up and down the fretboards of Reverend Gary Davis, Blind Boy Fuller, and Sonny Terry, and wailed through harmonicas blown by the likes of Brownie McGhee.

Today, Piedmont blues artists strut their sound at the Bull Durham Blues Festival, one of the Southeast's largest blues events. Etta Baker might ride over from her home in Morganton, at the foot of the Appalachians, to sing "Never Let Your Deal Go Down."

Other Piedmont artists—Moses Rascoe, John Dee Holman, Big Boy Henry, George Higgs, or Algia Mae Hinton—might share the stage at this two-day event with some of the world's best known blues artists: Bobby "Blue" Bland, Koko Taylor, Dr. John, Denise LaSalle, Otis Rush, Hank Crawford, Johnnie Clyde Copeland.

The September festival, at the old Durham Bulls Athletic Park, attracts growing crowds of blues lovers, who spread blankets in the outfield and dance themselves wild in the infield. *See page 354.*

■ BULL CITY ARTS

Thanks largely to Duke University, the arts make themselves at home in Durham, whose major festivals include the American Dance Festival (June and July); the International Jazz Festival (February through April); the Bull Durham Blues Festival (September); Centerfest, North Carolina's oldest street arts festival (September);

Festival for the Eno (July 4 weekend); and the Bimbé Cultural Arts Festival (June).

The American Dance Festival, held each June and July for more than 20 years, is one of the largest, most influential modern dance festivals in the world. It offers audiences a full slate of world-class performances, premieres of commissioned dance works, and behind-the-scenes tours.

Other arts organizations often join in this event. In 1997, for example, the festival presented a Dance on Film series in conjunction with the Carolina Theatre, and an art exhibit with the Duke University Museum of Art. (This museum, on East Campus, features a permanent collection of medieval sculpture, stained glass, and pre-Columbian art.)

The restored St. Joseph's Church, one of the nation's oldest autonomous African American churches, is today part of the Hayti Heritage Center, which showcases the work of local African American artists and sponsors the Bull Durham Blues Festival. *804 Old Fayetteville Street; 919-683-1709.*

■ DOWNTOWN DURHAM

The best way to see downtown Durham—the first commercial district to be designated a National Historic District—is on foot. Maps for a two-mile walking tour of the area are available at the **visitors center** at *101 East Morgan Street.*

You may also want to visit Main Street, noted for its Beaux Arts and Art Deco architecture. A block over, the Carolina Theatre, a splendidly renovated Beaux Arts theater, is now an auditorium for performing arts. Its marquee announces performances by the Durham Symphony and Triangle Opera. *For tickets, call 919-560-3030. For a listing of the city's excellent restaurants, see pages 330 to 332.*

Durham's old brick warehouses are reincarnating. Brightleaf Square, a resurrected 19th-century warehouse a block down from Ligget & Myers, welcomes antique and art lovers. You'll find three nationally reviewed restaurants in the area, too: AnotherThyme, Pop's, and Taverna Nikos. The best place to grab a dog, however, is the Durham Bulls' new park.

The Bulls have been punching them out of the ballpark in Durham since 1924. Their original home, where the movie *Bull Durham* was shot, is now home to the Durham Dragons—a women's professional fast-pitch softball team. The Bulls' new park, which opened in 1995, packs in around 400,000 fans a year.

NORTHERN PIEDMONT & DURHAM

■ DURHAM AREA PARKS AND HISTORIC SITES

Durham is home to 60 parks and recreation areas, including the popular **West Point on the Eno,** on Roxboro Road (501 N). This city park, on the Eno River, includes a reconstructed 1778 grist mill, a historic home and blacksmith shop, and the Hugh Magnum Museum of Photography. Picnicking, hiking, rafting, and canoeing are popular, as is the Festival for the Eno held each July.

The **Bennet House** is a reconstruction of the small farmhouse where Johnston surrendered to Sherman. *On Morreene Road as you head toward I-85 and Hillsborough.*

The **Duke Homestead State Historic Site and Tobacco Museum** is a living history museum where costumed players demonstrate the early farming techniques and tobacco manufacturing processes Washington Duke's family employed during the 19th century. *2828 Duke Homestead Road.*

Historic Stagville was once one of the largest plantations in the South. This historic site's 18th- and 19th-century buildings include original slave quarters. Seven miles north of Durham on the Old Oxford Highway.

Beth Woody demonstrates soap making at the Duke Homestead and Tobacco Museum (above).
(Right) A foot suspension bridge crosses the Eno River in the Eno River State Park,
just one of many popular parks in the Triangle Area.

BRIDGE RULES

DO NOT RUN,
SIT, JUMP, OR
PLAY ON BRIDGE

GRADUATION DAY

Thomas Wolfe, 1900-1938, is North Carolina's most famous writer. In his first novel, Look Homeward, Angel, *Wolfe's father, a stonecutter, is represented as Old Gant, and his mother, who ran a boarding house, as Eliza. Thomas Wolfe entered The University of North Carolina in 1916.*

Gant and Eliza came to his graduation. He found them lodgings in the town: it was early June—hot, green, fiercely and voluptuously Southern. The campus was a green oven; the old grads went about in greasy pairs; the cool pretty girls, who never sweated, came in to see their young men graduate, and to the dance; the mamas and papas were shown about dumbly and shyly.

The college was charming, half-deserted. Most of the students, except the graduating class, had departed. The air was charged with the fresh sensual heat, the deep green shimmer of heavy leafage, a thousand spermy earth and flower-scents. The young men were touched with sadness, with groping excitement, with glory.

On this rich stage, Gant, who had left his charnel-house of death for three days, saw his son Eugene. He came, gathered to life again, out of his grave. He saw his son enthroned in all the florid sentiment of commencement, and the whole of his heart was lifted out of the dust. Upon the lordly sward, shaded by great trees, and ringed by his solemn classmen and their families, Eugene read the Class Poem ("O Mother Of Our Myriad Hopes"). Then Vergil Weldon spoke, high-husky, deep, and solemn-sad; and Living Truth welled in their hearts. It was a Great Utterance. Be true! Be clean! Be good! Be men! Absorb the Negation! The world has need of. Life was never so worth. Never in history had there been. No other class had shown so great a promise as. Among other achievements, the editor of the paper had lifted the moral and intellectual level of the State two inches. The university spirit! Character! Service! Leadership!

Eugene's face grew dark with pride and joy there in the lovely wilderness. He could not speak. There was a glory in the world: life was panting for his embrace.

—Thomas Wolfe, *Look Homeward, Angel,* 1929

■ CHAPEL HILL

Most university towns, somewhere along the way, fostered universities. Here, a university fostered a town. Chapel Hill, which grew up solely to serve the nation's first state-supported university (1795) remains eternally young, eternally innovative, and eternally too liberal for many North Carolinians' tastes.

Although 45,000 people live here, Chapel Hill's business district, with its wide, tree-lined walkways, feels like a village. Franklin Street, which fronts the university, is lined with bookstores, small shops, restaurants, and clubs. The stone wall in front of the commons is a great perch for people watchers.

UNC-Chapel Hill's colonial campus, with its planetarium, arboretum, museums, botanical garden, and historic buildings provides Chapel Hill's main visitor attractions.

■ UNC CAMPUS TOUR

Borrow a Walkman at the Morehead Planetarium, located on Franklin Street—the main campus drag—and set off on a campus tour, following brick walkways

The University of North Carolina campus in 1861 was depicted by E. Valois in this lithograph. Left to right are New East, Old East, South Building, Old West, and New West bordering the grassy commons where Thomas Wolfe once daydreamed. (North Carolina Collection)

around the grassy commons where Thomas Wolfe once daydreamed and studied. Old East (1795), Person Hall (1797), the 1852 PlayMakers Theatre, and the Old Well are popular stops.

In **Wilson Library,** the Sir Walter Raleigh Rooms' rare maps would be familiar to the armchair explorer who misplaced the Lost Colony. The octagonal library of **Edenton's Hayes Plantation** includes most of the plantation's 2,000 books, and original furnishings. Another exhibit offers the low-down on Siamese twins Eng and Chang, who settled in Surry County in 1840.

Stargazers easily spend hours at the **Morehead Planetarium,** which once served as a training facility for Mercury, Gemini, Apollo, and Skylab astronauts.

The **Coker Arboretum,** next door, is more down-to-earth. Its collection of native and exotic shrubs and trees has been interplanted with daylilies and with daffodils, which add a dash of yellow to the landscape by early March.

Ackland Art Museum, on South Columbia, houses works by Rubens, Delacroix, and Degas, plus a collection of Indian art.

With 600 acres, the Southeast's largest natural botanical garden is located just southeast of campus. The **North Carolina Botanical Gardens** include trails, carnivorous plants, and herb gardens.

RATS AND ROUGE AT CHAPEL HILL?

University of North Carolina. The first state-supported university in the country to open its doors (1795) did not however accept women until more than a hundred years later—and then only if they wore hats and gloves to class and were accompanied by a chaperone. Males backed away in horror and fear; as one pioneer observed, "No matter how crowded the lecture room, a coed always has two benches to herself." In 1901 thirteen female students were not permitted to have their pictures in the yearbook, and years later, women were still not invited to their own graduation ceremonies. When a residence hall for these valiant scholars was being considered, the college newspaper headlines blared, "Shaves and Shines but no Rats and Rouge . . . Chapel Hill is a place inherently for men and men who desire no women around. . . women would only prove a distracting influence, could do no possible good, and would turn the grand old institution into a semi-effeminate college."

—Lynn Sherr, *The American Woman's Gazetteer,* 1976

Basketball—specifically men's basketball—is a passion in North Carolina and especially in the Triangle Area, where Atlantic Coast Conference (ACC) rivalries span generations. The UNC Tarheels play at the **Dean Smith Center,** locally known as the Dean Dome. UNC supports 27 varsity men's and women's teams. *For University information, call 919-962-2211.*

■ HILLSBOROUGH

Although tax collector Edmund Fanning may not have thought so in 1770 as he ran shrieking from Hillsborough's courthouse with outraged neighbors cracking a horsewhip at his heels, Hillsborough (just north and west of Chapel Hill and Durham) may be the prettiest town in North Carolina's Piedmont region.

If you drive into Hillsborough from Durham, you may think colonial North Carolina's summer capital took its name from the rolling hills of the countryside. Not so. This town of 5,000, once home to governors and Declaration of Independence signer William Hooper, was named for the Earl of Hillsborough.

Despite visits from British troops during the Revolution and Confederate troops during the Civil War, time has strolled these sleepy avenues unimpeded and unignited since 1754. Colonial, antebellum, Victorian, and modern homes with grassy English lawns settled here side-by-side. Over 100 Hillsborough homes and buildings are on the National Register of Historic Places.

To get your bearings, stop by the Alexander Dickson House, on East King Street. At this farmhouse, headquarters of CSA Major Wade Hampton, an orientation video prefaces the walking tour.

Hillsborough's best known for colonial history, but explorer John Lawson visited an Occaneechi Indian village here in 1701. Occaneechi artifacts and a village diorama reside at the Orange County Historical Museum, on Tryon Street.

In the cupola of the courthouse a 1769 English clock patiently bides Hillsborough's time. The rocking chairs on the Colonial Inn's wide verandah offer visitors a chance to do the same.

East of Hillsborough (south of Burlington) on NC 62 lies **Alamance Battleground,** where North Carolina's royal governor William Tryon and the Regulators had at it back in 1771, blasting away over taxes. This North Carolina State Historic Site orients visitors with a film and battleground monuments.

■ REIDSVILLE

Reidsville, an old tobacco town, is today home of the American Tobacco Company, a remnant of the monopoly James B. Duke created. Former North Carolina governor David Settle Reid's restored home is now the Chamber of Commerce building, downtown. (Follow the signs.)

Other signs lead to Reidsville's primary destination: **Chinqua-Penn Plantation,** outside town. It just may be the most unexpected stop along Tobacco Road.

This Guilded Age mansion is a three-dimensional mosaic of timeless religious icons, brazen folk art, delicate tapestries, Asian knickknacks, French furnishings, priceless paintings, murals, and entire rooms lifted from other countries and other centuries—all of it collected in the 1920s by Betsy and Thomas Jefferson Penn. The 27-room mansion defies description—not for lack of words, but for lack of ink. Anyone with a modicum of curiosity could spend a day touring the living room alone. (The ghost in the dining room, by the way, is Betsy's.)

Chinqua-Penn's 22-acre landscaped gardens, which are being restored to reflect their 1920s charm, are most popular in April, when 10,000 tulips burst into bloom. (The Tulip Festival runs the last three weeks of April.)

■ GREENSBORO

The population of metro Greensboro is more than 300,000 yet it looks and feels like a small town. The downtown business district, which is still reeling from the impact of malls on the outskirts of town, is just awakening to the idea of revitalization. Art galleries, a few small cafes, and museums are going up in the old downtown area, which, like most of North Carolina, pulls its shades at 5 PM.

The Carolina Lite Blues Festival, in May, and Eastern Music Festival, throughout June, are this city's most popular events. But Greensboro, which nurtures deep Quaker roots, is best known for starting the lunch counter sit-ins of the 1960s.

On February 1, 1960, four African American students from North Carolina Agricultural and Technical State College pushed through the glass doors of F. W. Woolworth Co. on Elm Street, taking seats at the whites-only lunch counter. "We had the confidence of a Mack truck," Franklin McCain later said. "I probably felt better that day than I've ever felt in my life."

The main entrance to the Chinqua-Penn Plantation.

In the next days, white and black students from other Greensboro schools—Bennett College, Guilford College, and Greensboro College—joined the protest at great personal and political risk. An anecdote from this period: Bennett College, at this time a school for black women, required its students to wear gloves when they went downtown. When the students requested permission to join the protest, it was granted on the condition that they *not* wear the gloves that identified them with the school. The sit-in began a movement that helped force integration throughout the South.

Today, that Woolworth's is slated to become a Civil Rights museum. Meanwhile, the lunch counter and its empty stools are the centerpiece of a curiously antiseptic Civil Rights exhibit at the **Greensboro Historical Museum,** a few blocks from the old Woolworth's. This museum also offers the best history overview, including exhibits on Greensboro natives Dolley Madison (wife of President James Madison), and short story writer Sidney Porter, or O. Henry.

South of Greensboro on NC 220B, a peaceful rural drive leads to the Richard Petty Museum, North Carolina's zoological park, a potters community and a Native American temple complex. *See "SOUTHERN PIEDMONT," pages 204–228.*

The Jefferson Pilot building (above) in downtown Greensboro reflects the light of the setting sun. (Right) This display at the Greensboro Historical Museum memorializes the Woolworth sit-in.

■ GUILFORD COURTHOUSE

North of Greensboro on Battleground Avenue, signs point to Guilford County Courthouse, the site of North Carolina's largest Revolutionary War battle. Today the only redcoats here belong to reenactors who storm the park each March, or to joggers and bicyclists who use the network of trails that connect the 220-acre park's grassy meadows, massive oaks, granite monuments, and statuary.

The Battle of Guilford Courthouse pitted Britain's Lord Charles Cornwallis's soldiers against Major General Nathaniel Greene's forces, which included 1,000 drafted North Carolina backcountry sharpshooters. To get those sharpshooters to line up behind a skimpy rail fence on the front line, Greene offered them a deal: if they squeezed off two rounds at the British, they could go home. If they didn't, he'd shoot them where they stood.

The British advanced. The sharpshooters fired once, fired twice, and ended their military careers with a heartfelt stampede. "To our infinite distress and mortification, the North Carolina militia took to flight," wrote Lighthorse Harry Lee.

This engraving made in 1780, claims to show the British attacking the Americans in the Battle of Guilford Courthouse, the largest Revolutionary War battle in North Carolina. (Anne S. K. Brown Military Collection, Brown University Library, Providence, RI)

"Every effort was made…to stop this unaccountable panic, for not a man of the corps had been killed or even wounded. . . . All was in vain; so thoroughly confounded were these unhappy men that, throwing away arms, knapsacks, and even canteens, they rushed like a headlong torrent through the woods." Still, the battle sent Cornwallis limping to surrender at Yorktown, Virginia.

The park's visitor center features a film on the battle, a bookstore, and self-guided auto and bike tours of the park. At Tannenbaum Park, next to Battlefield Park on New Garden Road, the cabin Joseph and Hannah Hoskins fled as the battle drew near is the heart of a backcountry farmstead.

The Old Mill of Guilford on Beaver Creek.

History's hand has scattered Quaker museums and meeting houses throughout the countryside, but most are open only a few hours each week. Look for brochures at area visitors centers.

■ WINSTON-SALEM—THE CITY OF THE ARTS

Tobacco put Durham and Reidsville on the map, but Winston-Salem was a major point on North Carolina's map long before Joe Camel loped onto the scene. Winston-Salem is now home to numerous artists, including author Maya Angelou. The city began in 1766 as a Moravian commune on the edge of America's wild, western frontier.

Today their restored 18th-century village, Old Salem, is one of the nation's most authentic colonial sites.

■ OLD SALEM

Old Salem, the literal and figurative heart of Winston-Salem, hasn't changed much since William Loughton Smith visited in May 1791:

> *A*fter traveling through the woods for many days, the sight of this little settlement of Moravians is highly curious and interesting. . . . The first view of the town is romantic, just as it breaks upon you through the woods; it is pleasantly seated on a rising ground, and is surrounded by beautiful meadows, well-cultivated fields, and shady woods. The antique appearance of the houses, built in the German style, and the trees among which they are placed have a singular and pleasing effect; the whole resembles a beautiful village, and forms a pastoral scene.

Today, nearly a half-million visitors a year explore Old Salem, now a living history museum where you can talk with costumed interpreters practicing 18th-century trades. You can see exactly what made this town so prosperous.

The Moravian Book Shop in the restored 18th-century village of Old Salem.

In the two-story, brick-and-log Single Brothers Home, guests stroll a stone-paved hallway lined with 18th-century shops. In one, a dye-maker explains the natural dyes Salem's craftsmen grew, harvested, and used. In another, a tailor holds needle and thread up to the light. Decorated Moravian pottery—the first art in "the City of the Arts"—lines the potter's shop walls.

Over in the Old Tavern—once Salem's link to the outside world—costumed interpreters discuss slavery. At Winkler Bakery, women in long, dark dresses and chaste white bonnets slide loaves of Swedish rye into the wood-fired oven as visitors line up to buy warm gingerbread and sugar cookies.

The statue of Richard J. Reynolds in front of the Wachovia Bank Building in downtown Winston-Salem.

Old Salem's guides know their stuff, and like to chat. The Old Salem Official Guidebook, available at the visitors center, is jam-packed with detail.

Salem was unique on the Carolina frontier. Moravians, a Protestant group from Germany, settled in Pennsylvania in the early 1700s and looked south for good, cheap land, explains Gene Capps, Old Salem's Vice President. In 1753, they bought 100,000 acres in the North Carolina backcountry for $35,000, and named it Wachovia.

They chose the Carolina tract for three reasons. First, for religious freedom. "Another reason would have been the richness of natural resources," Capps says. "And the third reason was its location on the Great Wagon Road, which meant there would be customers coming down the road who would buy their products."

Bishop August Spanenberg led a group of 11 men to North Carolina to choose a site for Salem. The Bishop must have thought he teetered on the edge of the world. In November of 1752, he wrote to friends in Pennsylvania:

> The land is very rich, and has been much frequented by buffalo, whose tracks are everywhere, and can often be followed with profit. The wolves here give us music every morning, from six corners at once, such music as I have never heard. . . .

Finally, the axes rang out and the brethren began a town—two large dormitories, a store, tavern, pottery, mill, sawmill, barn, four shops, and meeting hall.

Happily for historians, the Moravians recorded everything—dewfall, lovers' spats, slaves' behavior, religious rites—and socked their notes away in the church archives. Today, historians mine those archives, turning up nuggets of truth more precious than emeralds mined in the Appalachians.

Thanks to yesterday's note-takers and today's historians, Salem's 97 historic buildings and 30-some gardens rank among the most authentic restorations in the country. And we know some of Salem's early residents—white, slave, and free Blacks—almost as well as we know Salem's quiet streets.

Even Salem Tavern profits from the colonial Moravians' love for detail. Its ragout recipe comes from Winkler Bakery, tucked away by flour-dusted hands in the 18th century. The kraut hasn't changed since the day George Washington dropped by. And the recipe for lemon ice cream, a beloved delicacy from the early 1800s, was stored away at Winkler Bakery, too.

■ WINSTON-SALEM HIGHLIGHTS ■

R. J. Reynolds Company Tour

R. J. Reynolds Company, established in Winston as a plug factory in 1875, stunned the cigarette industry in 1913 when its Camel cigarettes lumbered onto the scene, sporting a name swiped from a Barnum & Bailey dromedary. In just over a decade, Joe Camel owned 45 percent of the cigarette market.

R. J. Reynolds Tobacco Company, now a subsidiary of R. J. R. Nabisco, still produces about one in three cigarettes smoked in the United States, including Winstons and Salems—named for the towns, of course, and not the other way around. (They also produce Camels, and Vantage cigarettes, among others.) R. J. Reynolds Tobacco's free 30-minute tour is the only one of its kind in the state. Tours (Monday through Friday, 8:00 AM until 8:00 PM) include exhibits on the company's history, and a trip onto the

Old Joe, photographed here with his trainer, was passing through Winston-Salem in 1913 as part of the Barnum & Bailey Circus when inspiration for a new ad campaign struck Richard J. Reynolds.

plant floor to see how 430 million cigarettes get a state-of-the-art start each day; *for directions and information call 336-741-5718.*

Museum of Early Southern Decorative Arts

MESDA, a collage of historic Southern roomscapes, is North Carolina's most interesting, most immediate history and art museum. This outstanding museum is located on the edge of Old Salem. Overlook the coma-inducing name, and step inside.

This museum's 19 fascinating rooms were dismantled in Maryland, Virginia, North Carolina, South Carolina, Georgia, Kentucky, and Tennessee, and reassembled here—woodwork, portraits, needlepoint, silverware, et al. Take Old Salem Historic District or Salem College exit off I-40 and follow signs to historic area. MESDA is at *924 South Main Street; 336-721-7360.*

Reynolda House

R. J. Reynolds, his wife Katherine Smith Reynolds, and their children once lived in this 100-room mansion designed by Charles Barton Keen. The museum's permanent collection, which spans three centuries, includes paintings, prints, and sculptures by Mary Cassatt, Andrew Wyeth, Georgia O'Keeffe, Thomas Hart Benton, John Singleton Copley, Frederic E. Church, Gilbert Stuart, Thomas Eakins, and Jacob Lawrence.

Built in 1917, Reynolda also retains many original furnishings and family memorabilia. In the basement, you can almost hear the Reynolds children playing handball, splashing in the pool, or sending a gutterball rocketing down a lane in the bowling alley. (Listen closely as you walk through the upstairs rooms, and you can almost hear them shooting the bulbs out of the chandeliers during less idyllic times.)

Reynolda Gardens—20 acres of wooded paths, vegetable gardens, and formal flower gardens—surround the home. The estate's servant's quarters, stables, and outbuildings have been converted into specialty shops and restaurants; *from I-40 take Silas Creek Parkway north to the White Forest University exit; continue to 2250 Reynolda Rd.; 336-725-5325.*

SECCA

The English-style manor house across the street from Reynolda House was the home of the late industrialist James G. Hanes, who put America in skivvies. Today, his mansion is the Southeastern Center for Contemporary Art, known for ever-changing exhibits by nationally known artists.

Piedmont Craftsmen Gallery and Shop

This outlet showcases quality crafts made by Southeastern craftspeople—many from North Carolina. Its Crafts Fair, the fourth weekend in October, features the work of around 120 artists. *1204 Reynolda Drive.*

Reynolda House Museum of American Art.

National Black Theater Festival
Produced by the North Carolina Black Repertory Company, this is a biannual event held in early August, in odd-numbered years, when theaters across Winston-Salem showcase original dramatic productions with widely varied African American themes.

North Carolina School of the Arts
Winston-Salem test-markets Broadway performances, which makes the Stevens Center, at the North Carolina School of the Arts, a good place to see the big shows before they're the big shows. The Stevens Center also hosts productions by the North Carolina School of the Arts and the Winston-Salem Piedmont Triad Symphony. *Call 336-770-3399.*

Tanglewood Park
Tanglewood Park was a gift from the Reynolds family to Forsythe County. The 1,100-acre park—home of the Manor House B&B—provides three golf courses, a steeplechase each May, tennis, swimming, equestrian trails, paddle boats, and ducks waiting at this moment for a crust of bread. *Nine miles west of Winston-Salem off US 158 in the town of Clemmons.*

Bethabara Colonial Gardens
On the outskirts of Winston-Salem, Bethabara Historic Park contains two of the most important colonial gardens in the United States. "Our community gardens are the only known, well-documented colonial community gardens in

*The Moravians at Bethabara palisaded their settlement for protection from Indians.
(Moravian Archives, Bethlehem)*

America," says director Rod Meyer.

For that, we can thank Moravian surveyor Christian Reuter, who dropped by with pens and ink in 1759 and 1761, to map the gardens row-by-row. Using his maps, archaeologists relocated the gardens in 1985. "They're reconstructed from actual garden maps that list what was planted in each one of the rows," Meyer says.

Planted in the spring of 1754, the Brethren's vegetable garden soon fed 300 people a day—the Moravians, plus refugees from the French and Indian War who fled into the palisade.

Today, this is a community garden of a different stripe. Around 30 Winston-Salem gardeners lease plots here each year, planting from Christian Reuter's 1759 plant list.

One bed grows heirloom vegetables, but most gardeners cultivate hybrid descendants of the Moravians' crops.

The Medical Garden, which includes medicinal herbs plus various vitamin-rich plants, wasn't difficult to relocate, Meyer says. The fennel still held its original ground.

Today, visitors stroll through these gardens, chatting with gardeners about colonial gardening techniques and the gardens' history. They rest in the cool, vine-covered arbor as martins swoop overhead, or explore the medical garden, which in June wears the hypnotic scent of roses. They explore the small museum, the restored Gemeinhaus (1788), the Potter's House (1782), and the Brewer's House (1803), and the reconstructed 1756 palisade fort. Gardeners sharpen their hoes around mid-April; *call for directions, 336-924-8191.*

■ SPECIALTY SHOPPING IN THE PIEDMONT

Greensboro's Replacements Limited

Replacement Limited's showroom and warehouse just north of Greensboro on I-85/40, make up a Never Never land of lost crystal, china, jelly glasses—even those eerily blank-faced plates and saucers that snuck into America's cupboards via laundry detergent boxes in the 1960s.

Shoppers with chipped pasts come here by the busload. Hollywood stars, royalty and first ladies phone in, too. (Their patterns are displayed along a back wall.) *Mt. Hope Church Road exit off of I-85, left at stop sign then left on Knox Road. 1089 Knox Road; 336-697-3000.*

High Point Furniture

High Point, which, began making furniture in 1880, carved a multi-million dollar industry out of the region's hardwood forests. Today, the area's 125 plants include the 15 largest furniture factories in the world. Over 40 area stores, showrooms, and outlets sell everything from discontinued furniture lines, to crystal chandeliers handmade in Eden, North Carolina.

Furniture Discovery Center, on the corner of Main Street and Green Drive, is the nation's only furniture manufacturing museum.

Kannapolis Textiles

Fieldcrest Cannon Textile Company, in Kannapolis, fulfills the linen fantasies of thousands of visitors via its outlet shop at Cannon Village, which includes specialty shops, an antique mall, and a free textile museum. *From Charlotte, exit 58 off I-85 to US 29. Follow signs to Cannon Village. 20 West Avenue; 704-939-2869.*

Hickory's Furniture

Highway 321 between Hickory and Blowing Rock is known nationally for its furniture showrooms and outlets. Hickory has been a major furniture producer since the 1800s.

Fine furniture-making has been a North Carolinian tradition for over a century. This Farm Security Administration photo from the 1930s shows a man crafting rocking chairs. (Library of Congress)

SOUTHERN PIEDMONT

"PIEDMONT" MEANS, LITERALLY, "FOOT OF THE MOUNTAINS." North Carolina's mountains have size-12 EEE feet.

The Piedmont plateau covers about 45 percent of the state, about the same as the Coastal Plain, and extends from the fall line in the east to the Appalachians in the west. "Soil" in the Piedmont means bright red clay.

In general, the Piedmont rises from about 500 feet above sea level in the east, to 1,500 feet in the west. Its stooped mountains, now the hearts of several state parks and a national forest, are the cores of North America's most ancient ranges.

They've melted away over the millennia, softened by time, winds, and rains. Today, remnant peeks overlook small towns set in a patchwork of corn fields and dairy farms, steam-billowing textile mills, the state's largest cities, and quiet communities of traditional potters who have found a time-honored use for the Piedmont's generous supply of clay.

■ SETTLEMENT

Unlike the Coastal Plain, where civilization seeped inland along languid rivers and streams, the Piedmont was settled by Germans and Scots who barreled into the area in the mid-1700s. European diseases had decimated the Catawba and other native peoples, leaving the clay hills ripe for the taking.

Settlers came first on foot and horseback, following the Indian Trade Path from eastern Virginia and the Great Wagon Road from Pennsylvania. Soon they rumbled along in Conestoga Wagons, pushing south along what is today the I-85. They came singly, in families, and as entire communities, searching for religious freedom, cheap land, and water that could irrigate a crop and spin a mill wheel.

Moravians from Germany became the first tradesmen. Their bustling mission towns included Salem, the heart of Winston-Salem, now a major tobacco center in the northern Piedmont. Quakers settled the hills around Greensboro, which became the home of North Carolina's Underground Railroad and the sit-ins of the early Civil Rights movement. To the south Salisbury, Charlotte, and other backcountry towns sputtered to life as trade centers.

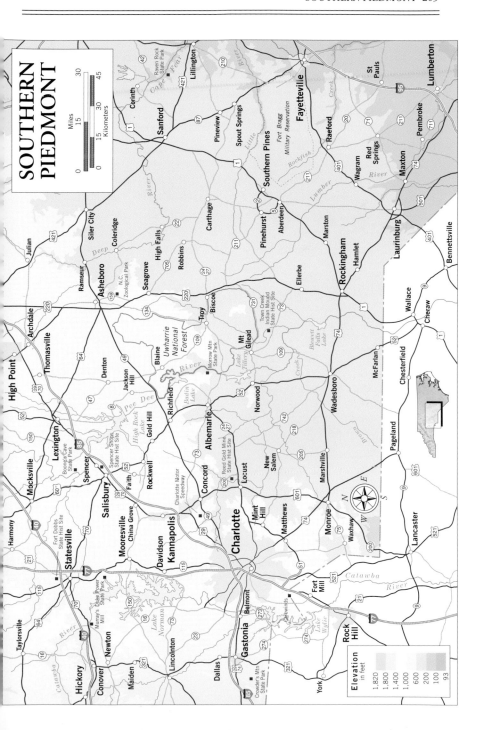

In 1770 backcountry Regulators traded lead with royal governor William Tryon's militia over unfair taxes. But the Revolution largely by-passed the Piedmont, not out of respect for its large, pacifist Quaker and Moravian populations, but because Piedmont clay held little military value. The only major battle fought here—at Guilford County Courthouse near Greensboro—was more than enough for the sharpshooters drafted to fight it.

After the Revolution, the state legislature stepped off a new capital city, Raleigh, and a university at Chapel Hill *(see "NORTHERN PIEDMONT," page170).*

Immigrants still rattled down the Wagon Road—though many followed Salisbury's son, Daniel Boone, west to Kentucky. Hessian soldiers, who came to America courtesy of King George, hung up their red coats and settled down. One of those soldiers was John Reed, whose boy Conrad stumbled across a 17-pound gold nugget near Charlotte in 1799, setting off America's first gold rush.

North Carolina seceded from the Union in 1861. Textile mills shifted gears, churning out oceans of grey material for uniforms. Men who'd never owned a slave enlisted to defend states' rights and their homes.

No major Civil War battles took place on this red soil, but industries and homes went up in smoke as Sherman's forces swarmed across the state in 1864. Following the Battle of Bentonville, to the east, Sherman accepted the surrender of CSA General Joe Johnston's troops at Bennet

A Carolina gold dollar from the 1830s. (Courtesy NCDA&H)

House, near Durham, ending North Carolina's war.

Now the state built new economic muscles around the railroad's iron skeleton. In Burlington, Kannapolis, Charlotte, and Gastonia, streams were collared to fuel textile mills, putting entire families to work. In High Point, Hickory, and Lenoir, furniture-makers carved an industry out of sprawling hardwood forests.

Beginning in the 19th century, textile mills became one of North Carolina's biggest industries.
(University of Maryland)

■ THE PIEDMONT TODAY

Today, the Piedmont remains a place of industry: tobacco, textiles, and furniture; pharmaceuticals, education, and banking. Charlotte, little more than a crossroads at the time of the Carolina gold rush, is the center of one of the largest urban areas in the nation.

In a smaller, more typical Piedmont city, you'll find a couple of museums downtown and a pleasant historic district nearby. You may also find a small district of cafes, shops, and coffeehouses near one of the Piedmont's many colleges or universities.

Malls ring Piedmont cities. Along I-85 and I-40, furniture and textile outlets are so popular that tour buses hover in the parking lots.

To get a true sense of the region, venture off the major highways from time to time, onto twisting lanes laid out by streams and jostling wagons. In sight of metro skylines and asphalt arteries, traditional Piedmont Carolina lives wrapped in the smell of Moravian wheat bread, the hum of a potter's wheel, the sigh of a long-leaf pine.

■ CHARLOTTE

If you're visiting Charlotte, you're probably in town on business. You're not alone. Most of Charlotte is in town on business.

Charlotte, the only place in North Carolina that moves like a city, claims North Carolina's most dramatic manmade skyline and the nation's second-largest banking community. Today Charlotte, with a population of 466,000, is the geographic center of one of the largest urban areas in the U.S.—a mid-sized city in a web of small towns. Within a 100-mile radius of the city live 5.6 million people.

(Left)
A lush canopy arches over Hertford Road in Charlotte's Dillsworth/Myers Park area.

(Right)
The Charlotte skyline is the most dramatic in the state.

■ CHARLOTTE HIGHLIGHTS ■

Discovery Place

700,000 people a year visit Charlotte's award-winning hands-on science and technology museum, known for its three-story rainforest, aquariums, and OMNIMAX Theater. The Kelly Space Voyager Planetarium honors North Carolina Astronaut Michael J. Smith, pilot of the fallen *Challenger* Space Shuttle. *301 North Tryon Street; 704-845-3882.*

Sports Teams

The NBA Charlotte Hornets and WNBA Charlotte Stings swish nets at the Coliseum, and the NFL Carolina Panthers set records in the new $160 million Ericsson Stadium. The train into Charlotte from points north delivers fans to the stadium door.

Mint Museum of Art

One of the state's best museums, the Mint Museum of Art is home to American and European paintings, Victorian silver, Pre-Columbian and African art, one of the nation's outstanding pottery and porcelain collections—and a complete set of Charlotte-minted gold coins.

Gold put Charlotte on the map during the North Carolina gold rush, with the first branch mint in the U.S. opening its doors here in 1836. The Charlotte Mint stamped raw Carolina gold into $5 million worth of coins, jump-starting the city's huge banking industry, which is today second only to New York's. (In Charlotte's Historic Fourth Ward, known for its Victorian architecture, you walk along shady streets originally paved with fill from Charlotte's early mines.)

The Charlotte Mint closed in 1861, and preservationists moved it to its current address, to save it from the wrecking ball. It reopened in 1936 as the Mint Museum of Art. *2730 Randolph Road; 704-337-2037.*

Blumenthal Performing Arts Center

The Blumenthal Performing Arts Center, *130 N. Tryon Street,* and Spirit Square, *345 N. College Street,* showcase opera companies, symphonies, choruses, dance and theater productions; *800-231-4636.*

Uptown's Dillworth Section

Charlotte's many restaurants include bistros, micro-breweries, barbecue houses, and everything in between. East Boulevard and Morehead Street, in the Dillworth Section of "uptown" Charlotte, are known for cafes, clubs, and shops.

To find out what's going on pick up a copy of *Creative Loafing* (free on the newsstands), or the entertainment section of the *Charlotte Observer.*

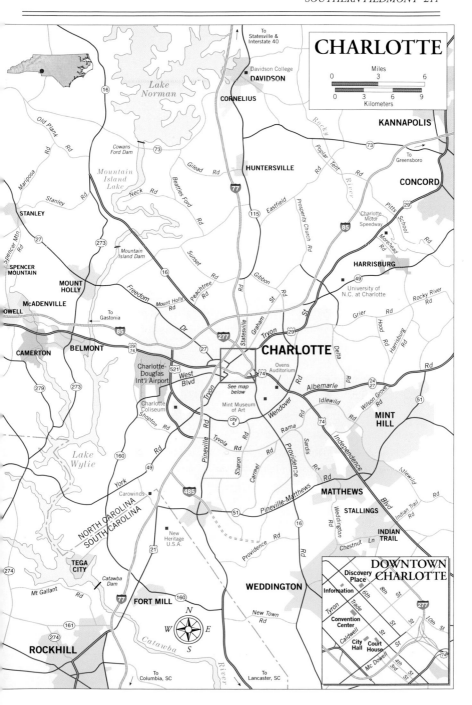

■ GASTONIA

Land-locked Gastonia, which lies west of Charlotte on I-85, is home to the best fish camps in the state—an unexpected spin-off of the textile mills that have kept this area in money since the mid-1800s.

The camps got their start during the Depression. In the 1930s, cooks boiled up kettles of Catawba River fish over open fires, spooning out fish stew to patrons who ate in sawdust-floored open-air eateries called "camps."

Over the years the camps evolved into restaurants, and the Catawba River fish gave way to fresh seafood trucked in from the coast. Today, textile workers with Friday paychecks still head for the fish camps' heaping plates of fried fish, shrimp, and oysters. Most camps welcome guests seven days a week, and a few even open for lunch.

The rule here is "good food and plenty of it."

Fish camp ambiance means yellow pine chairs, bare tables, and a waitress who calls you "sugar" and pirouettes from kitchen to table with plates of steaming seafood balanced on her outstretched arm. Come hungry, and order the lunch special: Fresh fried trout, cole slaw, fries, endless hushpuppies, and all the iced tea you can drink.

After lunch, head for the **Schiele Museum of Natural History & Planetarium**, one of the state's most visited museums. Exhibits include the Southeast's largest mounted land mammal collection, as well as geology, paleontology, archaeology, and anthropology exhibits. Outdoors, nature trails lead to a reconstructed Catawba Indian village and 18th-century backcountry farm. *Take the New Hope Road exit off of I-85 and follow the brown and grey signs to the museum; 704-866-6900.*

❖

🚗 From Gastonia, I-40 heads west to Asheville *(see pages 288–298)*. US 321 leads to Crowder's Mountain State Park, created in the early 1970s to keep two wizened old mountains out of the hands of kyanite-hungry strip miners.

■ CROWDER'S MOUNTAIN STATE PARK

Crowder's Mountain and Kings Pinnacle, which rise only 800 feet from the park floor—are remnants of an Appalachian chain that towered thousands of feet above sea level millions of years ago. Their quartzite-rich cores stood strong while their neighbors melted away.

When buffalo roamed these prairies, these mountains marked the boundary between Catawba and Cherokee hunting grounds. The buffalo are long gone but possums, foxes, raccoons, chipmunks, salamanders, and 160 bird species scurry among the red maple, pine, rhododendron, laurel, and oaks.

You can backpack into these secluded campgrounds, or picnic near no-name lake. You can also canoe the shoreline, or cast for bream and bass. Hikes range from easy to strenuous; Crowder's Mountain's sheer 150-foot vertical cliffs challenge even experienced climbers. (No pitons, bolts, or cliff-scarring devices allowed.)

🚗 From Charlotte head east on NC 24–27 to NC 200 which leads north to reach Reed Gold Mine.

■ REED GOLD MINE STATE HISTORIC SITE

One Sunday in 1799, 12-year-old Conrad Reed played hooky from church, wetting a line in Meadow Creek instead. For penance, he pried a pretty yellow stone from a creek bed, and lugged it to his family's cabin. It served as a doorstop until

This restored stamping mill is one of the exhibits at Reed Gold Mine State Historic Site.

SOUTHERN PIEDMONT & REED GOLD MINE

A gold mine tunnel at Reed Gold Mine State Historic Site.

1802, when a visitor took a gander at the 17-pound toe-stumper. "Gold!" he shrieked.

"Nein," muttered Conrad's father, who took the stone to a Fayetteville jeweler, just in case. Gold! Reed sold the ingot for $3.50, and raced home with the news. Gold in Cabarrus County!

Farmers dropped their plow lines, teachers shelved their books, merchants folded their aprons. Armed with picks, pans, and provisions, they poured into the Carolina gold fields around Cabarrus County. America's first gold rush was on, and eventually 115 pounds of gold enriched the Reed family's coffers. Today, at the Reed Gold Mine State Historic Site, the pay dirt surfaces in buckets from April to November, ready to be panned in flowing water. A modest fee buys the use of a pan, two pans of dirt, and a few pointers.

The visitors center, open year-round, offers a film and exhibits on gold mining. The park includes a restored mine area, 19th-century stamping mill, 1850s Engine House, and numerous trails.

Modern prospectors pocket gold here, but as for striking it rich: "If gold was that plentiful," drawls the owner of a nearby commercial mine, "I'd be down there panning it myself." (*To visit, take 24-77 east to 200, and follow the signs.*)

■ THE FAST LANE: NASCAR

As you head northeast from Charlotte on NC 49, if the traffic runs bumper-to-bumper and you're cruising among an inordinate number of drivers in black cowboy hats, you're headed for one of the biggest parties in the state: a NASCAR race at the **Charlotte Motor Speedway,** in Concord.

Over a half-million race fans surge to the Speedway each year to cheer their favorite drivers around the 1.5-mile track. For super events like Memorial Day weekend's Coca-Cola 600—the third largest sports event in the U.S.—they cruise in a day early and camp, living on hot dogs and beer until the races begin.

NASCAR racing wears the same blue-collared workshirt it's worn since North Carolina moonshine runners gunned the engine on the sport in the 1930s. During Prohibition, North Carolina bootleggers made deliveries up and down the East Coast, stocking bars from Connecticut to Florida. After unloading in Florida, they raced on Daytona's beach and circular track, creating a NASCAR tradition of going nowhere very, very fast.

■ SITES OF INTEREST TO NASCAR FANS ■

Richard Petty Museum
South of Greensboro on peaceful US 220B, is the Richard Petty Museum—the equivalent of Lourdes for NASCAR fans. The museum includes six race cars driven by the seven-time Winston Cup Champion. The cars are various makes and models, says the museum's director and curator. "Whatever went fast in that year is what he drove." *311 Branson Mill Road; 336-495-1143.*

Mooresville's Race Shops
This small town on I-77 is home to race shops that keep Ricky Rudd, Kyle Petty, and Rusty Wallace in the driver's seat. Many of the region's 48 shops welcome visitors. Call the Cabarrus County vis-

itors center for a schedule; *800-848-3740.*

The North Carolina Auto Racing Hall of Fame
Located in Mooresville, this hall of fame welcomes around 150,000 race fans a year to its 30-car museum. *Follow the state signs on I-77 to exit 36. 119 Knob Hill Road; 704-663-5331.*

Speedways
The Charlotte Motor Speedway is North Carolina's best known NASCAR track, but speedways in Rockingham and North Wilkesboro also host big NASCAR races, and the area is rife with smaller tracks.

Today, National Association of Stock Car Auto Racing drivers enjoy the status of country music stars. Fans spend millions on the products they endorse—from headache powders to chewing tobacco. Big race tickets go almost as fast as the cars themselves, selling out months in advance at up to $100 a seat. Humbler events are free for kids, and modestly priced for adults.

Speedway tour vans putter around on the track on non-race days. Half-day race car driving classes, including face-stretching laps in a stock car, begin at around $300.

■ SALISBURY

Salisbury grew up at the intersection of the Trading Path and the Great Wagon Road (now I-85 and Route 70), becoming a jumping-off place for pioneers, visionaries, fugitives, and frauds.

Walking Salisbury's peaceful tree-lined streets today, it's hard to imagine this was home to a notorious Civil War prison, but it was. Salisbury Prison was built for 1,000 men, but by late 1864 ten times that many languished within its walls. One of them, Maj. Abner Small, wrote, "I saw, shuddering as I looked, the dead-cart on its morning rounds, and in it God's images tiered up like sticks of wood."

Over 5,000 unknown Union soldiers who died here of disease, hunger, and cold rest at the Salisbury National Cemetery—the largest number of unknown dead from any Civil War prison.

The Confederates opened the prison gates in January 1865, but no one told the Union's Gen. George Stoneman. His calvary thundered into Salisbury, burning the prison, factories, businesses, and railroad facilities. But he spared the courthouse and homes, including the **Josephus Hall House,** home to the prison's chief surgeon. (It's now a museum.)

Thanks to Stoneman's restraint, Salisbury's 30 square-block west historic area located in the downtown area includes numerous pre–Civil War Greek Revival and Federal-style homes, and an 1855 Greek Revival county courthouse. The town offers walking tours year-round, and guided tours on the second weekend of October. Pick up information at Salisbury Station visitors center, *215 Depot Street; 704-636-0103. To reach the historic district take exit 76B on I-85 down Innes Street until Fulton Street.*

Salisbury National Cemetery contains the bodies of 5,000 unknown Union soldiers.

■ IN THE SALISBURY AREA

The hills around Salisbury are as thin-skinned and hard-boned as a ten-year-old's knobby knees. Here and there, slabs of grey slate and granite jut through thin, grassy pasture land. Among ranch-style brick homes and doublewides, old clapboard farmhouses stand back from the roads, surrounded by huge, hunkered-down old barns, silos, and milking sheds.

Not long ago, men pitched hay from the barn lofts, children ushered cows across pastures, and women urged cows into milking stalls. Today, dairy farming isn't so much a family operation as a corporate one. Most folks make a living in the area's growing factories.

Germans settled this area. Cleveland's and Rockwell's stately stone churches, which date from the 1700s, are among the staunchest architectural reminders of that ancestry. (Both welcome visitors.)

Place names here have a literal bent. **Rockwell** grew up around a rock well; **China Grove** was named for a grove of chinaberry trees. The area's oldest house is

A steam engine repair shop at Spencer's Transportation Museum.

the 1766 Old Stone House in Granite Quarry. Diamond Jim, legendary Manhattan financier, once lived in **Gold Hill**, a rowdy little mining town whose 19th-century prospectors lifted over $2 million in gold from the earth. The town, which nodded off for a century or so, is waking up. Parts are under restoration; the park contains three old gold mines and a small museum.

Faith, population 500, throws the state's biggest Fourth of July party. (It's just south of Granite Quarry.)

In **Spencer**, you can hop a restored steam-driven train at the North Carolina Transportation Museum, an in-progress museum in what was once the Southern Railway's largest repair facility. Inside the giant roundhouse, where a mammoth Lazy Susan spun wheezing engines and crippled cabooses over mechanic's pits, several old trains have been upfitted, painted, and polished one more time: pug-faced engines, bullet-fast silvery trains, elegant cars built for window-shade romance, highbrow cars that conveyed the royalty of a newly industrialized nation.

NC 801 winds southwest of Salisbury to White Road and **Thyatira Presbyterian Church**, the home of two eyewitnesses to a Revolutionary War scene.

In 1781, military lines seesawed so unpredictably here that Elizabeth Steele, who ran a popular Salisbury inn, never knew who might stop by for dinner. Her portraits of King George and Queen Charlotte smiled on Cornwallis's men when they were in town, and she turned the portraits' royal faces to the wall when Patriots bivouacked nearby.

One night, General Nathaniel Greene stopped by for dinner. When he described his soldiers' poverty, Mrs. Steele plunked down a sack of money. The grateful General scrawled on the back of the king's portrait, "O, George! Hide thy face and mourn." Today, the eyewitness portraits hang in Thyatira Church. Outside, a stone monument marks Mrs. Steele's grave.

From Salisbury, 150 heads west through farming communities and hardwood forests to **Mooresville**, known for its NASCAR garages, and **Lake Norman**. An early avenue of commerce, the Catawba River and its neighbor to the east, the Pee Dee, are today a stepped series of vast manmade lakes that help power the largest concentration of textile factories in the world. Lake Norman is North Carolina's largest inland body of water with 520 miles of shoreline. It's known for its boating, swimming, skiing, and commercial camping. The fishing here is outstanding.

■ FORT DOBBS AND VICINITY

Fort Dobbs State Historic Site lies north of Statesville, on SR 1930, but offers more nature than history.

The French and Indian War, in the 1750s, pitted Britain and her Native American allies against France and her Native American allies, with colonists catching hell from every direction. Many northerners experienced full-scale war, but settlers in the North Carolina Piedmont lived in relative peace once the Cherokee, in the Appalachians, formed an alliance with the English. Nobody was going to mess with the Cherokee. Not yet, anyway.

To visit Fort Dobbs, exit I-40 on US 21, head north one mile to SR 1930 and then west a half mile. The fort itself is off-limits, but excavations have turned up a moat, cellar, magazine, and well. The museum explains life around the fort. A half-mile nature trail rambles among hickories and oaks, over footbridges and fern-filled ravines.

West of Fort Dobbs on I-40, the Catawba exit leads to **Murray's Mill** (Highway 10 to Murray's Mill Road) where a working mill and museum stand near a serene pond. A gallery displays and sells local folk art.

At the harvest festival held at Murray's Mill Historic Site, a man adjusts an antique corn hopper (left) for use at the mill.

(Right) The grist stone at Murray's Mill.

Murray & Minges General Store.

Murray & Minges General Store, across the road, has stocked horseshoes, dry goods, and penny candy for over 100 years.

Head west, this time on US 70, to the **Bunker Hill Covered Bridge** two miles east of Claremont. The 85-foot bridge, which spans rock-strewn Lyles Creek, is one of of only two left in the state.

Further west on I-40, is Hickory, with its 20 miles of furniture outlets *(see page 203)*. The blue haze in the distance? The Appalachians.

❖

 To the east on Interstate 40 lie the big cities of the northern Piedmont, **Winston-Salem, Greens-boro, Durham,** and **Raleigh.** *(See the previous chapter, "NORTHERN PIEDMONT.")*

Away from the mall madness along I-40 and I-85 are pleasant side trips. Due south of Greensboro on NC 220B, a peaceful drive takes you to the Richard Petty Museum *(see page 215),* the North Carolina Zoological Park, an extensive potters' community, and a restored Native American temple complex.

■ NORTH CAROLINA ZOOLOGICAL PARK

Off Highways 220B and 159, south of Asheboro, is the **North Carolina Zoological Park**—the nation's third-largest zoo. A million visitors a year come here to see the creatures and habitats of Africa and North America, and habitats representing five more continents are planned for the remaining 950 of the zoo's 1450 acres.

The Africa habitats include a chimp exhibit Dr. Jane Goodall called the best in North America, and the largest African Plains exhibit of its kind.

Explore the natural habitat zoo on foot, or by tram. Spring and fall are the best times to visit, since animals (and humans) are more active in moderate temperatures. If you come in August, visit the arctic section of North America's Rocky Coast area at midday—it's air conditioned for the polar bears. *6 miles southeast of Asheboro. 159 Zoo Parkway; 336-879-7000.*

■ SEAGROVE

Seagrove is a little town at the intersection of NC 220 and 705, but when people mention Seagrove potters, they're referring to several small, very laid-back communities along 705. In fact, they're so laid-back, they're attitudinally horizontal.

The North Carolina Zoological Park is the third largest zoo in the nation.

Whynot, which went nameless for years, finally got its name from a community debate: "Why not this name?" "Why not that one?"

Whynot won by a landslide.

And, at Owens Pottery, near Westmoore, a sign in the shop reads, "If no one is here to wait on you, please come to the back porch and yell."

Clearly, you don't want to come to Seagrove in a hurry. Talk to people about their work and the weather, and expect a few easy delays as you explore NC 705 and its winding tributaries. They lead to potters' shops, tiny log-cabin museums, and groundhog kilns with walls of firewood neatly stacked nearby. You'll find scores of potters along these roads. In fact, you can easily spend a day carrying an inexpensive wealth of pottery to your car.

Several families of English potters settled this area in the mid-1700s, drawn by rich clay deposits and plenty of pine trees, which stoke up red-hot fires in the kilns.

Mildred Teague Moore, whose family has turned pots here since the 1700s, sells her wares from one of the several one-room shops lining 705 at Westmoore. "A hundred years ago, just men were potters," she says. "It was kind of a man's type thing."

Seagrove potters turned out oceans of utilitarian pots: storage jars for fruit, milk, pine tar, whiskey. They made butter churns, chamber pots, dinner-

(Left) At Owens Pottery in Seagrove, Boyd Owen mixes local clay by hand.
(Above) Earthenware made by Boyd's grandfather, Ben Owens, at Jugtown Pottery, ca. 1950.
(St. Johns Museum of Art, Wilmington)

Krisalys Hall throwing a ring pot at Earth Spirit Pottery in Seagrove.

ware. They even made grave markers.

Whiskey jugs were big business until Prohibition and Mason jars killed the market. "Years ago, it got down to where there weren't more than five or six potters here," Moore says.

The community has revised and revived, with a new generation of art-school-trained potters leading the way. "There has been a surge in the past ten or fifteen years," says Ben Owens III, who turned his first pot here at his grandfather's knee. Owens, who continues a family tradition of incorporating simple Asian forms and bold color into his art, earned his BFA at East Carolina University, in Greenville, North Carolina. Visit his studio on 705 near Westmoore.

Westmoore Pottery, around the corner on Jugtown Road, reproduces colonial designs.

At Jugtown Pottery, a couple of miles down Jugtown Road, the log cabin shop is filled with pottery, tapestries, and hand-blown glass. Beyond the small garden of old timey purple iris, yarrow, and phlox, in a small museum, pottery exhibits and photos explain the long life of Jugtown Pottery, created in 1921 by Raleigh artists

Jacques and Juliana Busbee to market North Carolina pots in their Greenwich Village Tea Room.

Their marketing skills marked the first revival of Seagrove pottery. The second was sparked by tourists driving up from Pinehurst and Southern Pines. Seagrove is known for traditional pottery. It has one nice restaurant, Jugtown, but you may want to pack a lunch. *Follow signs off Highway 220, exit 45 to Seagrove. Visitors center at 124 Main Street; 336-873-7887.*

■ UWHARRIE NATIONAL FOREST

The Uwharrie National Forest, which curls west of US 220, attracts people with a taste for solitude. Hikers come for the 20-mile Uwharrie Trail, and nine shorter hiking and interpretive trails. Nature lovers also know the park for its deer, quail, ducks, wild turkeys, fox, and rabbits. Fishermen know Badin Lake for its large-mouth bass, white bass, bream, perch, and sunfish.

The Uwharrie Mountains, which once towered thousands of feet above the park floor, have worn away to around 900 feet. Even their name, Uwharrie, is beyond memory—a word borrowed from the Suala Indians, perhaps, who once lived here.

Settlers plundered these hills' veins for gold, silver, lead, and copper, and exhausted the thin soil with their crops. The Civilian Conservation Corps

Pine trees along Parson's branch trail in the Birkhead Mountain Wilderness of Uwharrie National Forest.

reforested this land in the 1930s. Today, mountain laurel, pines, hardwoods, dogwood, sourwood, wildflowers, and ferns form a gentle canopy along the slopes and stream banks.

Family and primitive campgrounds, accessible by hiking and bridle trails, are open year-round. Enter the 46,888-acre forest through Troy.

■ TOWN CREEK INDIAN MOUND

NC 109 to Mt. Gilead and NC 73 wind east through fields and forests once tended by Creek Indians, who colonized this area around AD 1250.

The Creek lived in villages, pulled fish from stone fish traps at the river's edge, and hunted the forests here for 200 years. Where tractors rumble through cotton and soybean fields today, the Creek hoed corn, pumpkins, gourds, beans, squash, and grew bright yellow sunflowers.

The reconstructed temple at Town Creek Indian Mound.

On a sharp bluff overlooking the fork of Town Creek and Little River, they built a palisaded temple complex, placing a thatch-roofed temple on a stepped pyramid. They celebrated important feast days here, and played ceremonial ball games. Only priests lived here, to keep the temple.

The Creek vanished around AD 1450. Some researchers suspect they died from disease introduced by Spanish explorers. Others say their Siouan enemies drove them away.

At their rebuilt temple complex, Town Creek Indian Mound, an interpretive center and film introduce visitors to the Creek culture, and guided

An interior of the temple on the mound.

tours offer a first-hand look at the temple, priest's dwelling, and ceremonial grounds. *Follow signs off Highways 73 or 731; 910-439-6802.*

From Mt. Gilead, NC 73 continues west to Concord and NASCAR country *(see page 215). To visit the Sandhills and the Inner Coastal Plain see the following chapter.*

QUILTS

NORTH CAROLINA QUILTS

The quilts below are part of the North Carolina Quilt Project, which documents quilts and quiltmakers in the state. Over 10,000 quilts have been documented: those below represent seven varieties. *(Photos and text courtesy Ruth Haislip Roberson.)*

Tree of Life
(left) A masterpiece medallion quilt in chintz applique. By Sarah Alexander Harris Gilmer, 1826.

Double Irish Chain
(right) Made by a mother for her four-year-old daughter. By Amelia Rosetta Arey Rothrock, 1851.

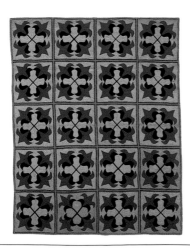

Tulip Quilt
(left) Made in a red and green pattern popular in the latter half of the 19th century. Made by machine and quilted one block at a time. By Joyce Shearin Coleman, 1880s.

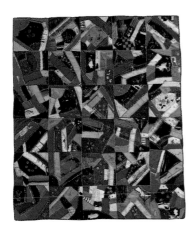

Crazy Quilt
(left) Scraps from a grandfather's carriage shop made into motifs of starfish, birds, butterflies, and flowers. By Laetitia Brown Gibbs, 1890.

Melon Patch Quilt
(right) A home-dyed quilt—this one made from home-dyed sugar sacks. By Mary Midgett Bridgman, 1902.

Friendship Basket
(left) This quilt has the names and birthdates of each person making a block. Made in the Stone Mountain Community for Sarah Royal, 1939.

American Eagle (right)
By Hazel Reece, 1967.

THE SANDHILLS

The Sandhills lie east of Charlotte, between the Cape Fear and Pee Dee Rivers. They owe their unique character to a prehistoric ocean whose receding tides and snapping winds left white sand dunes baking in the sun.

Early Scots farmers, who watched the sandy soil trickle through their fingers, named the area the Pine Barrens and moved on. Nothing, it seems, grew easily in the Sandhills except long-leaf pines. Today, the Pine Barrens are anything but barren, having given birth to three unique North Carolina cultures: Fayetteville's spit-and-polish military tradition; the golf-and-polo culture of Pinehurst, Aberdeen and Southern Pines, and the Lumbee tribe.

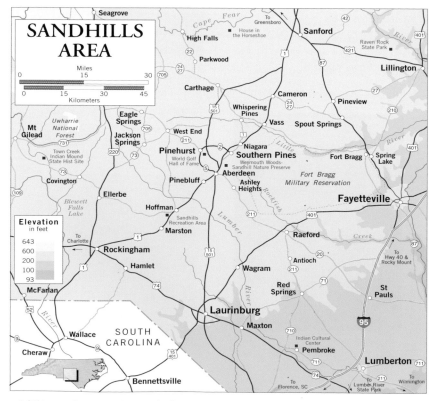

A hiking trail traverses the long-leaf pine forest in Weymouth Woods Sandhills Nature Preserve.

NC 211 takes you from the Seagrove area into Pinehurst and Southern Pines. You'll know you've crossed into the Sandhills when long-leaf pines begin crowding the roadside, growing in soil the color of ash and bone. This drive's dotted by unpainted board-and-batten houses and hills behind them rise and fall like the pale, prehistoric ocean floor they are. The pristine white stucco gas station with the cupola lets you know you've entered Pinehurst—"a whole 'nother world."

■ PINEHURST

Driving into Pinehurst, the transformation from sandhills to an oasis of golf greens is magical—especially in April, when azaleas and dogwoods turn the area's 40-odd golf courses into a scrollwork of manicured gardens.

That transformation is the legacy of Boston businessman James Walker Tuft, who hopped off the train one day in 1895 and bought 5,000 acres of stripped pine lands that were so inhospitable, even wild hogs didn't care to live on them. He called its remnant dunes "sand traps" and hired landscape architect Frederick Law Olmstead to turn his Sandhills into a New England-style village, Pinehurst.

Pinehurst Resort and Country Club is the world's largest golf resort.

Northerners flocked to the fresh-air resort, eager to trade blizzards for shirt-sleeve winters. Tuft added a golf course and in no time flat, Pinehurst was the bee's knees.

Amelia Earhart buzzed in for a landing. Annie Oakley headed up the Pinehurst Gun Club. The Rockefellers, Du Ponts, and Morgans swung by. So did Bing Crosby and Douglas Fairbanks.

Tuft's golf course was the first of the 40-plus courses that today make the Pinehurst region one of the world's top golf resort areas. His No. 2 course, the annual site of the North/South Amateur, still ranks among the nation's top 10 courses.

Today the area hosts top tournaments, and the Pinehurst Resort and Country Club is the world's largest golf resort. Golfers love Pinehurst for its history, and because they actually tee up on its tournament courses.

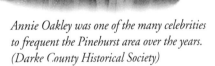

Annie Oakley was one of the many celebrities to frequent the Pinehurst area over the years. (Darke County Historical Society)

Golfers aren't alone in their regard for the Sandhills. Pinehurst's major tennis championships often include the U.S. Clay Court Championships. At Historic Pinehurst Racetrack, trainers take standardbreds through their paces year-round. Polo, fox hunting, harness racing, and Olympic trials are also staged here.

In addition, the 100-mile Tour de Moore, held each April, draws bicyclists from around the world. Olympic teams from the U.S. and Canada train here, but wobblier bicyclists take to the trails, too, crisscrossing parks on miles of gentle bike trails.

■ GOLFING IN SANDHILLS

With more than 30 courses in the Southern Pines–Pinehurst area, the Sandhills is the region to golf in North Carolina. Listed below are some of the finest courses in the area.

PUBLIC

Hyland Hills Golf Club. 4100 US No. 1 N; Southern Pines; 910-692-3752. Good course for average player.

Legacy. U.S. Hwy 15-501 S., Aberdeen; 910-944-8825; 800-344-8825. Great staff. Interesting layout by Jack Nicklaus, Jr.

The Pit Golf Links. Hwy. 5, Pinehurst; 910-944-1600. A unique course.

Talamore. 1595 Midland Rd., Southern Pines; 910-692-5884. Beautiful Sandhills course. Llama caddies available.

PRIVATE

The Club at Longleaf. 2001 Midland Rd., Southern Pines 910-692-6100 or (800) 889-5323. Some holes play through the old horse track. Semi-private.

Deercroft Golf and Country Club. 3000 Deercroft Dr., Wagram; 910-369-3107. Interesting, scenic, and challenging. Semi-private.

Foxfire Resort and Country Club. 9 Foxfire Rd., Jackson Springs; 910-295-4563. Two 18-hole courses.

Little River Golf Club. 500 Little River Farm Rd., Carthage; 910-949-4600. One of the newest courses in the area.

MidPines Golf Club. 1010 Midland Rd., Southern Pines 910-692-9362 or (800) 323-2114. Classic scenic course by Donald Ross stands the test of time.

Pinehurst Resort & Country Club. Carolina Vista St.; Pinehurst; 910-295-8141 or (800) 795-4653. Eight courses, particularly noteworthy are No.2 (Ranked 1st in North Carolina by Golf Digest). The crown jewel at Pinehurst, this course will be the site of the 1999 U.S. Open. No. 8 is the newest course built to celebrate the resort's centennial. Designed by Tom Razio.

Pine Needles. 1005 Midland Rd.; Southern Pines; 910-692-8611 or (800) 747-7272. A superb course, second only to Pinehurst.

Whispering Woods. 26 Sandpiper Dr., Whispering Pines; 910-949-4653 or (800) 224-5061 Excellent senior course. Semi private.

Woodlake Country Club. 150 Woodlake Blvd., Vass; 910-245-4686 or (888) 843-5253. A challenging course shaped around a lake.

■ IN THE PINEHURST AREA

The villages around Pinehurst are full of crafts shops, antique shops, cafes, and late-19th-century historic districts.

Ten miles off Carbonton Road, the bullet-riddled 1772 **House in the Horseshoe** is the area's most famous historic site. **The Malcom Blue Farm,** east of Aberdeen, includes an old mill and wooden water tower.

NC 2, a peaceful passage lined with long-leaf pines, connects Pinehurst and **Southern Pines,** a picturesque village with a viable downtown, restaurants, bookstores, and offices. Flowers bloom along the track leading into its clean, well-tended railroad station, right in the middle of town. Southern Pines has long been home to artists and writers.

A year-round program in the arts and humanities is available at the **Weymouth Center,** a Georgian-style house situated on 24 acres in Southern Pines. Many notable Carolina writers have been guests here.

The House in the Horseshoe is the region's most famous historic site. Bullet holes from the Revolutionary War are visible on the wall above the door and portrait.

At **Weymouth Woods Sandhills Nature Preserve,** on Ft. Bragg Road on the outskirts of Southern Pines, grows one of the Southeast's few remaining virgin, long-leaf pine forests. When the wind blows, this is a place of music. In fact, there's a special word just to describe a wind blowing through long-leaf pines: "susurrus." (The trees pronounce it, "soo-sur´-rahs.")

Explore this 168-acre forest by a mile-long loop trail that begins at the visitors center and museum, at the top of the hill. The forest slopes down along the gentle hillside. Large hardwoods—mostly black oaks and hickories—have taken root in the forest's upper meadow. "At the lower end of the meadow you'll start running into the big, old-growth trees," says park superintendent Scott Hartley. "They're anywhere from 200 to 400 years old. Height-wise, they're upwards of 70 to 100 feet." A former state champion long-leaf pine towers beside the trail. "It's really fantastic," he says. "You get two people, and you still can't hug it."

Farther down the hillside meadow, pines dominate. Sit beneath a pine, close your eyes, and listen. "It's almost like an instrument, the way the long-leaf needles sound when they move in the wind," Hartley says. "When the wind's real hard it sounds like a roar, almost like heavy surf."

🚗 From Pinehurst, NC 211 continues northwest to Uwharrie National Forest. A right at Eagle Springs takes you north on NC 705 to Seagrove *(see page 223).*

■ FAYETTEVILLE

Maybe it's the sky-high testosterone level. Maybe it's the World War II military housing standing at ease among the pines, or the lingering effects of a century's worth of good-byes.

Whatever it is, you feel it as soon as you exit I-95, cross the old bridge high above the Cape Fear River, and veer toward Fayetteville's downtown. Fayetteville—with its flashing neon, military-surplus shops, and platoons of topless bars—is a military town from the top of its well-shorn head to the toes of its spit-and-polish boots.

Even the name is military. Fayetteville, formed by the merger of Campbelltown and Cross Creek in 1783, was the first U.S. town named for Revolutionary War hero, the Marquis de Lafayette. Still, it didn't become a military town until 1918 when Congress put an artillery site on the edge of town, naming it after CSA General Braxton Bragg whose strategic errors hastened Wilmington's fall in 1864. In

1919 Congress added a landing field, naming it for a pilot who crashed in the Cape Fear River.

Despite the inauspicious beginnings, Fort Bragg and Pope Air Force Base today make up one of the world's largest military installations. In fact, Fort Bragg is the largest army base east of the Mississippi, supporting 146,000 active military people, dependents, and civilian employees. On base, the **John F. Kennedy Special Warfare Museum,** on Rifle Range Road, occupies what appears to be a 1960s-style elementary school. But that's just its cover. Inside is the stuff spy films are made of. Some of it, James Bond would have sent back for a refund—the 38-caliber glove, for instance, is about as subtle as an oven mitt with a pistol taped on top. In fact, it may be an oven mitt with a pistol taped on top. The harmonica-sized OSS mini-camera was a miracle of technology in the 1940s. So was the Stinger, a one-shot, 22-caliber, black-steel cigarette.

Fayetteville's historic district is reached from I-95 via exit 56 (I-95 Business) and Person Street, which leads into the small but fireproof downtown. Some 600 of the city's buildings went up in flames in 1831. The city rebuilt, only to be torched by Sherman in 1865. The few buildings that stood the heat generally aren't open to the public, or require reservations. If you'd like to look from the outside, the Fayetteville Area Convention and Visitors Bureau at 245 Person Street will get you pointed in the right direction. Follow Green Street off of Route 24 heading towards the military bases until Hay Street. The **Museum of the Cape Fear,** on Bradford and Arsenal, offers the best overview of area history.

Thanks to its military ties, Fayetteville is a multicultural community. Its diversity is most accessible via its restaurants, which offer everything from Eastern-style vinegar-dressed barbecue to tangy Thai food.

■ ROBESON COUNTY AND THE LUMBEE

South of Fayetteville, I-95 crosses the brooding Lumber River and travels into the world of the Lumbee, the largest Native American tribe east of the Mississippi.

The Lumbee (Lum-beé) have been a puzzle since 1755, when settlers found an English-speaking society of Native Americans living here in English-style houses. Most Lumbee believe the settlers stumbled on a melting-pot nation made up of displaced tribes. Catawba, Tuscarora, Creek, Waccamaw, and Cheraw people escaped into this dense swamp, they say, adopting English as a common trade language. Others believe the tribe included the English-speaking descendants of Sir Walter Raleigh's Lost Colony, and runaway slaves.

The Lumbee lived peacefully with their neighbors until the racially charged 1830s. To survive, they hid their culture underground.

Today the 40,000-member tribe has legal recognition from North Carolina, but not from the Bureau of Indian Affairs.

For Lumbee children growing up in a region known for poverty, drugs, and crime, the challenge is restoring a sense of culture, and of self. "First you've got to make people proud," says Tony Clark, who teaches traditional dances to young Lumbee. "I always tell them: you've got to believe in yourself."

■ PEMBROKE AREA FESTIVALS, SIGHTS, AND PARKS

At the **Indian Cultural Center** north of Pembroke in May, the parking lot's packed with cars and pick-up trucks sporting license plates from across the eastern U.S. Men, women, and children from various Native American tribes mill about the arena in traditional regalia—feathers, bone breastplates, face paint, turtle-shell

Ken Freeman of Pembroke, a member of the Lumbee tribe, stands by a painting depicting Lumbee history at the Lumbee Guaranty Bank which he manages.

rattles, and bells—waiting to dance at this annual powwow, hosted by the Lumbee. As the drums begin, the dancers begin their low, stately whirls.

The Lumbee host two powwows here each year—one in early May and one the second weekend in October. The Indian Wild Game Festival, held each November, invites guests to sample Native American foods, from venison to raccoon stew. Lumbee Homecoming on Fourth of July weekend attracts 15,000 to 20,000 visitors each year.

The Indian Cultural Center is north of Pembroke. *From I-95, take exit 14. Travel west 12 miles on US 74, and then follow the signs; (910-521-2433).*

The University of North Carolina campus at Pembroke was the first four-year college in the nation established for Native Americans (1887). It has an outstanding Indian Museum and began the first American Indian Studies B.A. degree program in the U.S.

The first weekend of each October, thousands of visitors take the high road to the **Flora MacDonald Highland Games** in Red Springs, called by the skirl of Scottish bagpipes and the swirl of the Highland Fling. The three-day event includes Scottish arts and crafts, traditional Scottish games, and a Revolutionary War battle re-enactment.

Red Springs is about 25 minutes northwest of Lumberton on NC 211. Between Lumberton and Red Springs, the **Humphrey-Williams-Smith Plantation** includes the 1856 Raft Swamp Post Office—the state's only known Confederate Post Office. *(Call first: 800-359-6971.)*

From Red Springs, NC 211 continues north to Pinehurst and Southern Pines *(see page 234).*

Lumber River State Park winds along the Lumber River, roughly from Wagram to Fair Bluff. The cypress-stained river is a state-designated Scenic River.

Park officials offer night hikes, birding tours, and guided canoe trips, but you can drop a canoe or small boat and explore the cypress-lined shores on your own. Move quietly, and you may see deer peeping over the riverbanks.

Fishermen with North Carolina licenses pull in black crappie, red breasts, bass and catfish. (Those without licenses land hefty fines.) Two rare minnow-sized fish, the sandhills chub and pinewood darter, haunt the waters in the northern park.

This park-in-progress includes drive-in camping, and canoe-in campgrounds. Bring your own canoe.

Drive south from Lumberton on NC 41 to Fairmont, 12 miles east on NC 130, turn onto SR 2225 south, to SR 2246 east. The park entrance lies two miles ahead.

THE APPALACHIANS

THE WESTERNMOST EIGHTH OF NORTH CAROLINA lies within the Appalachian Mountains, one of the oldest mountain ranges in the world. North Carolina's geologic braid of time-gentled mountain ranges is noted for broad vistas, pristine forests, thundering waterfalls, and vast tracts of protected lands.

The Blue Ridge Mountains, the easternmost range of North Carolina's Appalachians, runs parallel to the coast, northeast to southwest. Immediately behind the Blue Ridge, which rises sharply from the Piedmont floor, lies a mountainous tableland of forests, pastures, valley farmland, and clear, rushing streams.

Along North Carolina's border with Tennessee, the Great Smoky Mountains rise in ranges parallel to the Blue Ridge, like rails on the same geologic railroad. Both the Blue Ridge Mountains and the Great Smoky Mountains draw their names from the blue-grey haze that veils the mountains.

To the south, near Asheville, the cross-ranges begin. These short, choppy ranges—the Black Mountains, Craggy Mountains, Cowees, Nantahalas, Pisgah

Idyllic Mill Creek Valley is nestled in the Norton area of the Appalachian Mountains.

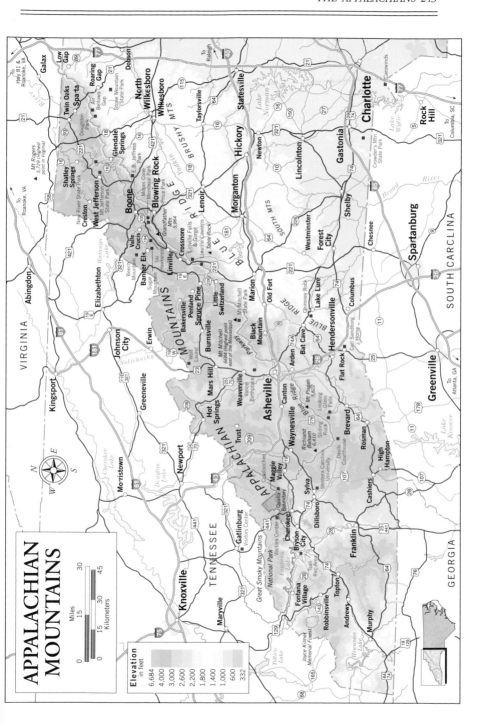

Ledge, Balsams, Plott Balsams—run perpendicular to the Blue Ridge, providing North Carolina's most rugged mountain scenery, and the tallest peaks east of the Mississippi.

Asheville, population 67,000, stands as the mountains' lone city. In general, this is a place of small towns, quiet hamlets, hardscrabble homesteads, and used-to-be villages.

■ GEOLOGY, HISTORY, AND A WAY OF LIFE

How did the Appalachians come to be here? The Cherokee, who have lived here for thousands of years, say that one day long ago, the Great Buzzard swooped low over the new earth. His wings brushed the impressionable earth, creating the mountains ranges that rise and fall, and then fade into the sky.

Geologists envision a wilder scenario.

About 450 million years ago, about the time the first fish darted through the sea, a drifting continental fragment collided with an underwater continent. Sheets of earth several miles thick skidded over the edge of the raw North American continent. As the earth folded, crumpled, broke, and steamed, the Appalachians rose shakily while beneath their feet, superheated rock changed the continent's very blood.

The land rose, dipped to become an ocean bed, and rose again. Twice more over the next 250 million years land masses collided, building mountains taller than today's Alps. Over the next 200 million years, time softened their edges. Freezing water sheered boulders and mountainsides, tree roots split stones, spring rains swirled away tons of pebbles and sand.

Today's Appalachians are the hearts of those towering peaks. Most are made of granite and greenstone. Some are remnants of the old continent: gneiss, schistose, and quartzite. Quartzite, the hardest of them all, forms the heart of the tallest mountains.

Earth forces have also given North Carolina more gems and minerals than any other state.

The Cherokee once mined mica in Mitchell County. Today commercial mines harvest mica, feldspar, and ultra-pure quartz in the same region, while rockhounds search for emeralds, rubies, garnets, amethyst, and sapphires that tumble from the earth's pockets.

Over the millennia, the myriad of streams and rivers have gradually worn the once towering Appalachians down to gentle peaks.

■ A MATTER OF ALTITUDE

Sky-side, these mountains support a wealth of life.

The mountains' unusual diversity of plant life has sent botanists into quiet frenzies since 1775, when William Bartram "discovered" the fiery azalea. (Part of Bartram's pathway is now a trail in Nantahala National Forest.) Botanists have recorded, named, and sketched oceans of flowering shrubs, wildflowers (1,500 species in Smoky Mountain National Park alone), lichens, and fungi species. Plus, they chortle, more tree species live in the North Carolina Appalachians than in all of Europe.

In the mountains, altitude determines two big environmental factors: temperature and rainfall. The temperature drops about three degrees for every 1,000-foot climb up a mountainside, and temperature helps define ecological communities.

Then there's rain. In North America, only the forests of the Pacific Northwest receive more rainfall than the southern Appalachians, though the amount of rain is uneven. Asheville, which lies in a valley, receives 40 inches of rain a year; a few miles to the south, Transylvania County's mountains receive 100 inches each year. (This helps explain why Transylvania County is home to the state's most spectacular waterfalls.)

Thanks to differences in temperature and moisture, a 6,000-foot mountain may harbor 16 different forest types—complete with trees, shrubs, ferns, wildflowers, fungi, and lichens—with the forest types stacked one on another as the altitude rises.

This lush plant kingdom supports an equally lush wildlife community, from black bears, to hawks, to rattlesnakes, to mud puppies, to trout, to fireflies and migrating Monarch butterflies. Volumes have been written on the plants and wildlife of the Appalachians.

■ THE CHEROKEE

The first known stewards of these mountains were the Cherokee, who once occupied the Appalachians from the Ohio River, south to Alabama. When Europeans first visited North Carolina's mountains in 1540, they found around 25,000 Cherokee living in a land the Cherokee called *Shaconage,* "The Land of the Blue Mist."

The Cherokee lived in villages of perhaps 50 small, log homes, centered on a town square and large council house. The seven-sided council house acknowl-

FLOWERS OF THE APPALACHIANS *AS MAY BE SEEN FROM THE PARKWAY*

Phlox bloom May through June near mileposts 4, 79–82, 163–4, 200–2, 219–21, 339, and 370-80.

Mountain laurels bloom late May through June near mileposts 130, 163, 348, 380–81.

Catawba rhododendrons bloom in June near mileposts 45, 77–83, 130, 239, 247, 267, 348-50, 364.

Black-eyed susans bloom in July and are common in fields and along roadsides.

Azaleas bloom May through June near mileposts 139, 144–5, 150, 164–6, 217–21, 308–10, 368–80, 412–23.

Trillium bloom April through May near mileposts 175, 200–16, 339–40, 365.

Carolina lilies bloom April through May near milepost 439.

Tulip poplars bloom April through May in low woods and coves.

edged the seven clans within a society where clan membership and property was passed down matrilineally. (A boy looked to his mother's brother for his sense of place in society.) Neighboring Shawnee occasionally skirmished with the Cherokee—over hunting lands rich with buffalo, deer, bear, and wild turkeys. For the most part, though, the Cherokee lived quietly, much of their sustenance coming from gardens planted in corn, melons, beans, and tobacco; and from wild plants gathered for food, as well as for medicine and trade. Cherokee women wove baskets of oak strips and reeds, and they cooked in pots of clay. They fashioned robes of animal skins, and ceremonial headdresses of sacred eagle feathers.

The Cherokee wove a mythology as intricate as their basketry, explaining their relationship to plants, animals, other tribes, a race of little people, and giants. When they fell ill, they consulted healers, who gathered herbs and talked with their god, who listened. And why not? The Cherokee believed themselves to be the *Yun Wiya,* the "real people" of the world.

Spanish explorer Hernando de Soto visited the Cherokee in 1540, lured by fables of gold and silver mines. His murders made an impression: As late as 1890, a Cherokee who killed an eagle immediately identified himself to other powerful eagle spirits as a Spaniard, in case they took revenge on him and his people.

Scots rather than Spaniards finally settled the North Carolina highlands, looking not for gold, but rich soil. From the mid-1700s on, Scots and Germans surged down the Great Wagon Road claiming valley lands farmed by the Cherokee, and pushing the Cherokee into the hills. A local boy named Daniel Boone soon blazed a Wilderness Road to Tennessee, leading settlers deeper into the mountains. The Cherokee struggled to change with the times. They adopted a legal code, and a Supreme Court. Sequoyah, a Cherokee silversmith, designed an alphabet for his language; within two years, most Cherokee could read and write. They published a newspaper, and wrote a constitution.

Sequoyah—Cherokee warrior, silversmith, and painter— invented the Cherokee alphabet in 1821. He created a system of 86 symbols, adapting letters from English, Hebrew, and Greek. (The Thomas Gilcrease Institute of American History and Art, Tulsa, Oklahoma)

PRIVATE BURNETT REMEMBERS

*T*his is my birthday, December the 11th, 1890, I am eighty years old today. . . . I grew into manhood fishing in Beaver Creak and roaming through the forest hunting the Deer the wild Boar and the timber Wolf. . . . On these long hunting trips I met and became acquainted with many of the Cherokee Indians, hunting with them by day and sleeping around their camp fires by night. I learned to speak their language. . . .

The removal of the Cherokee Indians from their life long homes in the year of 1838 found me a young man in the prime of life and a Private soldier in the American Army. Being acquainted with many of the Indians and able to fluently speak their language, I was sent as interpreter into the Smoky Mountain Country. . . . in the chill of a drizzling rain on an October morning I saw them loaded like cattle or sheep into six hundred and forty-five wagons and started toward the west.

One can never forget the sadness and solemnity of that morning. Chief John Ross led in prayer and when the bugle sounded and the wagons started rolling many of the children rose to their feet and waved their little hands good-by. . . .

❖

Being a young man I mingled freely with the young women and girls. I have spent many pleasant hours with them when I was supposed to be under my blanket, and they have many times sung their mountain song for me, this being all that they could do to repay my kindness. And with all my association with Indian girls from October 1829 to March 28th 1839, I did not meet one who was a moral prostitute. They are kind and tender hearted and many of them are beautiful.

—John G. Burnett, 2nd Regiment, 2nd Brigade, Mounted Infantry, 1838–39
The Cherokee Removal Through the Eyes of A Private Soldier

But by 1828, some 30 treaties with the Cherokee had been signed and broken, and North Carolina's Cherokee found themselves elbowed into the rugged, southwest corner of the state. Gold, which had lured De Soto to their land in 1540, now sealed their fate.

When prospectors struck gold in Georgia's mountains in 1828, settlers clamored for Indian land. President Andrew Jackson signed the Removal Act, demanding that all Native Americans east of the Mississippi move to the new Oklahoma Territory.

The Cherokee insisted on their legal right to stay. In Congress, Davy Crockett, Daniel Webster, and Henry Clay argued in their behalf. The U.S. Supreme Court ruled in their favor. Chief Junaluska, who had saved Jackson's life at the Battle of Horseshoe Bend in 1812, now asked President Jackson for help.

For the first and only time, a U.S. President turned his back on a Supreme Court decision. He forced the Cherokee on a 1,200-mile death march known as today The Trail of Tears. A few hundred Cherokee hid in the mountains, eking out a living until 1899 when Congress chartered the 56,000-acre Qualla Boundary, commonly known as the Eastern Cherokee Reservation. Today, around 11,000 descendants of its original 1,000 residents live there.

■ HARDSCRABBLERS AND HOLIDAY-MAKERS

With the Cherokee driven away or in hiding, white settlers claimed the Appalachian countryside. The rich bottomlands had been settled by traders, merchants, and farmers. Still settlers came—Scots, Germans, the Irish. These "hardscrabble farmers" clung to the high mountainsides, scrabbling to stay alive.

Another, wildly contrasting lifestyle emerged, too.

As early as the late 1700s, wealthy lowlanders summered in the North Carolina mountains, trading summer's deadly malarial fevers for the cool mountain air. As tuberculosis rates climbed in the lowlands, health resorts flourished, with Asheville leading the way. People came to the mineral springs, boarding houses, and spas, hoping to cure everything from hiccups to brain tumors.

The Civil War came and went, with the relatively slave-free mountains dressing sons in both blue and grey. Now the railroad puffed through the highlands. George Vanderbilt (1862–1914) hopped off the train in Asheville, brushed the cinders from his coat, and took a good look at the scenery. He liked what he saw. He built an opulent, 255-room chateau outside town, importing European artists, craftsmen, and forestrymen to create his 120,000-acre Biltmore Estate.

Suddenly everybody who was anybody wanted a place in the mountains. Mansions went up on mountaintops, gardens sketched themselves along mountainsides, geometric ponds lolled in the valleys. Cream-colored roadsters packed with well-heeled outlanders purred along the switchbacks leading to the old resort towns: Flat Rock, Cashiers, Asheville, Blowing Rock. But roads winding from those towns and high into the mountains crossed economic chasms as stunning as Nantahala Gorge.

The members of this Appalachian family, photographed in the 1930s by a Farm Security Administration photographer, are testimony to the "hardscrabble" life many of the state's mountain residents endured before and during the Depression. (Library of Congress)

The stock market crash of 1929 sent the resort economy into a downhill skid. Millionaires lost millions but across the economic chasm, where farm income averaged $86 a year, there wasn't much to lose. As banks drew their shades and resorts closed their doors, hardscrabble farmers planted their corn and carded their wool, and wondered what all the fuss was about.

■ THEN CAME THE PARKWAY

Over 25 million people drive the Blue Ridge Parkway each year, making it America's most popular scenic drive. In North Carolina, the Parkway meanders from the Virginia border, down along the rim of the Blue Ridge Mountains to Asheville. There it swerves west, past Cherokee and the Qualla Boundary, to the Great Smoky Mountains National Park.

Before the Great Depression, a description of that route would have been a real knee-slapper. The Parkway crosses regions then known for mud roads, oxen-pulled sleds, and mule-drawn wagons. Folks built their own cabins, ground their own corn, and shot their own squirrels.

So, why a Parkway? The National Park Service wanted to connect Shenandoah National Park, in Virginia, with the Great Smoky Mountains National Park, draped across the North Carolina–Tennessee border. More importantly, President Franklin D. Roosevelt wanted to put America to work, and a 477-mile project was bound to help in that regard.

In September, 1935 a blast of Red Diamond dynamite and a shower of mountain stones christened Parkway construction. The *Asheville Citizen* reported: "More than 100 men started work on the Parkway at the Carolina–Virginia line above Low Gap Monday morning, this being the first 12-mile section of the Parkway. . . . The men were secured from the relief and unemployment rolls of Allegheny County. . . ."

Of course, not everyone was glad to see FDR's steam shovels, trucks, and dynamite coming round the mountain. Most people who found themselves on the government's broad right-of-way had to move—lock, stock, and hen house. Caroline Brinegar, however, closed her cabin door and refused to budge.

(Above) The Brinegar Cabin, whose owner refused to budge when the Parkway was being built. (Right) Rhododendrons bloom beside the entrance to the Parkway's Craggy Pinnacle Tunnel.

How did the Federal government fare in a standoff with the aged mountain woman? You can still visit Mrs. Brinegar's mountain home, where for years she raised squash, potatoes, pole beans, corn, tomatoes, and mountain flax as tourists' Studebakers puttered along the Parkway, outside her back door. The Park Service now makes good use of the homestead. Today, the park's ubiquitous costumed interpreters demonstrate the chores and crafts Caroline Brinegar refused to do someplace else.

It took 52 years to complete the Parkway. Workers chiseled roads around, along, and through mountainsides; Italian stonemasons fashioned graceful arched underpasses, tunnels, and sweeping walls; engineers built spectacular roadside balconies from mountain rubble; and landscape architects artfully hid every inch of scar on the mountains' altered faces with rhododendrons, laurels, and wildflowers.

Hints of forgotten homesteads do remain. The apple trees that perfume April mornings are gifts from settlers who woke up here morning after morning, stretched, and snuggled back beneath their quilts, never dreaming a Parkway would bring millions of outland visitors to their cabin door.

■ DRIVING THE PARKWAY

Today, the Parkway includes a host of campgrounds, hiking trails of various difficulty (from stroll-alongs to puff-alongs), historic sites, orchards, fishing streams, nature walks, waterfalls, and overlooks.

The place is rich in wildlife. Groundhogs, or "whistle pigs" stand paunch-bellied and limp-wristed by the side of the road, like tiny, inquisitive old men. Bear and wild turkeys live in the forests; deer graze by the road as foxes, possums, skunks, squirrels, and other small fry scurry through the woodlands. In spring, over a hundred species of birds migrate through, or nest here.

The seasons stroll majestically up and down the North Carolina mountains, and the Parkway is a great place (but certainly not the only place) to watch their stately procession.

Spring awakens in the valley in early April, and wanders up the mountainside trailing naive greens, the pristine white of the flowering dogwood, and the pinks of service berries, redbuds, and mountain laurel. Summer climbs in lusher, deeper greens and the royal purple of the Catawba rhododendron.

In September, autumn brushes the mountaintops with a faint, reddish gold that descends to the valley like a long, voluptuous blush: sumac, dogwood, gums, and sourwoods; buckeyes, birch, tulip poplars, beech, hickory, and sassafras; mountain ash, maples, and red oaks.

Before autumn brushes her fingertips across the valley one last time, winter begins its slow, pale drift down the mountains, returning to the valley until spring is born again.

■ DIRECTIONS AND SIDEROADS

Parkway directions are easy, since all sites have a milepost number. Milepost 0 marks the northernmost point of the Parkway, in Virginia. Off the Parkway, directions can be trickier. But despite their lust for deadpan *(see page 292)*, most mountaineers give good directions. To understand the directions, you must know two things.

Number One: "Up" means uphill, not north. "Down" means downhill, not south. If someone tells you to "Go up Highway X," they mean drive up the mountain on Highway X even if you head south to do it.

Number Two: Roads are scarce. "Take the next paved right" may mean turn right a half-hour down (or up) the road. If this kind of uncertainty makes you nervous, ask for travel times.

Mountain drives come in three varieties: Parkway, Off-Parkway, and Off-Off-Parkway. Off-Parkway highways and roads twist and turn their way to tiny Carpenter Gothic churches with unexpected frescoes, general stores with pot-bellied stoves, barn dances with pot-bellied fiddlers, crafts fairs, gemstone mines, gourmet restaurants, gourmet trout streams, wildlife walks, and whitewater gorges.

Off-Off-Parkway drives are the dotted blue roads on the road map. They're usually graveled, two-lane roads—but, as one local explains, "sometimes the lanes lie on top of each other."

Use your horn before you enter a blind curve, and give the right of way to drivers coming downhill. (If you drive backcountry roads often, buy *North Carolina Atlas & Gazetteer*.) Courtesy counts. Nod to cows, wave to everybody else.

■ OUTDOOR RECREATION

About two-thirds of North Carolina's mountains lie within a tremendous patchwork of protected areas, including the Great Smoky Mountains National Park, the

(Following pages) Waynesville Overlook at Milepost 441 is typical of the many extraordinary vistas along the Blue Ridge Parkway.

Parkway, two national forests, and several state parks. In addition, the private economy is based almost entirely on tourism, and small businesses are eager to help you do just about anything you'd want to do in the mountains: from white-water rafting, mountain biking, and downhill skiing to enjoying the rocking chairs on the front porch of a cozy mountain inn.

For anglers, the North Carolina mountains are a promised land of fast-flowing, well-stocked, and wild trout streams. In fact, there are around 2,100 miles of public mountain trout waters in North Carolina, and they're loaded with brown, brook, and rainbow trout. You can get a complete list of those waters, with rules and regulations, from the North Carolina Wildlife Resources Commission; *919-733-3633.*

Fishermen need a license, available at area stores and via phone *(1-888-2HUNT-FISH).* Those under 16 can fish with a licensed adult, or carry the license of a parent or guardian. To fish on the Cherokee Reservation you need a tribal license, available at shops in and near Cherokee. Check the state and tribal regulations before casting your hand-tied fly upon the waters, or you may land more than a trout.

By the way, fishermen don't need a license to fish in a private pond. The mountains abound with ponds stocked with fat, easily duped trout sold by the pound.

■ THE LOST PROVINCES: ASHE AND ALLEGHENY, THE NORTHERN COUNTIES

Not long ago, the easiest way to get to North Carolina's northernmost mountains was to be born there. Today, most visitors take NC 89 from Mt. Airy instead.

Heading west from Andy Griffith's home town, the hillsides grow steeper, the soil grows thinner, afternoon's blue shadows lie flatter against the earth.

Life slows down, too. At **Dobson,** the drivers of mule-drawn carts "whoa" to chat in front of the general store. Down the road, a farmer has draped the mountainside with neat garlands of bright green Christmas trees. His neighbor devotes her felt-green pastures to horses and black-and-white Holsteins. By a white frame house in the bend, a seamstress advertises handmade quilts.

At Low Gap, NC 89 slips beneath the Blue Ridge Parkway's arched stone overpass, and heads into Allegheny County.

Saturday Night in the Lost Provinces

Mountain music is big in the Lost Provinces, especially on Saturday night, and especially in Tom and Nancy Burgiss's barn, home of the weekly New River Mountain Music Jamboree.

"Our purpose is to promote and pass on the tradition of mountain dancing and mountain music," says Tom Burgiss, who built the barn after Hurricane Hugo leveled a stand of timber on his farm, near Laurel Springs. "From lemons you make lemonade," says Burgess, running a hand through his white hair. "From Hugo, you make a barn."

Every Saturday night since, two top mountain bands—one bluegrass and one old-timey—have stepped up on stage, peered across the antique-filled barn, and gotten 150 or so dancers buck-dancing, flat-footing, clogging, and waltzing.

The difference between the bluegrass and old-timey bands? "A bluegrass band always has a fiddle, mandolin, banjo, guitar, and bass," he says. "Other instruments, like the autoharp, are optional." Old-timey bands, on the other hand, can be any number of instruments. Wooden spoons and a washtub bass qualify.

Folks dance from 8 until 11 PM—with a modest charge for adults, and polite children free. "They pay if they're not well behaved," Burgiss warns.

Square dance teams sometimes drop by, but most people dance alone or in couples. "In buck dancing, you just feel the rhythm, get up, and start dancing," Burgess says. Other dancers clog, or flat-foot.

"I'm more of a waltzing man," Burgiss adds. Not that that keeps him off the dance floor. "It's impossible to make a fool of yourself," he says. "Everybody's in their own zone."

Call 910-384-4079 or 800-233-1505 for directions.

Jeeter Gentry, Elmer Thompson, and Fiddlin' Bill get together for a bluegrass jam in the 1930s. (Library of Congress, Farm Security Administration)

Allegheny County remains innocent of ski slopes, artsy shops, and upscale restaurants. (In fact, Sunday drivers best pack a picnic.) The architecture tends to be frugal and hard-working, like the people, and constructed from materials close at hand: timber and stone.

Old settlements here include sixth-generation extended families. Newer houses sit with their backs nestled against hillsides, for warmth. Here and there older, plain-faced clapboard houses sit a ways up the mountain, their grey tin roofs pulled up into tight buns. In the valleys, tiny, white, steepled churches—most of them Baptist of one bent or another—dot the countryside.

Scots, Germans, and Brits settled this land in the late 1700s, drifting south along river valleys into hunting grounds claimed by the Shawnee and Cherokee. Most built one-room log cabins, with fieldstone chimneys and rear-shed kitchens.

They positioned their homes carefully, building halfway up a hill or in a valley to ward off winter winds, and near a stream or spring for water and power. They planted apple orchards, and named places so you'd know when you got there: Air Bellows, Roaring Gap, Low Gap, Laurel Springs.

A view over the New River Valley from Luther Rocks in Ashe County's Mt. Jefferson State Park.

In Allegheny and Ashe Counties, the main industries rely on the land: livestock, burley tobacco, Christmas trees, timber. The barns are sprawling affairs—broad, elegant structures with diamond-shaped vents near their peaks.

The Lost Provinces' 600-plus miles of unpaved, back-country roads wind along dancing rivers and up undeveloped mountains. Road posts with four-digit numbers are public roads; those without number-posts are private drives.

■ ROARING GAP AND SPARTA

Roaring Gap, east of the Parkway on US 21, was settled in 1780 by a runaway servant, Absalom Smith, and his ex-boss's daughter, Agnes. They named their new home Roaring Gap, because the rock formations amplify the howl of the winds. (The private golf resort, built in 1926, also carries the name Roaring Gap.)

West of the Parkway, Sparta's townscape benefits from the work of an Italian stonemason who came to build the Parkway and settled in Allegheny's county seat. Much of the cut stonework throughout the mountains reflects the skill of Parkway stonemasons, or locals who learned the art from them.

Sparta Industries, Inc. makes Doctor Grabow smoking pipes from the mountain laurel on low-elevation mountainsides.

■ ALONG NC 93

US 221 heads west from Sparta. Veering north on scenic NC 93, you'll see Stratford Road on your left; **Mangum Pottery's** small sign is down Stratford a ways, on your right. The steep gravel path winds up through the rhododendrons, poplar, oaks, and dogwood, to the shop of Bet Garrison and Robin Mangum. Mangum Pottery is best known for its red glazes and autumnal raku, but the work here is extremely diverse. Visitors watch these artists throw pots, and build sculptures from the feet up.

Backtracking to NC 93, this country road wanders past a tractor graveyard, where ancient metal skeletons rust away, putters along the twisting section of road tended by the Piney Creek Dirty Fingers Garden Club, and then cuts over to **New River State Park.**

This 26.5-mile Scenic River, the heart of North Carolina's newest state park, offers some of the best easy canoeing in the mountains. The New is actually one of

North America's oldest rivers. Thomas Jefferson's father, who surveyed the western North Carolina–Virginia line, apparently named it after a Mr. New, who drowned here.

The New River, on the western side of the Eastern Continental Divide, flows north. Its clear, greenish water rolls through a valley of rhododendron, pines, and dogwood. Paddlers have taken a shine to the New, which offers a relaxed paddle— Class I rapids with a couple of Class II runs near the Virginia line. Private outfitters along the river offer canoes, shuttle service, etc.

■ THE SPRINGS

South on NC 16 lie Ashe County's mineral springs—popular health resorts from the late 1800s until the Depression.

A left on **Healing Springs Road** leads along a mountain stream and a row of easy-going, 1930s-era cabins. Folks stop by the springhouse to trade gardening tips and load up on the free, mineral-rich waters. (Three ladies from Tennessee cruise in regularly with exactly 52 gallon jugs—the record for jugs packed, precisely, into one car. Don't distract them.)

A little farther down NC 16, at **Shatley Springs,** the water's free but the jugs will cost you. Martin Shatley discovered Shatley Springs in 1890, when a dip in its waters cured a life-threatening skin disease. Thousands have flocked to the springs since, to cure skin diseases, digestive problems, rheumatism, and nervous twitches.

People still come to take the waters, but more drop by to hike the buffet line. Shatley Springs' huge 1930s-style restaurant serves its Southern cooking to about 10,000 visitors a month. Breakfast—a banana muffin and cup of coffee—costs 50 cents. Lunch—chicken pie, fresh baked apples, sweet cabbage, homemade biscuits, and tea—is also moderately priced.

NC 16 and US 221 lead to the New River General Store, a 1928 mercantile with sassafras candy, a hand-cranked coffee-grinder, brass spittoon, canoes, and a defunct two-seater outhouse in the back room, overhanging the river.

■ AIR BELLOWS GAP

If you hook beneath the Parkway onto Air Bellows Road, and take the gravel drive winding down into the valley and sharply up the side of the mountain, you'll find

Air Bellows Herb Gardens. If you're not familiar with mountain wildflowers and herbs, these theme gardens will get you oriented.

Back on the Parkway, Caroline Brinegar's cabin—the one she refused to vacate for the Parkway—bustles. Caroline, a well known weaver, used "tromp as writ" patterns for her four-poster loom. This "sheet music" told her which foot treadles to tromp to create a specific pattern. (Docents will demonstrate it for you.)

Doughton Park bears the name of the U.S. Congressman who helped finagle the Parkway out of Tennessee's mountains and into North Carolina's, bringing Depression-era jobs and a long-term tourism industry with it. Nature lovers know Doughton Park for its campfire programs, and nature walks.

■ GLENDALE SPRINGS

It's no accident the Parkway runs so near Glendale Springs Inn's front door. Congressman Doughton, who helped route the Parkway, was part owner of the inn.

Colonel D. W. Adams built this National Registry inn in 1895. Some visitors' Model Ts did wheeze up the cutbacks on Old 16 (now a very scenic, one-lane gravel drive with more back-and-forth than a belly dancer). But the resort never quite caught on.

Instead, it's been a bit of everything for Glendale Springs, population 350: inn, post office, circuit courthouse, general store, wedding chapel (the preacher lived upstairs), and moonshine-stocked dance hall.

From 1935–38 the mildly scandal-ridden inn headquartered Parkway engineers and stonemasons. The inn has recently re-opened—restored rooms, gourmet dining, and ghosts included. The most popular destinations for guests? The frescoes in two tiny churches—one within walking distance, the other in West Jefferson, nine miles down the road.

■ WEST JEFFERSON

West Jefferson is also home to Ashe County Cheese, North Carolina's only cheese manufacturer, and to Mt. Jefferson State Park, named for Thomas Jefferson. The park offers hiking and nature trails.

NC 163 deposits travelers on the Parkway near Horse Gap, and slips south through E. B. Jeffress Park, and Deep Gap. US 421 heads west to Wilkesboro, a Piedmont town known for NASCAR races. US 221 heads east to Boone.

ASHE COUNTY'S FRESCOES

In 1973, Faulton Hodge came to Ashe County to pastor two tiny Episcopal churches. He found Holy Trinity, in Glendale Springs, standing empty, one wall caved in. Nine miles away, in West Jefferson, St. Mary's 13 members worshiped in a church badly in need of repair. To make matters worse, Hodge had a budget the size of a mustard seed.

Then, at a party, he met artist Ben Long who suddenly announced he wanted to paint a fresco in Hodge's church—for free. To create a fresco, Long explained, the artist places a thin mixture of lime and sand on a wall, and brushes pigments into the wet wall. While studying the technique in Italy, Long said, his spirit had been told to paint a church fresco in North Carolina. And since he and Hodge had crossed paths. . .

Long began his work. For St. Mary's, he wanted to paint an expectant Mary. He scanned every face he met, searching for a model. One day, he spied a barefoot girl walking along a road. "That's her!" he thought, and asked to sketch her. When he had finished, he finally asked her name. "Mary," she said, walking away.

As people came to watch Long paint, the church took on new life. He began a second work, "John the Baptist." Then, as people filed into the church to pray, he created a tremendous crucifixion/resurrection scene, "The Mystery of Faith."

While Long finished his work at St Mary's, Hodge stood in Trinity's churchyard, wondering if he should destroy the Glendale Springs church he couldn't afford to repair, and sell the property. A car pulled up and a stranger got out, saying he'd come to see his mother's childhood church. He looked at the tumbled down wall. "What do you reckon it would take to fix her?" he asked. Hodge guessed: $1,500. The man wrote a check, hopped in his car, and drove away. The repairs cost $1,400, leaving $100 for supplies for Long's finest fresco, "The Last Supper."

Long worked on this piece for three months, using locals as models for all the figures except Christ and Judas. Even a dog who dozed in the church found a home in the fresco.

Some people see Ben Long's frescoes as miracles of faith, some as a revival of a Renaissance art. One thing is certain: his art resurrected these beautiful old Carpenter Gothic churches.

From the Parkway, take Route 163 to Ashe County. Holy Trinity Church in Glendale Springs is off Route 16, about two and half miles north of Route 163; 828-982-3076. Nine miles farther on Route 163 is West Jefferson. St. Mary's Church is only about a half mile off the highway on 400 Beaver Creek School Road; 828-246-3552.

A fresco titled "The Last Supper" adorns a wall in Holy Trinity Episcopal Church in Glendale Springs.

■ BOONE

Boone, the home of Appalachian State University, is a right-this-minute college town from its ski goggles to its hiking boots. Set tight in a mountain valley and surrounded by forest, it is a compact town of brick buildings, wide sidewalks, and lush vegetation. (Its less appealing condo and mall area is southeast of town on Hwy. 321 going toward Blowing Rock.) Drive up to **Howard Knob,** the county park in the middle of town, and get out for the view of Boone and its surrounding evergreen and deciduous forest, filled with mountain laurel and rhododendron.

At the center of downtown are King Street's student-oriented shops that post signs boasting, "FAMOUS SINCE APRIL," and "ESTABLISHED LAST YEAR." It's fitting, actually, since the town's named for the quintessential restless youth: Daniel Boone.

As a gateway to North Carolina's best ski resorts, Boone is more visitor conscious than small towns to the north. Something's always going on, from arts festivals, to crafts demonstrations, to June's Firefly Festival. The *Southern Farmer's Almanac* has christened Boone the Firefly Capital of America. Glow-worm watching (there are thirty varieties) is one form of Boone nightlife, June through July. Another form of nightlife can be found in King Street's pubs—Murphy's and the Caribbean Cafe, which has darned good food for darned little money. The Blue Planet Map Company next door is one of the best on the planet. Nearby is an old Mast General Store, not the original, but one of the oldest, as you can tell from its creaky floors and old-fashioned counters. The *Mountain Times,* a free tabloid available in local businesses, explains what's going on.

Daniel Boone Native Gardens is a lovely place to get out of your car and walk around. Paths meander beneath an arbor trailing clematis, and through a sunken garden, rockery, sweet-smelling fern garden, and several other small gardens. The log hunting cabin with the mossy roof once belonged to Daniel Boone's father, Squire Boone. Near his cabin, you can picnic on a broad lawn, or browse through the trillium, jack-in-the-pulpit, beech, wild roses, wild larkspur, and bloodroot.

The surrounding park area includes Daniel Boone Native Gardens, Hickory Ridge Homestead, and "The Horn in the West," an outdoor drama that dramatizes the role Daniel Boone and other North Carolina mountaineers played in the Revolutionary War. *(Late June through mid-August; 828-295-9627.)*

■ Skiing in the Appalachians

There are eight ski resorts in North Carolina, four of which are in the high country. **Appalachian Ski Mountain** (800-322-2373) in Blowing Rock is popular with families and beginners. The outdoor ice-skating rink, with its spectacular views, is an appealing alternative to skiing. **Sugar Mountain Resort** in Banner Elk (800-784-2768) is the largest, with 18 slopes and 1,200 foot vertical drop. **Ski Beech** in Beech Mountain (800-438-2093) is a lively resort with restaurants, shops, and an ice-skating rink. The smallest ski area is **Hawksnest Golf and Ski Resort** in Seven Devils (800-822-HAWK) which has two beginner runs, an expert run, and a large area for snowboarders.

High Country Host, a visitors center in Boone, has general ski information (828-264-1299) and a 24-hour ski line from mid-November to mid-March (800-962-2322).

Further west, **Cataloochie Ski Area** (800-768-0285) in beautiful Maggie Valley is a good place for beginners, families, and groups. It has a top elevation of 5,400 feet and nine slopes, some of which are quite challenging. **Wolf Laurel Ski Area** in Mars Hill (800-817-4111) has snowboarding and a ski school. **Ski Scaly Mountain** (800-929-7669) has recently added a tube run.

The Unaka Mountains in Pisgah National Forest.

Hickory Ridge Homestead, next door, includes 18th-century buildings typical of a Watauga County farm. Demonstrators cook over the cabin's fire, hang hams in the smokehouse, pitch hay in the barn, and create traditional homespun in the weaving house. The museum sells local crafts; *828-264-2120.*

■ APPALACHIAN STATE UNIVERSITY

Boone, population 13,600, welcomes 12,000 ASU students each year. The Appalachian Museum, on campus, is the region's best overview museum, tracking the area from geologic to modern times. The Appalachian Summer festival, in late June and July, includes chamber music, jazz, popular singers, and arts workshops.

The restored 1875 home of an Appalachian Training School founding trustee, Edward Francis Lovill, has been reincarnated as one of the area's nicest inns *(see accommodations, page 324).*

Appalachian State has a fine geography department, and one of its graduates, Mark Stroud, has designed most of the maps in the Compass American Guides, including those in this book.

(Left) Toy maker Bob Miller demonstrates a handmade top. (Above) Twenty to 40 inches of snow may be expected to fall each winter in the mountains around Boone.

THE APPALACHIANS & BOONE

■ TWEETSIE

Tweetsie—a gussied-up old steam engine that once huffed through these mountains, has retired to a modest track just outside Boone on 421. The East Tennessee & Western North Carolina Railroad, or ET&WNC, laid tracks through this region in the mid-1880s, bringing in visitors and supplies as it tugged iron ore out, to market. Local wits soon renamed the ET&WNC the "Eat Taters & Wear No Clothes." The nickname Tweetsie, honoring the engine's two-toned whistle, stuck instead.

Today Tweetsie puffs serenely along three miles of track through an "Old West" amusement park. *(Open mid-May through October; admission; 800-526-5740.)*

■ VALLE CRUSIS

The biggest thing south of Boone is the Mast General Store in Valle Crusis. This is the first Mast General Store, founded in 1883, the sire of the Mast Generals scattered through the mountains. You'll know it by its oak floors, glass-fronted show-

The Natural Blend Honor Market in the Bryson City area sells honey, sweets, and condiments, using the honor system; payment is made through a slot in the door. The Appalachians are host to a number of rural general stores and specialty shops.

cases, wooden nail bins, coffee barrels, splay-toed rakes, beehives, and wire fly swatters.

Near the pot-bellied stove in the middle of the store, a checkerboard stands between two chairs, ready for a game: red Coca-Cola bottlecaps squared off against the gold caps snapped from bottles of Blenheim Ginger Ale.

Of course, times change. This venerable old mercantile stocks some tourist items, and the old-timey cash register disguises a computer screen. But that sweet, dusty odor in the back room isn't the smell of $200 hiking boots, it's chicken feed. And the trap door by the cash register? Owner W. W. Mast once took chickens in trade for the hardware, coffee, and salt on his shelves. He dropped his squawking, wing-flapping profits through the trap door before his customer could back out of a done deal.

Speaking of wing-flapping and squawking, for a few weeks each summer Valle Crusis is also home to a bagpiping school, the North American Academy of Piping. You might find its students, along with crews of stout-legged hikers and other relaxed visitors, at the 19th-century Mast Farm Inn, whose excellent dishes rely on fresh vegetables from its garden.

■ BANNER ELK

 To reach Banner Elk, head south on NC 194—a Scenic Highway so relentlessly twisted you can read road signs meant for cars going in the opposite direction. After 12 miles of emerald-green pastures, broad-shouldered barns, and old stone churches you will have wound your way into Banner Elk.

❖

This peaceful hamlet on the Elk River is noted for the massive ski resorts on nearby mountaintops, and for picturesque **Lees McCrae College**, which was willed into existence by Edgar Tuft, a Presbyterian minister who arrived in the valley in 1895 and made its people's welfare his life's work.

Tuft rolled up his starched shirtsleeves, beginning a church during his first summer's work, and finishing it during his second stay. Over the next years, the indefatigable minister and founded and funded an orphanage, and Lees McCrae College, whose dressed-stone buildings adorn a lovely, small campus area.

Elk River, which runs along one side of the campus, offers more than scenic landscape, says Dean Barnett who now owns the Tufts' old home. This river also offers good trout fishing—one of the most serene couples activities in the area. "It's not about the fish," Barnett explains. "It's more like a religion. You walk up the river together, away from everybody. It's about being out here, by the water, together. Most people throw the trout back."

Tuft's old home, now a B&B, rests on the edge of town.

Edgar Tuft would have little trouble recognizing Banner Elk today—unless he visited in mid-October. The Woolly Worm Festival, which attracts about 15,000 humans and scores of prancing caterpillars each October, is Banner Elk's answer to the National Weather Service.

Mountain legend says the 13 stripes on the back of an Isabella moth caterpillar foretell freezes, snowfalls—even high-low temperature patterns. In fact, farmers once moved their cattle from upland pastures after reading the crawlers' fluffy hides.

Since thousands of caterpillars patiently putter about the countryside in October, each wearing distinctive stripes, the big question is, which worm wears the truth?

In Banner Elk, they figure fastest is truest.

They race the contenders in heats, allowing early winners to soak up the festival's entertainments and crafts until one glossy beauty inches its way to victory in the final heat. Weather Channel fans take note: The winning worm's stripes, as deciphered by a qualified "worm reader," are on the money 80 percent of the time.

■ BLOWING ROCK

Blowing Rock shocked missionary Edgar Tuft, who visited in 1895:

> *I* never was more surprised than when I saw [Blowing Rock]. I thought my work would be almost altogether among country people. But Blowing Rock has four or five big hotels and they say sometimes there are as many as a thousand people there, from all parts of the country. . . .

Blowing Rock, a resort village across the Parkway, is still known for those old resorts, fine restaurants, golf courses, and for Blowing Rock. Winds sweep up the 3,000-foot cliff overhanging Johns River Gorge, creating an updraft that returns handkerchiefs and other light objects tossed over the cliff. *Fee; 828-295-7111.*

■ MOSES B. CONE MEMORIAL PARK

There are two great places to buy crafts on the Parkway, and **Parkway Craft Center** at Cone Park is one of them. (The other is near Asheville.)

This brilliant white mountaintop mansion and its graceful grounds were once home to textile magnate Moses Cone and his wife, Bertha. You've probably never heard of Moses Cone, but you know his work. In fact, you may be sitting on it. Cone put the "blue" in blue jeans. The denim that rolled from his North Carolina textile mills earned him millions and the title, "Denim King."

In 1897, drawn by the mountain air, the Cones raised the roof on a 20-room mansion, crowning their 3,516-acre estate. Moses also built 25 miles of carriage trails for Bertha, threading them through extensive rhododendron and mountain laurel plantings. He added white pines and hemlocks to their forests, transported enough New England sugar maples to make the mountains crimson in October, and added an orchard of 40,000 apple trees.

The Cone Manor House near Blowing Rock.

The Cones' guests rocked on the porch, admiring the view. Today, tourists rock on the same porch, admiring the same view, and chatting with a guild craftsman who weaves a delicate basket, using white oak strips cut days before. Out on the carriage trail, two denim-clad young men clip-clop by on Tennessee Walkers, the horses' gait as smooth as the rocking chairs'.

Most of this house, with its Tiffany windows, hardwood floors, and magical angles, is closed to visitors. No matter. The art of the Southern Highland Handicraft Guild, on the first floor, more than makes up for it.

Don't expect hillbilly jokes and Taiwan-made "mountain crafts" here. As you wander through these high-ceilinged rooms you'll find pottery of subtle design, hand-blown glass, textiles in ancient mountain patterns and in colors that would make Joseph drop his coat of many colors and kick it behind the door.

Fine jewelry, wooden toys, hand-stitched quilts, and Cherokee baskets line the shelves. In one room a weaver talks with inquisitive travelers as she overspins three handspun fibers on her spinning wheel, creating a vibrant multi-textured yarn.

You can buy a thousand dollars worth of art in this shop or simply browse through, enriching your life with the clear, earthbound arts inspired by highland life. *Located at milepost 294; 828-295-7938.*

The pottery of Michael Sherill represents the vibrant style of contemporary Appalachian art.

Whitewater rafting is one of the more popular recreational activities in the region.

■ RUNNING THE NOLICHUCKY

Adventurous travelers can sign up for a whitewater rafting trip with one of several well-known outfitters in the Appalachians. Blowing Rock's High Country Mountain Expeditions caravans rafters west through Erwin, Tennessee (a little town where folks either once hanged a circus elephant for murder, or tell tall tales), to a put-in on the rambunctious Nolichucky River.

The "Chucky" slices through protected lands in North Carolina and Tennessee, periodically roaring and then drifting through a beautiful, forested gorge. Nature regulates the waterflow on this undammed river, so rafters get the fastest ride in early spring when melting snows send the river's Class IV–V rapids cartwheeling along.

After a safety lecture and a few practice paddles—forward, back, and rest—rafts of four or five paddlers each launch themselves upon the Nolichucky.

Whitewater rafting brings with it definite risks and a stack of release forms. It also offers views you'll never see through a windshield, and a feel for the rivers that sculpted this land.

In whitewater, you travel at the speed of change.

At your elbow, the water molds itself into a perfect emerald sculpture, poised to dive across a boulder. At your side, a stone's smooth, freckled face peeps through parted waters. Behind you, rapids hang in the air like hawks with windswept wings.

By the end of a five-hour paddle, folks who hunched and lurched their way over the first rapids ride like swivel-hipped cowboys on wild horses, leaning slightly back, relaxed, sensing the river's dance. *For information on outdoor expeditions see page 355.*

■ PISGAH NATIONAL FOREST

Now the Parkway heads south into Pisgah National Forest, the oldest of North Carolina's four national forests.

On a map, the main section of Pisgah's nearly half-million acres look like a child's footed pajama pants tossed to the floor. One rumpled leg dips and folds along the North Carolina–Tennessee border; the other leg, bent at the knee, follows the Parkway.

Travelers who simply drive the Parkway may notice little difference heading into Pisgah National Forest, since the Parkway remains undeveloped. But travelers who venture Off-Parkway will find themselves in a land of rich, mountain forests and tiny, picturesque towns.

National forests offer travelers fewer amenities than national parks, and more backcountry access. Pisgah National Forest maintains 40 recreation areas. Hiking, fishing, camping, and nature study are perennially popular. (Thirty-nine of North Carolina's 55 species of wild orchids live within this park.) Bicycle access, limited to paved auto routes in parks, include designated trails, abandoned railroad beds, and old logging roads. *For information: 828-877-3350.*

■ JULIAN PRICE MEMORIAL PARK

Today, this park offers easy hiking trails, trout fishing, nature walks and boat rentals. During the Civil War, it provided a hideout for bushwhackers, draft dodgers, and escaped Union POWs making their way to Union-held Tennessee— often with the help of the fairly infamous Keith Blalock and his wife, "Sam." Together, the Blalocks wrote an odd chapter in North Carolina history.

Keith, a Union sympathizer, was drafted into the Confederate Army. His dedicated wife stuffed her hair under a soldier's cap and reported with her husband, joining Col. Zebulon Vance's 26th Regiment. The tentmates made good soldiers. The trouble was, given their political sensibilities, they were fighting on the wrong side.

So, after a respectable time, Keith rolled in poison oak, convinced army doctors he had an incurable skin disease, and went home to die. A few days later, the nimble-fingered "Sam" needed only 15 seconds and three buttons to convince startled physicians her enlistment had been a mistake.

The Blalocks moved into a cabin on Grandfather Mountain and lived happily ever after, cheerfully skirmishing with pro-South neighbors and helping Union soldiers to safety until war's end.

■ LINN COVE VIADUCT

Linn Cove Viaduct, the last section of Parkway to go into place in 1983, is one of the most sophisticated bits of environmental engineering on the planet.

The viaduct snakes along the side of Grandfather Mountain without disturbing the protected habitat below. To achieve that end, engineers designed 153 different pre-cast highway segments, each 8.6 feet long and weighing 50 tons, and extended the highway piece-by-piece over the 90-foot drop. (From the trail below you can look up at this state-of-the-art construction.)

Down a ways, US 221 leads to Grandfather Mountain, a privately owned quartzite giant whose trails, nature preserve, and swinging bridge make it a popular stop; *admission fee.*

■ GRANDFATHER MOUNTAIN

The Cherokee called Grandfather Mountain "Tanawha," for the golden eagles that rode its wind currents. Europeans, who settled the valleys, named the quartzite giant for the bearded man they saw profiled in its ridges.

Andre Michaux scrambled up Grandfather in 1794, scouting the bounds of France's New World. "Reached the summit of the highest mountain in all of North America," he wrote in his journal, and burst into song.

His song, as it turns out, was about 40 miles off-key. Mount Mitchell, to the south, is actually the highest peak east of the Mississippi. Nonetheless Grandfather—the highest on the Blue Ridge—has been a favorite hiking spot since Michaux's day.

❖

Grandfather Mountain provides habitat for more globally rare species than any other mountain east of the Rockies.

Its abrupt rise from the valley floor creates climates supporting 16 distinct ecological communities. In them live 42 rare and endangered species, 17 of them globally imperiled—including the peregrine falcon, funnelweb tarantula, Heller's blazing star, Blue Ridge goldenrod, bent avens, and Gray's lily.

Black Rock Nature Trail is a favorite with birdwatchers, who have spotted 147 bird species on the mountain. The cliffs host one of the South's largest flocks of ravens.

The Cherokee believed ravens were burned glossy black as they tried to steal fire from the gods. These ebony acrobats, which nest two-thirds of the way up sheer cliff faces, swoop, spin, dip, and back-flip from the mountainsides.

❖

A nature museum, cafeteria, and gift shop are located halfway up the mountain. At the outdoor wildlife habitats, a mountain cougar with smoke-grey face and soot-lined eyes leaps gracefully to a rock ledge, and his mate. Deer, otters, eagles, woodchucks, and bears busy themselves in other habitats. (This is one place you can feed the bears. In fact, they demand it.)

Continue up the mountain to reach the Mile High Swinging

A mountain cougar on Grandfather Mountain.

Bridge, the country's highest suspension footbridge. Winds gusting through this 80-foot ravine keep the green-plank bridge rocking. In the ravine below is a perfect wind-created bonsai garden of grey stone, pale lichens, sand myrtle, and dwarfed red spruce, which bow and shield their faces from the wind. From the other side of the bridge, high on a black rock riverbed wrenched sideways a billion years ago, is a fine view of the countryside thousands of feet below.

The trails that lead from Grandfather's upper parking area make for challenging hiking and backpacking. Some take a few hours, some take days. All require good boots. Follow the park's safety rules and regulations, and watch the weather; *800-468-7325.*

Grandfather Mountain, at 5,964 feet, is the tallest peak in the northern half of the state's Appalachians.

Each July the sweet, wild drone of the bagpipe swirls across the face of Grandfather Mountain as Campbells, MacLeods, MacRaes, Stewarts, MacDonalds, and scores of other Scottish clans file into the meadow, tartans unfurled, for the country's largest Highland Games.

Thousands of spectators and competitors pour in for the torchlight parade, traditional Highland athletic events, Highland dancing, piping, drumming, Scottish fiddling, sheep herding, and Scottish harp playing.

The Highland Games are held the second full weekend of July, with everyone invited "be ye Scot or be ye not." *(Call 828-733-1333. Make arrangements early.)*

Other annual events include Singing on the Mountain, a free, day-long gospel music convention founded in the 1920s.

■ SOUTH OF GRANDFATHER MOUNTAIN

From **Lost Cove Cliffs,** at nightfall, you can look for the Brown Mountain Lights. These mysterious star-like lights appear low on the horizon, twinkle brighter as they move near, and then fade away only to reappear and repeat their hesitant dance. Scientists have attributed the lights to Tweetsie (a theory that bit the dust when the train stopped running), and to refracted automobile lights. Others point the finger at mythical moonshiner Posey Slewfoot.

Just beyond Lost Cove Cliffs: **Linville Falls.** Poet A. M. "Chucky Joe" Huger probably blazed the first trails to the most dramatic set of falls on this stretch of the Parkway.

An easy trail from the River Bend parking area leads to the base of the falls, where sycamore, butternut, and ironwood shade the riverbanks. Slightly more difficult trails lead up through an old-growth forest of hemlock and pines to a series of overlooks that show off the falls and the 14-mile forested gorge that descends to the Catawba Valley.

Erwin's View—where pale pink rhododendron lean over the outcroppings to face the white waters below—offers the best view of the river, which curves and tumbles down the broad upper falls, pools, and somersaults down a narrow chasm. Catching its breath, it scrolls 30 feet down the grey cliffside, into a deep, emerald pool.

Just south of the falls, the Parkway again crosses US 221. If you love textiles, follow the signs west to the **Weavers Room at Crossnore.**

■ LINVILLE GORGE WILDERNESS AREA

To reach this well known hike follow Old NC 105. Here, hiking is a whole 'nother ballgame.

This extremely strenuous 11.5-mile trail scrambles 2,025 feet down into Linville Gorge. Getting down into this spectacular canyon is relatively easy; climbing out is a challenge for very experienced hikers. You need a special hiking permit, available at the U.S. Forest Service office in Marion.

Linville Cavern, North Carolina's only public-access cavern, lies three miles west of the Parkway on US 221.

■ LINVILLE CAVERN

"Here is one of the few chances of a lifetime to observe openly one of the usually hidden, but almost irresistible, forces of nature: the work of underground water. This water, often in mere traces, is the silent sculptor producing patterns of great beauty in stone," writes geologist Henry S. Brown.

Fishermen, not geologists, discovered these caverns. When their prey swam upstream into a mountainside, they followed, finding a vast maze of water-carved corridors and chambers. Their torchlight danced across geologic formations that resembled draperies, grape clusters, the capitol dome, giant bats with spread wings. They squeezed through narrow walkways, and edged along the rim of a bottomless pool as tiny Eastern Pipistrelle bats fluttered overhead.

Trout still occupy the cavern, but their waters are now lit by guides' flashlights as visitors explore this work-in-progress.

The cavern's dolomite stone—the compressed exoskeletons of tiny sea creatures—was deposited here when this was the sea floor, millions of years ago. After the earth shifted, fresh groundwater ran through the earth, carving the cavern.

(Dripping groundwater shapes more than caverns; it also creates a frizzled hair style known as "cave hair." Wear a hat. Admission fee.)

Linville Cavern doesn't provide the only access to underground treasures. Down the Parkway lie North Carolina's richest mineral and gem deposits—and an easy way to have at them. (*See Gemstone Mining essay, page 283.*)

■ SPRUCE PINE AREA

The little **Mineral Museum of North Carolina,** at the intersection of the Parkway and 226, offers solid, uninspired information about North Carolina's vast mineral wealth. Good background, true, but the most exciting introduction waits in gemstone "mines" near Spruce Pine and Little Switzerland.

In North Carolina's rocky soul rest more minerals than in any other state, and you'll find most of them—57—in the **Spruce Pine Mineral District,** one of the richest districts in the country. Some mines contain as many as 45 separate minerals and gems, gifts from a young earth's uneven temperament.

Today commercial mica, feldspar, and ultra-pure quartz mines dot this rugged countryside. Mitchell County yields around 35 percent of the feldspar produced in the United States—and used in everything from toilet bowls to false teeth.

Native Americans mined mica here—using the glittery, reflective mineral for personal ornaments and grave decorations—but mica's not the only pretty mineral in these hills. Tiffany's ran Crabtree Emerald Mine for years, beginning in 1883. Since 1884 Wiseman Mine has brought to light some of the best-colored aquamarine in the United States. The area produces buckets of gem-quality emeralds, aquamarine, clear quartz, amethyst, citrine, rose quartz, smoky quartz, tourmaline, garnets, and sapphires—mostly by-products of commercial mines.

Rockhounds can't visit the commercial mines directly, but gemstone mining operations buy their ore by the truckload, doling it out bucket-by-bucket to customers who search through it at the outfits' flumes. Most evaluate your find for free, and cut your stones for a fee.

Blue Ridge Gemstone Mine, near Little Switzerland, has a reputation for rich, local pay dirt and qualified, no-pressure advice about the stones visitors find. Part of its flume flows through a greenhouse-type building, offering solar heat and shelter from the elements; part is under the sky.

To get there, leave the Parkway at Little Switzerland. Chestnut Grove Church Road loops under the Parkway. Take the first paved left.

The earliest known illustration of mining in the state dates to 1833 and shows men digging for gold. At that time North Carolina was sometimes called the Golden State. (North Carolina Collection)

GEMSTONE MINING

Haven Peaden scoops a trowel of dirt and stones from her white, ten-gallon bucket onto her screen, and lowers the screen into the flume's fast-flowing stream of water. Ignoring the water's chill, she gently joggles the screen, watching a cloud of clay and sand drift away, and leaving a jumble of stones from tennis ball size, to the size of a pinhead.

She props the screen on the side of the flume, like a school book, and discards a few chunks of granite. When an amethyst the size of a golf ball rolls to the bottom of the screen, she plunks it into the plastic bag at her side.

Now she lifts the screen, tipping it to the sunlight. There's an emerald! A ruby the size of a pencil eraser, a three-inch quartz crystal. . . . And what's that? Uncertain, she drops the stone into her bag. She'll check it out when she goes back inside.

An hour later, Haven leans against Dick Johnson's counter, watching the gemologist divide her find onto three saucers. "We have three kinds of stones in the mountains," says the owner of Blue Ridge Gemstone Mine. "Gems worth cutting, gems that aren't worth cutting, and real pretty rocks."

The find evens out as you might imagine. "It would be well worth your while to have these cut," Johnson says, scooping two rubies, a small sapphire, an emerald, and a piece of citrine into a small plastic bag.

The gemstones not worth cutting—because of their size or uneven quality—include the amethyst, a piece of rose quartz, a silver opal, an angular chunk of tourmaline, and a handful of tiny rubies, emeralds, and garnets. They get their own bag, too.

"And these are your pretty rocks," he says, smiling as he pushes a small avalanche towards her. These rocks are bound for a flatland terrarium, but occasionally pretty rocks have more glamorous destinations. Down the counter, a woman who plucked a pretty rock from the flume sits down—hard—after learning the black-blue stone she nearly tossed away is a 477.5-carat sapphire.

Few will strike it rich at a gemstone mine, but most will strike it pretty. And if you count the calming of the mind, the joy of discovery, and a realization of the earth's generosity so crystal-clear you can put it in your pocket, more people strike it rich at these flumes than you might imagine.

To get to Blue Ridge Gemstone Mine, exit the Parkway at Little Switzerland, where the view explains the name. Take Chestnut Grove Church Road under the Parkway, then the first paved left and go two miles.

■ ALONG HIGHWAY 226

As Highway 226 and its smaller tributaries wind through Mitchell County, they pass a host of tiny towns with odd names. "It was easy to name a town in those days," Muriel Earley Sheppard wrote in *Cabins in the Laurel,* in 1935. "When the government in Washington was ready to establish a post office, whoever filled out the application blank wrote in whatever name occurred to him." Loafer's Glory needs no explanation. Relief was named for a tonic sold at Squire Peterson's store.

Sheppard noted others: "Ledger, Daybook, Wing, Bandana, Lunday, Hawk, Plumtree, Staggerweed, Poplar, and a host of like names are scattered through Toe River Country." (Toe River's name, which she didn't seem to find odd, echoes the Cherokee capital, Estatoh.)

Bakersville's Rhododendron Festival, in June, coincides with the blooming of the 600-acre Rhododendron Gardens on Roan Mountain. At **Spruce Pine's Mineral and Gem Festival,** some 50 dealers offer everything from geodes to cut gems to fossils. The August festival also includes gem-cutting demonstrations and mine tours.

Last but not least, the name **Penland** is synonymous with art-quality crafts worldwide. Miss Lucy Morgan founded Penland School in 1929 in a little build-

(Above) A display of glass and ceramic works in the Penland Gallery.
(Right) Unpaved backcountry roads in the Appalachians are ideal for hiking and bicycling.

ing of donated logs. In it, she helped local women rekindle the art of hand weaving, and marketed their work to the "outside world."

Today Penland, on NC 226 between Ledger and Spruce Pine, offers classes in textiles, printmaking, ceramics, glass, metal, wood, photography. Studios stand open; the student at the potter's wheel or loom may be a great-grandmother, or an artist who just pocketed his first driver's license.

Miss Lucy's is now an international school; its graduates' work resides in museums all over the world.

■ MT. MITCHELL

South of Penland, the Parkway heads into the Black Mountains, a mighty quartzite cross-range of North Carolina's highest peaks—including Mt. Mitchell,

the highest peak east of South Dakota's Black Hills. The range's name springs from the shadow-green hemlock, spruce, and pine tinting the mountainsides.

Mt. Mitchell State Park, an island within the Pisgah National Forest is, like Grandfather Mountain, a UN-designated Biosphere. (To gain this status, an area

This 1857 lithograph shows Elisha Mitchell, namesake of the highest mountain in the eastern United States. The mountain was named as a memorial to Mitchell who fell to his death near the falls. (North Carolina Collection)

Rime ice coats a tree along the Appalachian Trail in Yancey County.
Mt. Mitchell rises in the distance to a height of 6,684 feet.

must already be protected, have unique ecological significance, a history of scientific study, and provide for scientific education.) To visit, take NC 128, which climbs five miles almost to the mountain's summit.

An easy trail from the parking area leads to the summit of this 6,684-foot peak. The observation tower on top overlooks the cloud-draped Black Mountains, and surrounding countryside.

Treks of varying difficulty make up an 18-mile trail system. You may notice evergreens dying at higher elevations; scientists don't yet know exactly why, but some suspect pollution, others, natural causes. North Carolina's oldest state park incudes a seasonal campground, restaurant, concession stand, and interpretive center.

Just down the Parkway, the town of **Black Mountain,** experienced a "New Age" boom in the 1980s. This small town's restored historic district has become a busy neighborhood of antique shops, crafts shops, boutiques, and cafes. Stop in for a great lunch at My Father's Pizza on Cherry Street. The town is also known for the artistic and intellectual community that once hovered around Black Mountain College. Buckminster Fuller developed the geodesic dome while teaching here.

■ ASHEVILLE

Asheville, population 67,000, has been a resort town since almost forever.

Low country plantation owners began summering here in the late 1700s, trading malaria's fevers for the Cherokee's cool, untainted air. By the mid 1800s, Asheville was known for its middle-class boarding houses and fresh-air tuberculosis "cures." (Author Thomas Wolfe grew up in one of those boarding houses.)

With the opening of the railway in 1880, Asheville welcomed a more sophisticated set of visitors—among them George Vanderbilt, who fell in love with the countryside and stayed, importing architects and craftsmen to build a 255-room chateau and gardens at his Biltmore estate.

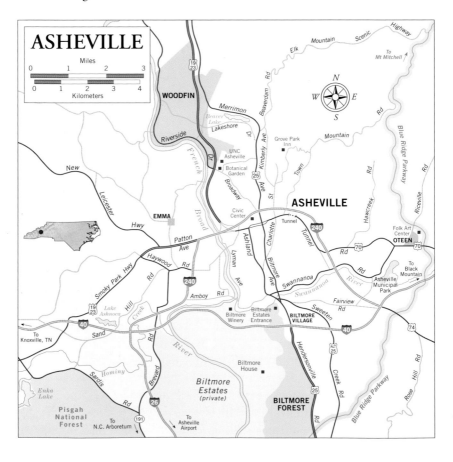

A crowded stagecoach stands in front of the Eagle Hotel in Asheville, circa 1880.
(Courtesy Pack Memorial Library, Asheville)

As the Vanderbilts' friends visited, Asheville's fortune shot skyward. By the 1920s Asheville was, irrefutably, the Cat's Meow. It looked the role.

With Biltmore complete, architects, stonemasons and other craftsmen turned to other projects: St. Lawrence Catholic Church, a domed basilica with Spanish baroque towers; an Italian-influenced Art Deco Baptist church; the stately Cathedral of All Saints. Influential guests promenaded in front of the mammoth Battery Hotel. Inspired by an infusion of culture and cash, city fathers sank a fortune into Art Deco skyscrapers and public buildings.

Then came the fall. The crash of 1929 stifled the city's luxury-based economy, saddling Asheville with the highest per capita debt in the nation. After the furor of the Roaring 20s, the silence was deafening. For nearly a half-century, civic leaders could barely afford to swing a wrecking ball. As a result, much of Asheville's fine old architecture still stands.

■ VISITING ASHEVILLE TODAY

To visit the most interesting part of Asheville, take the Parkway south to 70 (Tunnel Road) and head east to I-240 which circles north of town. From I-240 exit 5A leads to the visitors center at 151 Haywood, where you can pick up a map of the the self-guided urban trail and other materials. Exit 5B takes on the name Broadway as it takes you into the heart of town. From Broadway, you can hook a left on Woodfin to visit Thomas Wolfe's boyhood home or continue into a downtown noted for its parks, arts, and architecture.

Pack Square, downtown, has been a good place for travelers to stretch their legs since the early 1800s when the stagecoach deposited travelers here to mill about among townsfolk, innkeepers, and drovers, who filled the square with livestock en route to other markets. Today, Pack Square's architecture is a patchwork of old and new. Like many historic buildings on the square, Pack Place which now houses an arts and crafts center, is a relic of the early 1900s, Asheville's boom years. It illustrates Asheville's adaptive use policy (recycling older buildings), but all the square hasn't been so lucky. A blank-faced 1970s highrise bank that pre-dates Asheville's adaptive use policy, looms above the area.

From Pack Square you can stroll east on Patton Street to City/County Plaza, an area noted for its beautiful and sharply contrasting Art Deco and classical architecture.

If you walk west a few blocks to Haywood Street and turn right you'll find yourself in a lively downtown area of restaurants, bars, alternative movie houses, and specialty shops. Biltmore Avenue is at the heart of this district, which is popular with students from UNC-Asheville and other schools.

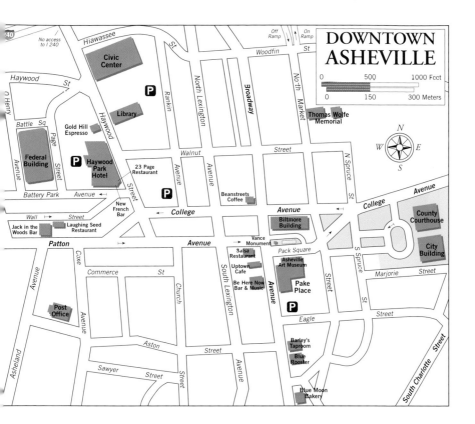

DOWNTOWN ASHEVILLE

0   500   1000 Feet

0   150   300 Meters

■ THOMAS WOLFE MEMORIAL

Walk up the steep front steps at 92 Woodfin, cross the porch, knock on the door, and step into the pages of Thomas Wolfe's autobiographical first novel, *Look Homeward, Angel*. Asheville's most famous son, Thomas Wolfe, grew up in this somber boarding house, run by his ruthlessly entrepreneurial mother, Julia Westall Wolfe. Today, Julia's 29-room Old Kentucky Home is known as the Thomas Wolfe Memorial.

These days Asheville hosts a four-day Thomas Wolfe Festival in early October, with workshops, tours, and theatrical works celebrating his birthday. But when *Look Homeward, Angel* first hit the bookstores in 1929, Asheville went pale with fury. Wolfe, who assumed Ashevillians would be delighted to find themselves described down to their imperfect belly buttons, was startled by his neighbors' death

(Opposite) The Buncombe County Courthouse is one of the classic Art Deco buildings that surround City Hall Plaza.

The most tranquil time to visit: early in the morning. See the house first and then the grounds. *(Pricey admission fee; 800-543-2961)*

Biltmore Village, a cluster of shops and galleries, occupies the stately old employees' quarters outside the Biltmore gates.

Take NC 25 off I-40 south of downtown; 800-543-2961.

■ GROVE PARK INN

While Vanderbilt boosted land prices on the south side of town, Edwin Wiley Grove looked north, toward Sunset Mountain. Later he recalled, "The dream of an old-time inn came to me—an inn whose exterior, and interior as well, should present a home-like and wholesome simplicity. . . . " The Midwesterner had the bucks to back the dream. With the catchy slogan, "Makes Children & Adults Fat

Relaxing on the verandah at the Grove Park Inn not long after the resort opened in 1913. (Courtesy Grove Park Inn)

as Pigs," his Grove's Tasteless Chill Tonic had made millions.

Grove's son-in-law designed Grove Park Inn and 400 builders signed on at $1/day to build it. They scoured Grove's properties, rolling boulders onto mule-pulled sleds, and "gee and hawed" them to a Packard-pulled train of wagons. Stonemasons—many of them Biltmore veterans—began construction, making sure only uncut stone faces showed, inside and out.

The 156-room inn went up in a little over a year. Workers hoisted 120 tons of boulders into the 36-foot-wide chimneys standing like granite musclemen at each end of the 120-foot Great Room. As exterior walls rose, workers rolled wheelbarrows of stones up wooden ramps, and roofers capped the building with a swooping, red tile roof.

Roycroft craftsmen hammered out copper lamps and light fixtures, and no-nonsense Arts and Crafts furniture. A bowling alley, indoor pool, and billiards room took shape.

Since 1913, when U.S. Secretary of State William Jennings Bryan officially opened the inn, its doors have swung open for heads of state, inventors, performers, and everyday travelers. Harry Houdini, Bela Bartok, and Enrico Caruso stayed here. So have Presidents from Woodrow Wilson to George Bush. Thomas Wolfe, who hated the place, never slept here. But in a page that could have been ripped from one of his own Jazz Age novels, a besotted F. Scott Fitzgerald began haunting the inn in 1935. Between visits to a local asylum, to visit his wife Zelda, he romanced any young woman who happened across his path.

Some suspect the pink-clad ghost haunting the inn's Palm Atrium, near Fitzgerald's old room, is Zelda. Others say the ghost's the ill-fated lover of another famous guest. (Besides, they say, the diva of the Jazz Age wouldn't be caught dead in pink.)

Whoever she is, she's oft-spotted, and known for pranks.

The Grove Park Inn suffered several humiliating renovations over the years but the restored inn now shows off all of its old stonework, and many of its original furnishings.

Visitors are encouraged to sign the guest register and drop by the Great Room for a drink and a look around. The Grove Park Inn Resort is home to the world's largest collections of Arts and Crafts furnishings, and to highly rated Horizons Restaurant. *The resort is located at 290 Macon Avenue (reached from the Asheville Loop off exit 5 and Charlotte Street); 800-438-0050.*

■ FOLK ART CENTER

As you're coming down the Parkway from the north toward Asheville you'll pass the center a half mile east of town. Remember Cone Memorial Park, near Blowing Rock, the first great place on the parkway to buy crafts? Well, this is the second great place. It, too, features the work of the Southern Highland Handicraft Guild.

Inside this modern building, you'll find crafts made in the highlands of nine southern states, along with a museum of modern, creative adaptations in craft media.

Appalachian craft designs, which immigrated to America with Scots, English, German, and Irish settlers, remained virtually unchanged in isolated, hardscrabble communities until the late 1800s. In 1895, when missionary Frances Louisa Goodrich accepted a hand-woven coverlet as a gift from a mountain woman in Madison County, the gift inspired an industry.

The vegetable-dyed Double Bowknot coverlet convinced Goodrich to begin Allanstand Cottage Industries, and to revive and market the mountaineers' crafts.

In 1908 Goodrich opened an Asheville showroom. Allanstand Shop, which the Southern Highland Handicraft Guild has operated since 1931, is a vital part of today's Folk Art Center.

Today, the Southern Highlands' multi-million-dollar crafts industry preserves and expands on traditional Appalachian crafts. This shop offers great browsing, and wonderful art.

The Southern Highland Handicraft Guild sponsors two crafts fairs at the Asheville Civic Center each year, one in July, and one in October. The guild also sponsors a shop called Guild Crafts, on Tunnel Road in Asheville. *Located half a mile east of Asheville on the Parkway; 828-298-7928.*

■ OUTDOORS

Upon the French Broad River, which strolls through Asheville, you can enjoy gentle rafting, kayaking, and tubing. (Area outfitters also arrange trips to wilder waters.)

Chimney Rock Park rates high with those who appreciate gorgeous views, wheeze-free hiking, and easy access. (An elevator inside the granite mountain zips visitors to its crest.) An easy trail leads to the bottom of its 400-foot waterfall. *Located 25 miles southeast of Asheville on Hwy. 74; admission fee; 800-277-9611.*

The new 400-acre **North Carolina Arboretum** takes advantage of the moun-

The view from Chimney Rock reveals Lake Lure.

tains' diverse environments, creating gardens at different altitudes to showcase the flora of the entire state. *Call for directions; 828-665-2492*

The NC Arboretum, which opened in 1997, includes theme gardens, wildflowers, a greenhouse, overlooks, and an Appalachian quilt garden laid out in patterns that duplicate traditional quilts.

◼ HENDERSONVILLE

Hendersonville, located southeast of Asheville on US 25, is a 19th-century resort town, whose small downtown historic district is loaded with antique shops.

The best place to browse and catch up on hearsay: The Curb Market, known for great-grandma entrepreneurs who make and sell hand-labeled jars of watermelon preserves, bread-and-butter pickles, apple butter, pickled beans, chutney, and heaven knows what else.

They also sell aprons, rugs woven from stocking toes, fresh vegetables, wheat bread, Indian corn, dried gourds, grapevine wreaths, birdhouses, fresh apples, even buckeyes.

G. L. Nolan displays her Christmas miniatures at the Whittier community center.

🚗 US 64 leads east to resorts on Lake Lure; US 25 goes south to Flat Rock and Connemara, Carl Sandburg's home.

■ FLAT ROCK

Flat Rock has been an upscale resort from birth, conceived of by Charlestonians as an elite summer retreat from the heat of the Southern lowlands. The town's history shows in Flat Rock's inns, B&Bs, old homes, and golf courses; and at St. John in the Wilderness Church, where headstones bearing prominent low-country surnames pepper the cemetery. (The church is less than a mile north of Carl Sandburg's home, Connemara, on US 25.)

Flat Rock Playhouse, aka the State Theater of North Carolina, stages Broadway and London hits and consistently rates as one of the ten best summer stock theaters in the United States.; *828-693-0731.*

Carl Sandburg, one of America's greatest poets and biographers, spent the final 22 years of his life on the outskirts of Flat Rock. He and his wife, Lillie, lived in a rambling, white clapboard house, **Connemara,** which they bought from the family of Charles Memminger, the first Secretary of State for the Confederacy. The center of a 240-acre farm, it overlooks rolling pastures, ponds, a barn for Lillie's prize-winning goats, and the Blue Ridge.

This National Historic Site offers almost-free guided tours of the house every day except Christmas. The grounds, trails, and farm are open at no charge; the goat barn lies within bleating distance of the house. *Located on Little River Road off US 25. (From the south take US 26 to exit 22 and follow signs.) 828-693-4178.*

■ THE LAND OF WATERFALLS

Route 64, as it heads west into Nantahala National Forest, unites a strand of picturesque resort towns: Etowah, Brevard (known for its white squirrels), Lake Toxaway, Sapphire, Cashiers, and Highland. This is the Land of The Waterfalls, which travelers can also access from the Parkway south of Asheville.

More than 250 spectacular waterfalls make Transylvania County's Parkway and Off-Parkway drives among the most popular in the Appalachians.

Why so many waterfalls? Two reasons.

These mountains are the first to greet heavy rain clouds rolling north from the Gulf of Mexico. They trap the clouds, which drop around 100 inches of rain here each year before they lighten up and pass on. (Picture your yard eight feet deep in water, and you'll have the idea.)

This flood splashes down on mountains that rise nearly 5,000 feet in elevation from one side of the county to the other. The result? "From upland coves water rushes headlong in leaps and splashes to the valley floor below, over countless cascades, cataracts, chutes, falls, jumps, runs, shoals, slides, slips, and spills," writes Transylvania County photographer Jim Bob Tinsley in his book, *The Land of the Waterfalls.*

Those falls include the 411-foot Whitewater Falls, highest in the eastern United States; Bridal Veil Falls, famous for its lacy cascades; and Sliding Rock, where visitors slide like playful otters along a 60-foot natural waterslide, plunging into a breathtakingly cold pool below. Caution: Always stay on the marked trails or in areas designated as safe.

■ SOUTH ON THE PARKWAY INTO NANTAHALA FOREST

South of Asheville, beyond the Cradle of Forestry, the Parkway enters **Nantahala National Forest.**

This forest, North Carolina's largest, includes over 517,000 rugged acres in the southeast corner of the state. The Nantahala means "Land of the Noon Day Sun"; if you drive or raft down the Nantahala Gorge, you'll understand why. Sunlight slips in only at noon.

This national forest offers a wealth of backcountry adventure—hiking, rafting, horseback riding, camping, and mountain biking.

Tsali Recreational Area, with around 40 miles of biking trails, is one of the nation's most popular mountain biking spots. Commercial outfitters in Asheville and Nantahala make good use of the Nantahala National Forest, too. *For information on the forest, call 828-479-6431.*

Devil's Courthouse, a marked stop on the Parkway, inspires legends. Settlers swore the Devil judges souls in a cavern beneath this rocky summit. The Cherokee believed this cavern to be the dance hall of a sensitive, slant-eyed giant named Judacalla, who lived in this secluded hideaway with a Cherokee woman.

If the Cherokee were right, Judacalla had some view. His roof offers a 360-degree look at the French Broad, Tuskaseigee, and upper Pigeon River valleys. (The Cherokee called Pilot Mountain, visible from here, *Tsuwahtuldee.* In a village inside the mountain, they said, people lived a life of song, dance, and feasting.)

■ To Cherokee

From Devil's Courthouse, the Parkway turns west toward **Cherokee,** a land increasingly rich in Cherokee history and tradition. On **Tanasee Bald,** travelers can still see where the giant Judacalla cleared the mountain for farmland. (Tanasee Bald borrowed its name from the Cherokee village, Tanasi. So did the State of Tennessee.)

Bears were once plentiful in the North Carolina mountains. The Cherokee believed the first bears were lazy men, transformed into animals for punishment. The names of a string of Parkway stops—Bear Pen Gap, Bear Trap Gap, and Bear Trail Ridge—are reminders of the once-plentiful bruin loafers. At **Flat Gap** and **Rabb Knob Overlook** you can see the sites of what used to be Cherokee villages. Both villages were decimated by U.S. troops in the 1700s.

❖

 At Balsam Gap, US 74 leads south to Sylva, and into crafts country; US 23 leads north to Waynesville, named for General "Mad Anthony" Wayne.

❖

Waynesville, home of the **North Carolina Handicraft Museum,** offers access to a little-used loop drive that can be a welcomed respite from heavy Parkway traffic.

(Preceding page) Whitewater Falls measures 411 feet—the highest in the eastern United States.

EXPLAIN *THAT* TO YOUR FATHER

He had met Swimmer the summer they were both sixteen. Inman had been given the happy job of escorting a few heifers to graze the last grass of summer in the high balds on Balsam Mountain. . . . He expected solitude and self-reliance. But when he got to the bald there was a regular party going on. A dozen or so men from Catalooch had made camp at the crest of the ridge and had been there for a week or better, lazing in the cool air of the uplands and joying in the freeing distance from hearth and home. . . .

❖

Soon, a band of Cherokee from Cove Creek had come up the other side of the divide with a rawboned herd of spotted cows of no singular breed. The Indians made their camp a short distance away and then cut tall pines and crafted goals from them and marked off boundaries for their vicious ball game. Swimmer, an odd big-handed boy with wide-set eyes, came over and invited the Catalooch party to play, hinting darkly that men sometimes died in the game. Inman and others took up the challenge. They cut and split green saplings to make their own ball racquets, strung them with strips of hide and bootlace.

The two groups camped side by side for two weeks, the younger men playing the ball game most of the day, gambling heavily on the outcomes. It was a contest with no fixed time of play and few rules so that they just ran about slamming into each other and hacking with the racquets as if with clubs until one team reached a set number of points scored by striking the goalposts with the ball. They'd play most of the day and then spend half the night drinking and telling tales at fireside, eating great heaps of little speckled trout, fried crisp, bones and all.

❖

After many days wet weather set in, and none too soon, for on both sides they were all worn out, hung over, and beat up. . . . The Catalooch party had lost to the Indians everything they could do without and some things they couldn't—fry pans and dutch ovens, sacks of meal, fishing poles, rifles and pistols. Inman himself had lost an entire cow, a fact he could not figure out how to explain to his father.

—Charles Frazier, Cold Mountain, *1997*
A novel about the Civil War–era in North Carolina

■ GREAT SMOKY MOUNTAINS NATIONAL PARK

More than nine million people a year visit the Great Smoky Mountains National Park, the best-used national park in the country. It's also the end-point (or begin-point) of the Blue Ridge Parkway. The 520,408-acre park lies draped across the state border, with 60 percent of its land falling within North Carolina, and 40 percent in Tennessee. The Oconaluftee Visitor Center, two miles from Cherokee, provides maps, and general information for visitors entering from North Carolina. This is also the place to pick up permits for the campgrounds, or backcountry camping.

You won't walk alone.

More than 1,500 species of flowering plants, 200 species of birds, 50 fish species, and 60 species of mammals occupy the park's forests, balds, historic sites, streams, and rivers. A whopping 27 species of salamanders scurry through the park, among 2,000 varieties of mushrooms. But bears still get all the glory.

❖

Five hundred black bears live here—fishing by a stream, plundering through a rhododendron slick, ambling along a berry-rich trail. Black bears, which weigh 200–400 pounds, may be black, brown, reddish, or even a cinnamon color. Of course you know not to feed them, but you might not know it's not wise to tempt them, either.

Park bears have come to like packaged foods. If they spot a snack, they want it; if they want it, they get it. Unless you want a convertible, don't leave canned food, cookies, or coolers stored in sight in your car. (Bears, who are not wily consumers, will also go for anything that looks like packaged foods. Put cans of tennis balls, cooler-shaped cases, etc. in the trunk.) Follow park suggestions for storing food when you camp or park. And if a bear does swipe a snack, don't try to get it back.

■ HISTORIC SITES

The park has several interesting historic sites. To see the best, cross into Tennessee. In the 19th-century village of **Cades Cove** complete with its churches, homes, and businesses—you can almost see settlers strolling along the one-lane road that loops through the valley. You can almost hear them joking as they trudge up the mountainside, or bustle about the fireplace getting dinner on the table. At dusk, when herds of white-tail deer saunter down to graze in the cove's rich bottomland, this is the most peaceful spot in the park.

(Following pages) Autumn descends on Deep Creek Valley in
Great Smoky Mountains National Park.

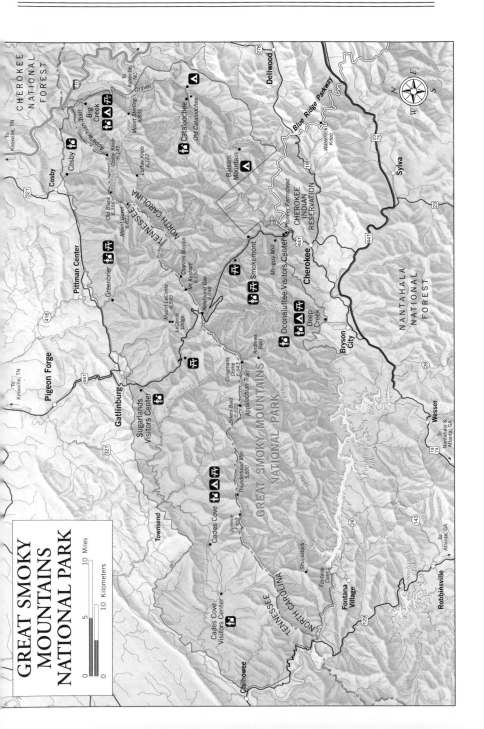

GREAT SMOKY MOUNTAINS NATIONAL PARK

On the less-developed North Carolina side of the park, interpreters reenact farm life at Pioneer Farmstead near the Oconaluftee Visitor Center, and at nearby Mingus Mill. Sadly, Cataloochee Village, one of the largest 19th-century villages in the Smokies, has wasted away to a few buildings. It's still worth the trip: Visit via the unpaved road at the junction of I-40 and US 276.

■ HIKING AND CAMPING

More than 800 miles of trails lead to the park's waterfalls, meadows, and overlooks. They range from strenuous climbs to easy, quarter-mile quiet walkways.

The Appalachian Trail, which dips along the North Carolina–Tennessee border, passes along 68 miles of the park's highest ridges on its 2,100-mile stretch from Georgia to Maine. Each year, around 100 hikers make the entire 2,100-mile trek, but most opt for a smaller slice of the outdoors.

Hikers can step onto the Appalachian Trail at Clingman's Dome, Newfound Gap, Fontana Dam, or Big Creek Campground. The most popular stretch is the eight-mile walk from Clingman's Dome to Charlie's Bunion and back. This trail,

A section of the Appalachian Trail as it rises over a summit in Madison County.

which explores a spruce and fir forest with outstanding vistas, has an elevation gain of only 980 feet.

Ten developed campgrounds are tucked away in the park. (Three take reservations: *800-365-CAMP*.) You'll find 100 primitive campsites on the ridges.

The Great Smoky Mountains National Park's popular scenic drives mosey along bumper-to-bumper during peak seasons. Those who seek serenity should visit at other times.

■ BRYSON CITY AREA

US 19 wanders along the Great Smoky Mountain's southern boundary to easy-going Bryson City, the home of Horace Kephart, who wrote *Our Southern Highlanders* and helped preserve Great Smoky Mountains National Park from lumber companies gnawing their way across the mountainsides.

Bryson City is also the departure-point for "The Road to Nowhere," a highway that simply stops enroute to the resort community, Fontana Lake. The Great

A conductor and engineer of the Great Smoky Mountains Railway take a break at the train depot in Dillsboro. The train runs from Dillsboro to Bryson City and back, and from Bryson City to Natahala Outdoor Center and back.

Smoky Mountains Railway, on the other hand, chugs all the way to Murphy, tugging passenger cars through remote, spectacular scenery.

US 19 continues south through the tiny community of Nantahala (the best place to catch a backcountry excursion or rafting trip). US 129 cuts northwest to Robbinsville, a conservative, no-frills little town a world apart from the area's many vacation centers.

■ ROBBINSVILLE

Cherokee Chief Junaluska rests, at last, near the small town of **Robbinsville.** When President Andrew Jackson forced the Cherokee from their homeland, Chief Junaluska—like other Cherokee—walked 1,200 wintry miles to Oklahoma, along the Trail of Tears. Thousands of his people died of exposure and exhaustion along the way. Many years later Junaluska walked back to North Carolina, to live his last years in his homeland.

A highway marker on Main Street reads:

JUNALUSKA
CHEROKEE INDIAN CHIEF, BRAVE WARRIOR UNDER
ANDREW JACKSON AT HORSE SHOE BEND, IN CREEK WAR, 1814.
GRAVE ONE MILE SOUTHWEST.

🚗 From Robbinsville, you can head southwest on US 129 and then NC 141 to the crafts-rich area known as Brasstown, and John C. Campbell Folks School. Or, you can follow the unsurpassed twists and turns of the new Cherohala Highway (TN 165 and NC 143) between Robbinsville, North Carolina and Maryville, Tennessee. If highways can be double-jointed, this one is. Ninety-nine of its twists exceed 90 degrees. Most of its elevations exceed 4,000 feet; many rise above 5,000, making it one of the region's loftiest drives.

Drive this highway with a sunset softening the sky ahead of you and a full moon rising at your shoulder, and you feel like Tanawah—a golden eagle soaring between two worlds.

(Left) At 6,643 feet, Clingman's Dome is the tallest peak in the national park, and only 41 feet shy of Mt. Mitchell.

■ JOYCE KILMER MEMORIAL FOREST

The Dragon writhes within three miles of Joyce Kilmer Memorial Forest, whose virgin forest is the largest in North Carolina.

This wilderness area is known for its giant tulip poplars, hemlock, sycamore, oak, basswood, maple, birch and beech. Spruce, pine, and cedars dwell in this forest, whose understory is a mosaic of wildflowers, ferns, mosses, lichens, rhododendron, laurel, and flame azalea.

This forest, unlike most North Carolina forests, has never been "harvested." This is the same, uninterrupted forest the Cherokee walked through hundreds of years ago.

It holds an ancient spirit.

Virginia Russell measures the largest hemlock in the state of North Carolina located in Joyce Kilmer Memorial Forest.

When plants were first made by a force now forgotten, the Cherokee believed, the Great One told them to stay awake for seven nights, as young men did when praying for their medicine. Nearly all stayed awake the first night, but on the second night they began falling asleep, one by one. After seven nights, only the cedar, pine, spruce, holly, and laurel remained. To reward their endurance, the Great One made them evergreen, and made them plants of healing.

Today, people come to Joyce Kilmer Memorial Forest to follow gentle paths along tumbling streams. They come to lean against the cool, strong trunks of giant poplars, and to rest beneath the gnarled, muscled arms of ancient oaks.

Most of all, they come to feel the enduring rhythm of uninterrupted life. Nowhere is that rhythm clearer than in the cathedral of this ancient forest.

The sun sets over the Smoky Mountains as viewed from Heintooga Overlook.

AREA CODE & CLIMATE

PRACTICAL INFORMATION

■ AREA CODE

As of April 1998 six area codes serve North Carolina. The Triangle Area uses 919. The northern Coastal Plain and Outer Banks use 252. The southern Coastal Plain and the southern Piedmont use 910. Northern Piedmont is served by 336; the Appalachians by 828; and Charlotte and surrounding counties by 704.

■ METRIC CONVERSIONS

1 foot = .305 meters
1 mile = 1.6 kilometers
Centigrade = Fahrenheit temp. minus 32, divided by 1.8

■ CLIMATE

The best time of year to visit North Carolina is entirely dependent upon which region you are planning to visit. On the **Coastal Plain** and **Piedmont**, summers are hot and oppressive, the air heavy enough to cut with a knife. The best season to visit these regions is spring, late March to mid-May, and the fall period between late September and early November. Winters are cool to cold with an occasional snowstorm every few years. On the **Barrier Islands** summers are cooler than inland thanks to ocean breezes, and winters are milder, but still windy and raw much of the time. Mid-March through mid-November is the best time to visit. **The Appalachians** are the only part of the state to experience a prolonged winter season. Snow falls every year increasing in intensity with altitude. The summers are relatively cool and pleasant with temperatures rarely reaching 90°F. May through September is the best time of year to visit.

TEMPS (F°)	AVG. JAN.		AVG. APRIL		AVG. JULY		AVG. OCT.		RECORD	RECORD
	HIGH	LOW	HIGH	LOW	HIGH	LOW	HIGH	LOW	HIGH	LOW
Hatteras	53	38	67	50	84	72	71	59	97	6
Wilmington	57	35	73	50	90	72	76	55	104	0
Raleigh	50	29	71	47	89	68	71	49	105	-9
Charlotte	50	31	71	48	88	69	71	50	104	-5
Asheville	48	26	68	42	84	62	70	45	101	-16
Mt. Mitchell	32	17	52	33	66	52	55	36	87	-34

PRECIPITATION (INCHES)	AVG. JAN.	AVG. APRIL	AVG. JULY	AVG. OCT.	ANNUAL	
					RAIN	SNOW
Hatteras	5.2	3.5	5.0	5.0	56	2
Wilmington	3.6	2.9	7.9	2.9	54	2
Raleigh	3.4	2.9	4.4	2.9	42	8
Charlotte	3.6	3.0	3.9	3.2	43	6
Asheville	3.1	3.4	4.2	3.3	45	14
Mt. Mitchell	5.8	5.8	7.0	5.1	74	58

■ HURRICANES

Ocean breezes create a generally pleasant summer climate on the islands, but occasionally the breezes escalate and a hurricane slams ashore. If this happens, you want to be elsewhere.

Meteorologists track hurricanes from the moment the storms spin to life, many days offshore. In case of a hurricane, island authorities call for a voluntary evacuation first, primarily because the bridges and ferries can't handle everyone leaving at once. Leave, and let others sweat their way off when the evacuation becomes mandatory, probably the next day. You can always come back if the storm turns.

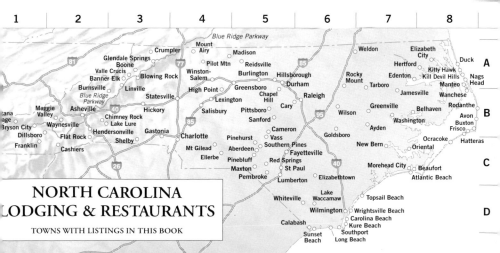

RESTAURANTS & ACCOMMODATIONS

■ RESTAURANTS AND ACCOMMODATIONS

■ ABOUT ACCOMMODATIONS

In general, the barrier islands are known for beach cottages. To rent a cottage, contact a realtor well in advance. Camping is also popular, but hot in summer. Chain hotels abound in most areas. For a list of small hotels and B&Bs throughout the state contact the **NC Bed and Breakfast and Inns Association**, 800-849-5392.

Along the coast, high season is Memorial Day to Labor Day. In the mountains, rates are usually lower in spring. In the golf country around Pinehurst and Southern Pines, high season is spring and fall.

> *Room rates:*
> Per night, per room, double occupancy:
> $ = under $60; $$ = $60–94; $$$ = $95–124; $$$$ = over $125
>
> *Restaurant prices:*
> Per person, not including drinks, tax, and tips:
> $ = under $10; $$ = $10–20; $$$ = over $20

Aberdeen *map 5-C*

☵ **Inn at the Bryant House.** 214 N. Poplar St.; 910-944-3300 or 800-453-4019. AAA-rated 1913 Colonial Revival inn listed on National Historic Register. Located near antique shops and golf courses of the Pinehurst area. Nine rooms, Continental plus breakfast. $-$$

✗ **Thai Orchid.** 1404 Sandhills Blvd.; 910-944-9299. Thai family restaurant with wonderful service and food. $-$$

Asheville *map 2-B*

☵ **Abbington Green B&B Inn.** 46 Cumberland Circle, 800-251-2454. This 1908 Colonial Revival home in Asheville's historic district features five rooms with fireplaces, antiques. Full breakfast; carriage house suite. $$$-$$$$

☵ **Acorn Cottage B&B.** 25 St. Dunstans Circle, 828-253-0609 or 800-699-0609. This 1922 Arts and Craft period granite bungalow/cottage style inn offers four rooms and full breakfast. $$$

☵ **Albemarle Inn.** 86 Edgemont Rd., 828-255-0027 or 800-621-7435. AAA three-diamond Greek Revival inn with carved oak staircases, paneling, and balconies. Ten rooms, one suite, full breakfast, pool. $$-$$$

☵ **Carolina Bed & Breakfast,** 177 Cumberland Ave., 828-254-3608. Circa 1900 home in the heart of Asheville features fireplaces, gardens, parlors, and porches. Six rooms, full breakfast. $$$

☵ **Corner Oak Manor,** 53 St. Dunstans Rd., 828-253-3525. This 1920s Tudor home, a half-mile from Biltmore Estate, has three rooms, one cottage, full gourmet breakfast. **$$-$$$**

⚏ **Dogwood Cottage Inn.** 40 Canterbury Rd. North; 828-258-9725. Rustic 1910s brown-shingle lodge. Pets allowed. Four rooms, country-style breakfast. Wheelchair access. **$$$**

⚏ **Flint Street Inns,** 100–116 Flint St.; 828-253-6723. Two early 20th-century homes filled with antiques and collectibles. Eight rooms, Southern breakfast. **$$-$$$**

⚏ **Grove Park Inn.** 290 Macon Ave.; 828-252-2711 or 800-438-5800. This inn, which opened in 1913 and is listed on the National Register, has welcomed Presidents, entertainers, and inventors. Championship golf course, indoor pool, sports center, ball room, Grand Hall, Arts and Crafts furnishings, porch with a view of Asheville and the valley below. **$$$$**

GROVE PARK INN

⚏ **Haywood Park Hotel and Promenade.** 1 Battery Park Ave.; 828-252-2522 or 800-845-7638. Very modern suite hotel. Computer hook-ups, fitness center. **$$$$**

HAYWOOD PARK HOTEL

⚏ **The Inn on Montford.** 296 Montford Ave.; 828-254-9569 or 800-254-9569. Four rooms, verandah. Full gourmet breakfast. **$$$-$$$$**

⚏ **The Lion and the Rose B&B.** 276 Montford Ave.; 828-255-7673 or 800-546-6988. Restored 1895 Queen Anne includes a fireplace in the parlor, and a verandah overlooking the gardens. Four rooms, one suite. Full gourmet breakfast. Near Biltmore Estate. **$$$-$$$$**

⚏ **North Lodge on Oakland.** 84 Oakland Rd.; 828-252-6433 or 800-282-3602. 1904 stone building with cedar shake roof. Four rooms; adults, non-smoking environment. **$$-$$$**

⚏ **The Wright Inn & Carriage House.** 235 Pearson Dr.; 828-251-0789 or 800-552-5724. Queen Anne home furnished with heirlooms. Eight rooms, one suite, carriage house. **$$$-$$$$**

RESTAURANTS & ACCOMMODATIONS

Asheville *cont'd*

✗ **Barley's Tap Room.** 42 Biltmore Ave.; 828-255-0504. Located in a cavernous downtown storefront with its original pressed tin ceilings, Barley's offers delicious microbrews and very good food, especially pizza. Families, downtown types, and artists alike come here. The photographer of this book recommends a lunch of calzone and a Highland Gaelic Ale. Music Wednesday through Sunday. Lunch and dinner. $

✗ **Blue Moon Bakery.** 60 Biltmore Ave.; 828-252-6063. Tasty baked goods, and a lunch menu which includes not-to-be-missed focaccia sandwiches. $

✗ **Flying Frog Cafe.** 76 Haywood St.; 828-254-9411. At this happening hotspot, the kitchen turns out interesting fusions of Indian and Caribbean food. You'll find both jerk chicken pasta and tandoori dishes on the menu. $$

✗ **Gabrielle's.** 87 Richmond Hill Dr., 828-252-7313. Dress up, relax, and enjoy gracious service in a Victorian dining room. If home-grown Southern cooking is often too heavy for you, come here for Southern dishes that have been transformed into classic entrees without losing their roots. There's a splendid view of Asheville from the wrap-around porch. Reservations. Dinner, Sunday brunch. $$$

✗ **The Greenery Restaurant.** 148 Tunnel Rd.; 828-253-2809. A bit of the Chesapeake emerges as fresh seafood, duck, and Maryland crabcakes dominate the menu. Impressive wine list. $$-$$$

✗ **Horizons.** Grove Park Inn Resort, 290 Macon Ave.; 828-252-2711. Exceptional food here, especially the wild game dishes. One of the most elegant dining establishments in town. Dinner, closed Sundays. Reservations. $$$

✗ **The Laughing Seed.** 40 Wall St.; 828-252-3445. After exploring downtown Asheville, this just might be the topper of the evening. Creative health-conscious and vegetarian menu at lunch and dinner. Chances are, this place will be packed, so if you've some time to kill, head downstairs to the Jack in the Woods and grab a seat on a couch. $

✗ **The Market Place,** 20 Wall St.; 828-252-4162. The Continental menu changes daily. Reservations. Dinner, Monday through Saturday. $$-$$$

✗ **Mountain Smoke House.** 20 South Spruce St.; 828-253-4871. Best known for its entertainment: mountain music, bluegrass, cloggin', square dancing. A must-go. Call for schedule. Dinner. $-$$

✗ **Possum Trot Grill.** 8 Wall St.; 828-253-0062. Mountain folks tend to be friendly, and so is the staff here. Cajun/Creole dishes, among the ethnic offerings. $-$$

✗ **Salsa's.** 6 Patton Ave.; 828-252-9805. The Venezuelan chef-owners here cook up Mexican food with a twist, adding uncommon ingredients like fried plantains to the burritos. A colorful place for a fast, inexpensive lunch. $

✗ **Spirits on the River.** 571 Swannanoa River Rd.; 828-299-1404. Ready to try something wild and different? Come here for chopped buffalo sirloin, or pasta with rabbit. This little place offers dishes not often served in North Carolina—or anywhere else, for that matter. $ $$

✕ **23 Page at the Haywood Park,** 1 Battery Park; 828-252-3685. This downtown restaurant serves innovative versions of American dishes, often with an Asian twist. The fresh mountain trout is always a winner. After dinner, head upstairs to the New French Bar, with its lovely copper bar. Lunch and dinner, Monday through Saturday. $-$$$

✕ **Windmill European Grill–Il Pescatore.** 85 Tunnel Rd.; 828-253-5285. The mountains surrounding Asheville attract people from all over, and the Windmill attempts to serve them with its eclectic mix of international dishes—mostly German, Indian, and Italian—on one menu. $-$$

Atlantic Beach *map C-7*

✕ **Franco's.** Ft. Macon Rd. and Kinston Ave., NC 58; 252-240-3141. Even beachgoers need a break from seafood, and Franco's provides it in the form of homemade bread, pasta, sauce, and desserts. Specializes in Italian fare but also serves steak, chicken, and seafood. Very popular. $-$$

Avon *map 8-B*

✕ **The Froggy Dog.** NC 12; 252-995-4106. Varied menu, live entertainment most nights summer months. $$

Ayden *map 7-B*

✕ **Skylight Inn.** Follow Lee St. to the edge of town; 252-746-4113. Owners Jeff Jones and his Uncle Pete have won the National Barbecue Cook-off in Washington D.C. two consecutive years. In acknowledgment of triumph in the capital city, the Skylight is crowned with a replica of the U.S. Capitol dome, made entirely of what looks suspiciously like tin cans. *National Geographic* has also chose Skylight's BBQ as "the world's best." Jones attributes their success to old-timey technique. "This has been in our family since 1830," he says. "We use the same recipes, the same methods. "It's all got to be done by hand. It's done with oak chips and coals. We burn the wood in a chimney, and take the live coals and [put them] around the pig while it's cooking." The Skylight serves its barbecue on paper trays, another family tradition. "We're one of the very few people that still do it the old fashioned way." $

Banner Elk Area *map 3-A*

⌂ **Archer's Mountain Inn.** Beech Mountain Pkwy.; Banner Elk; 828-898-9004. This inn has a stunning view of Elk River Valley and the neighboring mountains. Near Beech Mountain's ski areas. Outstanding restaurant. 14 rooms, fireplaces, some with private balconies and whirlpools. $$$-$$$$

Banner Elk Area *cont'd*

⊤ **Rainbow Inn B&B.** 317 Old Turnpike Rd., Banner Elk; 828-898-5611. In this 100-year-old farmhouse you'll find patchwork quilts on antique beds, and crackling fires in the gathering room fireplace. Four rooms, two with private baths. **$$**

⊤ **Tuft's House Inn.** 254 Edgar Tufts Rd. Banner Elk; 828-898-7944. This small, historic stone and wood B&B overlooks Elk River Valley. Pleasant walking trails, a stream to rest by, chickens clucking out back, hot tub, fireplace in the den. Emphasis on tranquility: no TV or phone in rooms. Breakfast. **$$-$$$**

✕ **Fred's General Mercantile Company.** Beech Mountain Pkwy, Beech Mountain; 828-387-4838. The mercantile's been upfitted, but the locals stop in to gossip anyway. (Fred's the mayor) Backyard cookouts on Saturdays, occasional concerts on the front lawn in summer. **$**

✕ **Jackalope's View at Archer's Mountain Inn.** 2489 Beech Mountain Pkwy, Banner Elk; 828-898-9004. Outstanding gourmet cuisine, eclectic menu, and a stunning view. This is where locals like to take their out-of-town guests. Breakfast and dinner. **$$-$$$**

✕ **Morels Restaurant.** One Banner St., Banner Elk; 828-898-6866. This elegant bistro serves inventive luxuries: pan-seared salmon in tamari, grilled house-made sausages. Dinner. **$$-$$**

Beaufort *map 8-C*

⊤ **Captain's Quarters Bed & Biscuit.** 316 Ann St.; 252-728-7711 or 800-659-7111. Victorian B&B furnished with heirlooms and antiques. Two rooms, one suite. Continental, English-style gourmet breakfast. **$-$$$**

⊤ **Cousins B&B.** 303 Turner St.; 252-504-3478. 1855 home with a Caribbean-style sunroom. Four rooms, full gourmet breakfast, weekend cooking classes. **$$**

⊤ **Delamar Inn.** 217 Turner St.; 252-728-4300 or 800-349-5843. 1866 inn furnished in period antiques. Four rooms, continental-plus breakfast. **$$-$$$**

DELAMAR INN

⊤ **Langdon House.** 135 Craven St.; 252-728-5499. Restored colonial home, four rooms, gourmet breakfast. **$$-$$$**

⊤ **Pecan Tree Inn.** 116 Queen St.; 252-728-6733. 1860's Victorian home; seven rooms and two bridal suites. Continental plus breakfast. **$$-$$$**

✕ **Beaufort Grocery Company Restaurant.** 117 Queen St.; 252-728-3899. Fanciful deli items by day, and wide-ranging, fresh-tasting specialties by night. Grilled yellowfin, free-range chicken at night. Reservations for dinner, Sunday brunch. $$-$$$.

✕ **Loughry's Landing.** 502 Front St.; 252-728-7541. Waterfront dining: seafood, steaks, and candlelight. $$

✕ **The Net House.** 133 Turner St.; 252-728-2002. Seafood restaurant known for its steam and raw bar. Dinner. $-$$.

✕ **The Royal James Cafe.** 117 Turner St.; 252-728-4573. A respite from the antique shops: hamburgers, cold beer, and pool tables. $

Belhaven *map 7-B*

⌂ **River Forest Manor Country Inn.** 600 E. Main St.; 800-346-2151. A wonderful, relaxed old mansion on the Pongo River. Crystal chandeliers, marina, tennis courts, dining room. You'll be prepared to see a sea captain walking up the steps, cap tucked under his arm. $$

✕ **River Forest Manor.** *(See address above)* is well known to land travelers and boaters for its 56-dish evening buffet, and Sunday brunch. $$

Blowing Rock *map 3-A*

⌂ **Chetola Resort.** North Main St.; 800-243-8652. The old stone hotel overlooks Lake Chetola. Hiking, tennis,

CHETOLA RESORT

racquetball, boating, fishing, pool. Hotel rooms and condos. $$$-$$$$

⌂ **Cliff Dwellers Inn.** US 321 Bypass; 828-295-3121 or 800-322-7380. Rooms in this cliffside inn overlook Lake Chetola. Rooms, suites, pool, spa. $$$-$$$$

⌂ **The Inn at Ragged Garden.** 203 Sunset Dr.; 828-295-9703. Stone house with gardens. Eight rooms, fireplaces, some Jacuzzis. Full breakfast. $$$-$$$$

⌂ **Maple Lodge B&B.** 152 Sunset Dr.; 828-295-3331. Built in 1946 as a village inn, and furnished with antiques and family heirlooms. Eleven guest rooms, comfortable parlors. Non-smoking. Near galleries, shops, and High Mountain Expeditions (rafting excursions, hiking, caving, etc.). $$$-$$$$

✕ **The Best Cellar Restaurant.** Off US 321 Bypass; 828-295-3466. This very popular restaurant hides out in a 1938 log cabin off the highway. (Call for directions.) Imaginative food, and a vast wine list. Reservations. Dinner Monday through Saturday; in winter dinner on Friday and Saturday only. $$-$$$

Blowing Rock *cont'd*

✕ **Crippen's.** 239 Sunset Dr.; 828-295-3487. Few local natives ever cooked or ate food like the "mountain cooking" served at this delightful little restaurant: New York strip stuffed with mozzarella, or grilled lobster in a cognac-butter sauce appeared on a recent menu. While the food may not be typically Appalachian, the friendliness of the waitstaff and the appealing old farmhouse location are. Certainly worth a stop. $$$

✕ **The Farm House Inn and Dining Room.** 1975 S. Main St.; 828-295-7361. Open only in summer, the large dining room, on top of a mountain, has seating for 500. While views, ambience, and cuisine are excellent, most diners remember the muscial performance provided by the 30 or so servers, college music students from all over the East Coast. $$-$$$

✕ **The Riverwood.** Hwy 321; 828-295-4162. A longtime favorite for those seeking "fine dining" in the area, Riverwood strives to provide an alternative to typical American cuisine with innovative culinary creations. Great wine selection. Make reservations. $$

✕ **Village Cafe.** Behind the ice cream stand on Main St.; 828-295-3769. No one knows why Blowing Rock hides its restaurants; this one serves gourmet breakfasts, lunches, and dinners. Closed Wednesdays, closed winters. $$-$$$

✕ **Woodlands.** US 321 Bypass; 828-295-3651. Where the locals go for barbecue and live bluegrass/folk music. $

Blue Ridge Parkway *map 8-C*

(Usually, you must exit the Parkway for accommodations. There are two exceptions.)

🛏 ✕ **Bluff's Lodge.** Milepost 241 (about 17 miles south of Sparta); 336-372-4499. Built in 1949, rustic, great views. Gift shop, service station, coffee shop, no TV in rooms. May through October. $$

🛏 ✕ **Pisgah Inn.** Milepost 408.6 (about 20 miles south of Asheville); 828-235-8228. Rustic atmosphere, great views. Gift shop, service station, restaurant. May through October. $$

Boone *map 3-A*

🛏 **Lovill House Inn.** 404 Old Bristol Rd.; 828-264-4204 or 800-849-9466. A restored 1875 farmhouse on 11 peaceful, wooded acres. A stay at this AAA four diamond inn includes PPP—"perpetual porch privileges." Five rooms, full breakfast, sane travel information. $$-$$$

✕ **The Caribbean Cafe.** 489B W. King St.; 828-265-2233. Good Caribbean food (try the catfish), very informal atmosphere and informal service. Lunch and dinner. $-$$

✕ **Howard Street Grill.** 179 Howard St.; 828-264-7111. Southwestern/New Mexican burritos with fillings like grilled chicken or blackened salmon. Students love this place. The Cottonwood Microbrewery is part of the restaurant. $-$$$

✕ **Sam and Stu's.** 115 New Market Center; 828-265-0500. This relatively unknown three-star bistro serves excellent French-influenced northern Italian dishes. $$

Bryson City *map 1-B*

Fryemont Inn. Fryemont Rd.; 800-845-4879. On the National Register of Historic Places, this inn boasts stone fireplaces, hardwood floors, and views of the Great Smoky Mountains Nat'l Park. $$$

FRYEMONT INN

Nantahala Village. 9400 Highway 19 West (just down the road from Nantahala Outdoor Center); 828-488-2826. Scheduled to reopen after extensive renovation in June 1998. Fifty cabins, open air cafe (casual, three meals). The lodge has 23 rooms and an excellent restaurant. Rafting, mountain biking, etc. available nearby at the outdoor center. Open mid-March through Thanksgiving. $$$

✕ **Nantahala Village.** *(See address preceding),* Reopens June 1998. Eclectic country gourmet cuisine served in a gentle, relaxed atmosphere. Breakfast, lunch, dinner; Sunday brunch. $$-$$$

Burlington *map 5-A*

✕ **The Cutting Board.** 2619 Alamance Rd.; 336-226-0291. The smell of burning coals adds to the downhome atmosphere of this lively restaurant. Savory grilled beef, chicken, and seafood. $-$$

Burnsville *map 2-B*

Nu Wray Inn. Town Square; 828-682-2329 or 800-368-9729. Listed on the National Register of Historic Places, this inn has hosted guests—among them O. Henry and Thomas Wolfe—since 1833. Hearty country breakfast included. $$

✕ **Nu Wray Inn.** Town Square; 828-682-2329 or 800-368-9729. Family dinners served Monday through Saturday (weekends only in winter): ham, roast beef, barbecue, vegetables, homemade breads all served to guests at long tables.

NU WRAY INN

In summer, there's a bluegrass barbecue on Thursday nights. $$

Buxton *map 8-B*

⌂ **Cape Hatteras B&B.** Old Lighthouse Rd.; 252-995-3002 or 800-252-3316. In the shadow of the historic Cape Hatteras Lighthouse. Surf, charter fishing, canoeing, windsurfing nearby. Five rooms, one suite. Gourmet breakfast. Closed December through March. $-$$

✗ **The Great Salt Marsh Restaurant.** Osprey Shops, NC 12; 252-995-6200. This California-style eatery fits right in on the Outer Banks. $$

Calabash *map 6-D*

This village is known for its Calabash-style, fried seafood just off the boats. A whole "school" of seafood restaurants occupy most of the main street. Get in line. They're all good.

Cameron *map 5-B*

✗ **Dewberry Deli.** 129 Carthage St.; 910-245-3697. The rumor is that the Dewberry Deli may be the last place in the country that serves dewberry (a form of blackberry) pie. This little sandwich shop, tucked away in the basement of an antique store, is open only for lunch. All offerings are homemade and are named for a town historic sight. Fountain drinks complement the sandwiches;

good wines accompany classic cuisine. Antique shoppers from all over the country mix with locals to wait for the next table. Don't miss it. $

Carolina Beach *map 6-D*

⌂ **The Beacon House Inn B&B.** 715 Carolina Beach Ave. North; 910-458-6244. 1950s beach house across the street from the Atlantic Ocean. Nine rooms and a three-bedroom cottage. Full gourmet breakfast. $$

✗ **The Cottage.** 1 N. Lake Park Blvd.; 910-458-4383. Grilled food and a good wine selection make this an excellent dining option while visiting the beach. Many locals are regulars. $$

✗ **The Marina's Edge.** 300 North Lake Park Blvd.; 910-458-6001. Fresh seafood and raw bar. Dinner every night, plus lunch on weekends. $$-$$$

Cary *map 5-B*

✗ **Fox & Hound Restaurant & Pub.** MacGregor Park; 919-380-0080. How many authentic English pubs feature an Irish folk singer? Wednesday nights that's what you'll find at this popular bar. Try the Yorkshire pudding or shepherd's pie. $ - $$

Cashiers *map 2-C*

⌂ **Millstone Inn.** Highway 64 West; 828-743-2737. Rated one of the top inns in the nation by *Country Inns Magazine.* Hiking, waterfalls, seclusion. Eleven rooms, full breakfast. $$$-$$$$

MILLSTONE INN

Chapel Hill *map 5-B*

☲ **The Inn at Bingham School.** NC 54 @Mebane Oaks Rd.; 919-563-5583 or 800-566-5583. A secluded Greek Revival/Federal style historic inn. Ten acres of grounds. Five rooms, full breakfast; gourmet dining nearby. $$-$$$.

☲ **The Carolina Inn.** 211 Pittsboro St.; 919-933-2001 or 800-962-8519. This 1924 landmark, located on the UNC campus, was renovated in 1995. $$$$

☲ **The Siena.** 1505 E. Franklin St.; 919-929-4000. 80-room hotel, full breakfast. $$$-$$$$

✗ **Carolina Brewery.** 460 W. Franklin St.; 919-942-1800. A handsome storefront pub in the downtown shopping district,

the Carolina boasts a more adventurous (if pricier) menu than other brewpubs. The house brews are English-style. $-$$

✗ **Crook's Corner.** 610 Franklin St.; 919-929-7643. Imaginative Southern cuisine—collards, hopping John, shrimp and grits—characterize the work of the masterful chef at this attractive restaurant. Local artists provide art to complement the upscale decor. $$

✗ **411 West Italian Cafe.** 411 W. Franklin St.; 919-967-2782. College students from UNC flock to this cafe for pizzas baked in a wood-burning oven. Sandwiches are tasty, as is the beef tenderloin appetizer, served with horseradish. $-$$

✗ **Il Palio, In The Siena.** 1505 E. Franklin St.; 919-918-2545. This highly rated restaurant serves northern Italian food. Lunch and dinner. $$

✗ **La Residence.** 202 W. Rosemary; 919-967-2506. The menu changes every day here, but this restaurant specializes in French cuisine. Extensive wine list. Dinner, Tuesday through Sunday. $$-$$$

✗ **Ma Dip's Country Kitchen,** 405 W. Rosemary; 919-942-5837. Downhome Southern cooking. $-$$

✗ **Pyewacket.** The Courtyard, 431 W. Franklin St.; 919-929-0297. College towns usually exhibit an eclectic character, and so do the restaurants in them: Pyewacket blends nicely with Chapel Hill's unique personality. Seafood and vegetarian dishes dominate the menu. Fashionable surroundings. $$

RESTAURANTS & ACCOMMODATIONS

Charlotte *map 4-B*

The Dunhill Hotel. 237 N. Tryon St.; 704-332-4141. This 1929 "Uptown" European-style hotel includes rooms, deluxe rooms, and penthouse. The staff chauffeur tools guests around town in the hotel Rolls Royce. $$$-$$$$

The Elizabeth B&B. 2145 E. Fifth St.; 704-358-1368. Located in Charlotte's second oldest historic neighborhood. Four rooms, one with a private entrance to the garden. Full breakfasts. $$-$$$

The Inn Uptown. 129 N. Poplar St.; 704-342-2800 or 800-959-1990. A stylish hotel with six rooms, fireplaces, and whirlpool baths. Full gourmet breakfast. Cookies in the evening. $$-$$$$

The Park Hotel. 2200 Rexford Rd.; 704-364-8220. This intimate hotel in the trendy South Park neighborhood is Charlotte's poshest lodging. Elegantly appointed with marble and brass fixtures, the hotel is known for its excellent service and careful attention to detail. The rooms are attractive, but many are quite small. $$$-$$$$

Still Waters Bed and Breakfast. 6221 Amos Smith Rd.; 704-399-6299. Lakefront log resort home with two bedrooms, a suite, and a cottage. Gardens, pool, deck, sports court. Three rooms, one cottage. Full gourmet breakfast. $-$$

Alexander Michael's. 401 West Ninth St.; 704-332-6789. Located in the historic Fourth Ward. Dinner features fresh seafood and pasta dishes. Lunch and dinner. $-$$

Bistro 100. Founder's Hall, 100 N. Tryon St.; 704-344-0515. An evening with someone special should be spent at a place like this. American cuisine with enough French flair to make dinner more intriguing. Lunch and dinner every day; brunch on Sunday. $$-$$$

Bravo Ristorante. Adam's Mark Hotel, 555 S. McDowells St.; 704-372-5440. Charlotte is in many respects like a gangly adolescent boy tryng to be grown up and sophisticated, but finding it difficult to leave the carefree days of childhood. The restaurants here reflect this. Bravo serves upmarket food, but the atmosphere's still fun: servers are professional singers, and entertain diners with opera as well as show tunes. $$-$$$

The Cajun Queen. 1800 E. Seventh St.; 704-377-9017. Cajun, of course, and live jazz. No reservations accepted weekends. Dinner. $$-$$$

Cino Grill. 6401 Morrison Blvd.; 704-365-8226. Earthy and robust Southwestern cuisine served in cantina-like surroundings. The menu changes frequently, so locals keep coming back. $$

Dilworth Brewing Co. 1301 East Blvd.; 704-377-2739. Looking for a locally made beer with dinner? A casual, pleasant atmosphere to enjoy consistently prepared pastas, meat, and fish, as well as excellent beer. $-$$

The Fishmarket. 6631 Morrison Blvd.; 704-365-0883. Most seafood restaurants in the Carolinas emphasize Southern casual. Not so here. This is one of the most elegant seafood restaurants in the state. $$$

✗ **La Bibliotheque.** 1901 Roxborough Rd.; 704-365-5000. An elegant French restaurant offering both classic French and American entrees. Extensive wine list. $$$

✗ **The Lamplighter Restaurant.** 1065 E. Morehead St.; 704-372-5343. This restaurant, which has won the Distinguished Restaurants of North America Award, serves continental American cuisinc. Dinner. $$$

✗ **McNinch House Restaurant.** 511 North Church St.; 704-332-6159. Fine dining, reservations only. Dinner Tuesday through Saturday. $$$

✗ **Ranch House.** 5614 Wilkinson Blvd.; 704-399-5411. Casual, rustic, and very popular, the Ranch House serves delicious steak and a shrimp cocktail that's hot and spicy. $$

✗ **Sonoma on Providence.** 801 Providence Rd.; 704-377-1333. Great for a change of pace. An old Southern home with a menu more typical of California's Napa Valley than of the American South. $$

✗ **Southend Brewery and Smokehouse.** 2100 South Blvd.; 704-358-4677. Trendy microbrewery with grill. Lunch and dinner. $-$$

✗ **30th Edition.** 301 S. Tryon, Two First Union Plaza, 30th Floor; 704-372-7778. Steak and fresh seafood anchor this lofty restaurant; the menu features items for the health-conscious, too. Panoramic view of rapidly expanding Charlotte. $$-$$$

✗ **The Townhouse.** 1011 Providence Rd.; 704-335-1546. This eatery has been providing locals and visitors with sophisticated fowl, seafood, and meat since 1939. But the menu today is thoroughly up-to-date: American eclectic with a dash of French. $$$

Chimney Rock *map 2-C*

☎ **The Dogwood Inn B&B.** Highway 64/74A; 828-625-4403 or 800-992-5557. This inn's porches overlook Chimney Rock Mountain and the Rocky Broad River. Full gourmet breakfast. Closed January and February. $$

THE DOGWOOD INN B&B

Crumpler *map 3-A*

✗ **The Shatley Springs Inn.** 407 Shatley Springs Rd.; 336-982-2236. Story goes that FDR used to eat here. Family-style meals emphasizing old-fashioned, mountain-style cooking—and plenty of it. Country ham, fried chicken, vegetables, and mouth-watering desserts insure that no one leaves hungry. $$

Dillsboro *map 1-B*

✕ **The Jarrett House.** 100 Haywood; 828-586-0265. The Jarrett House opened in 1882 as a fancy, three-story hotel. It's famous for Southern cooking served family-style, and for vinegar pie. Open for breakfast, lunch, and dinner, except Sunday dinner. **$$**

Duck *map 8-A*

⌂ **Advice 5¢, a B&B.** 111 Scarborough Lane; 252-255-1050 or 800-ADVICE5. A half-mile from the beach. Five rooms, one suite, continental-plus breakfasts. **$$-$$$$**

⌂ **Sanderling Inn.** 1461 Duck Rd.; 800-701-4111. Rooms and suites with private porches, indoor and outdoor pools, health club, sun deck, tennis courts, and private beach. Continental breakfast and afternoon tea. **$$$-$$$$**

SANDERLING INN

✕ **Elizabeth's Cafe & Winery.** Scarborough Faire; 252-261-6145. *Wine Merchant* rates this French bistro's wine list

among the top 250 restaurant lists in the U.S. Lunch and dinner; live jazz some nights. **$$-$$$**

✕ **Sanderling Inn Restaurant.** (above) 252-261-3021. This restaurant occupies the old Caffey's Inlet U.S. Lifesaving Station No. 5. Southern cuisine, freshly baked breads and desserts. The Sanderling also cranks its own ice cream. **$$-$$$**

Durham *map 5-A*

⌂ **Arrowhead Inn.** 106 Mason Rd.; 919-477-8430. Outside 919: 800-528-2207. Founded in 1775, this B&B tucks guest rooms in the manor house, carriage house, and a two-room log cabin. Five rooms, two suites, one log cabin; full breakfast. **$$$-$$$$**

⌂ **The Blooming Garden Inn.** 513 Holloway St.; 919-687-0801. 1892 Queen Anne–style home in Durham's historic district. Three rooms, two suites. Gourmet breakfast, gardens. **$$-$$$$**

⌂ **Brownstone Guest House Inn.** 2424 Erwin Rd.; 919-286-7761. Large, quiet rooms, VIP floor. Indoor pool and sauna, near Duke University Hospital. **$$**

⌂ **Old North Durham Inn.** 922 N. Mangum St.; 919-683-1885. Early 1900s Colonial Revival home in historic neighborhood. Period furnishings, fireplaces, whirlpool tubs. Three rooms, one suite, gourmet breakfast. **$$**

⌂ **Washington Duke Inn & Golf Club.** 3001 Cameron Blvd.; 919-490-0999.

WASHINGTON DUKE INN & GOLF CLUB

Beautiful old hotel overlooking Duke University Golf Course. 171 rooms furnished with antique reproductions. Lounge and restaurant. **$$$$**

✕ **AnotherThyme Restaurant.** 109 N. Gregson St.; 919-682-5225. Even meat-eaters will be happy at this higly rated vegetarian restaurant. Multi-cultural cuisine, the finest and freshest ingredients, and an impressive wine list will please anyone. Lunch and dinner. **$$**

✕ **Bullock's Bar-B-Cue.** 3330 Quebec St.; 919-383-3211. Bullock's has won fans world-wide for its hickory-smoked pork barbecue and fantastic hush puppies. Lunch and dinner Tuesday through Saturday, cash on the barrel head. **$$**

✕ **Cafe Parizäde.** First Union Building, Erwin Square, 2200 W. Main St.; 919-286-9712. Mediterranean dishes get a formal treatment at this radiant dining facility, with its colorful decor and charismatic owner. Expect rich pastas, roasted fowl and meats. **$-$$$**

✕ **Fairview Restaurant.** 3001 Cameron Blvd., inside the Washington Duke Inn; 919-490-0999. Classy restaurant noted for crab cakes, corn chowder, shrimp. Lunch and dinner. **$$$**

✕ **Magnolia Grill.** 1002 Ninth St.; 919-286-3609. A national magazine wrote that the chef here "is still stirring things up, putting a global spin on the flavorful memories of his Carolina childhood." Locals love this award-winning place. **$$-$$$**

✕ **Nana's.** 2514 University Dr.; 919-493-8545. Food critics praise chef/owner Scott Howell for his outstanding renditions of Southern regional cuisine, most of which reveal strong Italian and French influences. Dinner. **$$**

✕ **Neo-China Restaurant.** 4015 University Dr.; 919-489-2828. Many locals swear that the best Chinese food in the city is served here. Ranked as one of Durham's favorite eateries: a four-star authentic Chinese restaurant. **$$**

✕ **Pop's: A Durham Trattoria.** 810 W. Peabody St.; 919-956-7677. *Bon Appetit* named this northern Italian restaurant one of the top new restaurants in the nation. In a restored tobacco warehouse downtown, the visible stainless steel, large windows, and old factory equipment recall the industrialized Italian north. The seasonal menu reflects the chef's use of the freshest locally grown and gathered ingredients. Lunch and dinner. **$$**

✕ **Taverna Nikos.** 905 W. Main St.; 919-682-0043. Located in a former warehouse, this popular spot is a fun place to go for satisfying sandwiches. **$-$$$**

RESTAURANTS & ACCOMMODATIONS

Edenton *map 7-A*

☒ **Captain's Quarter Inn.** 202 West Queen St.; 252-482-8945 or 800-482-8945. 1907 inn three blocks from the Albemarle Sound. Dinner cruises, bicycles, wrap-around porch. Eight rooms, one suite. Full gourmet breakfast, dinner. $-$$

☒ **Dram Tree Inn.** 110 Water St.; 252-482-2711. Waterfront inn; suites. $$

☒ **The Lords Proprietors Inn.** 300 North Broad St.; 252-482-3641. Three historic buildings and a restored tobacco barn were combined to create 20 guest rooms, three parlors, library; antiques and reproductions. Tea, full breakfast. Supper Tuesday through Saturday. $$$$

THE LORDS PROPRIETORS INN

Elizabeth City *map 8-A*

☒ **The Culpepper Inn.** 609 W. Main St.; 252-335-1993. Fireplaces, garden tubs, pool. Corporate and government rates. Eleven rooms, full breakfast. $$$

☒ **Elizabeth City B&B.** 108 East Fearing St.; 252-338-2177. On the National Register of Historic Places. Four rooms, gourmet breakfast, evening candlelight dinners. $-$$

✕ **Mulligan's Downtown Grille.** 400 S. Water St.; 252-331-2431. Friendly, comfortable, tavern-like environment, good food, and a terrific view of the Pasquotank River. $-$$

Elizabethtown *map 8-C*

✕ **Melvin's.** 133 W. Broad St.; 910-862-2763. Many people in southeastern North Carolina swear that Melvin's makes the best hamburgers in the country. The cooks here use fresh beef round and chuck that is ground every three hours. $

Ellerbe *map 4-C*

✕ **Ellerbe Springs Inn and Restaurant.** US ☒ 220; 910-652-5600/800-248-6467. Good food, and lots of it, is served in the ambience of an old Southern resort inn. This is the place to please your palate without draining your bank account. $-$$

Fayetteville *map 5-C*

☒ **Radisson Prince Charles Hotel and Suites.** 450 Hay St.; 910-433-4444. This restored 1924 hotel is listed on the National Register of Historic Places, and is a member of the Historic Hotels of America. Fitness room, continental breakfast. $$

✕ **Bella Villa.** 201 S. McPherson Church Rd.; McPherson Square; 910-867-1199. The son of a Sicilian butcher is the owner-chef at this excellent restaurant. His extensive menu of two dozen seafood and chicken Italian entrees, plus his veal and handmade pizzas, are made from old Neapolitan and Sicilian recipes. $-$$

✕ **Chris's Open Hearth Steak House.** 2620 Raeford Rd.; 910-485-2948. The menu at this old favorite lists non-beef entrees, but why go to Chris's and not order some of the best steak or prime rib in the city? Dinner. $$

✕ **DeLafayette Restaurant,** 6112 Cliffdale Rd.; 910-868-4600. Cajun and Creole entrees are served in this upscale restaurant, which occupies a restored gristmill. Tasty and nicely presented entrees are the norm. Try to get a table overlooking McFayden Pond. This is the sort of place where couples celebrate their anniversaries. Reservations. Dinner, Tuesday through Saturday. $$-$$$

✕ **Haymont Grill and Steakhouse.** 1304 Morganton Rd.; 910-484-0261. Downtown Fayetteville is changing, but Haymont Grill has always turned out some of the best homemade soup in the region. This eatery is leading Hay Street in its evolution from seedy to upscale. $-$$

✕ **Hunan Garden Restaurant.** 2726 Raeford Rd.; 910-323-3778. Consistently high-quality entrees and appetizers make this one of Fayetteville's favorite Chinese restaurants. $

✕ **Vicenzo Lobster House.** 448 Person St.; 910-485-8866. This popular downtown restaurant specializes in (surprise!) seafood: best are Maine lobsters, Italian dishes, and charcoal-broiled steaks. A Fayetteville Landmark Restaurant. Dinner, Monday through Saturday. $$-$$$

Flat Rock *map 2-B*

⊞ **Flat Rock Inn B&B.** 2810 Greenville Hwy.; 828-696-3273 or 800-266-3996. This 1888 inn, listed on the National Register, provides easy access to the Carl Sandburg Home and to Flat Rock Playhouse. Four rooms, wonderful country breakfast. $$$

⊞ **Old Teneriffe Inn.** 2531 Little River Rd.; 828-698-8178 or 800-617-6427. Secluded 1850 Tudor-style mansion. Four rooms. Afternoon tea, tennis court, croquet court, trails on 22 acres. Full gourmet breakfast. $$$$

⊞ **Woodfield Inn.** Hwy. 25; 828-693-6016 or 800-533-6016. Established in 1852 as a stagecoach stop. Victorian bedrooms (all with private baths), antique furnishings, three dining rooms. Full breakfast. $$-$$$

✕ **Highland Lake Inn.** Highland Lake Rd.; 828-696-9094. This gourmet restaurant is known for its fresh ingredients, including vegetables from the garden out back. Dinner Tuesday through Saturday, Sunday brunch. Reservations. $$-$$$

Flat Rock *cont'd*

✕ **Woodfield Inn.** *(see address preceding)*, 828-693-6016. This inn opened in 1852 as a stagecoach stop. Varied menu, homemade desserts. Dinner daily, lunch Wednesday through Sunday. $$

Fontana Village *map 1-B*

☷ **Fontana Village.** 828-498-2211 or 800-849-2258. This resort community developed around housing left behind by the builders of Fontana Dam in 1945. The dam created a mountainside lake that stretches 31 miles. In the village is an inn with 94 rooms (some with fireplaces), 250 cottages, casual restaurants. Hiking, horseback riding, fishing, boating, crafts classes, etc. $$-$$$$

FONTANA VILLAGE

Franklin *map 1-C*

✕ **Gazebo Cafe.** 103 Heritage Hollow; 704-524-8783. In the wild, wonderful mountains of western North Carolina, it's miles between eating places (thankfully the fast-food chains have not blanketed the landscape), so this little refuge is a welcome sight. Stop in and enjoy lunch in an open-air gazebo overlooking a pretty mountain creek. $

Frisco *map 8-B*

✕ **The Gingerbread House.** NC 12; 252-995-5204. Excellent baked goods all day; open for dinner Tuesday through Saturday. $

✕ **The Quarterdeck,** NC 12; 252-986-2425. This informal, family-run restaurant serves fresh seafood and Italian dishes. Lunch and dinner. $$

Gastonia Area *map 3-B*

✕ **North Star Fish Camp.** 3150 High Sholis in Dallas; 704-922-7715. Outstanding fresh seafood fried up and served fish-camp style. Lunch and dinner, closed Sunday. $

Glendale Springs *map 3-A*

☷ **Glendale Springs Inn & Restaurant.** 7414 NC 16 (on the Blue Ridge Parkway at Milepost 259, 30 mins east of

Boone); 336-982-2103 or 800-287-1206. Authentic country inn with old fashioned parlors, period furnishings, and gardens. Nine rooms. $$

✗ Glendale Springs Inn & Restaurant. *(See address above)*. Gourmet restaurant serves "New American" cuisine. In summer, you can dine on the porch. Breakfast, lunch, dinner. Reservations. $$-$$$

Goldsboro *map 6-B*

✗ Billie's Backstreet Restaurant. 620 N. Madison St.; 919-736-4406. Tired of barbecue? Those seeking gracious hospitality will find that Billie's has an atmosphere that makes diners feel at home while enjoying fine food. $$

✗ Scott's Famous Barbecue. 1201 N. Williams St.; 919-734-0711. One of the state's oldest barbecue restaurants. Founder Scott claims that the recipe for his sauce came to him in a dream. *Food & Wine* magazine once ranked Scott's sauce second in a national competition. $

✗ Wilber's Barbecue. 4172 US 70 East; 919-778-5218. Wilber's is a typical eastern North Carolina barbecue house, serving a pepper-and-vinegar-based pork barbecue, pork sandwiches, Brunswick stew, and fried chicken. $

Greensboro *map 4-A*

🕌 Greenwood B&B. 205 N. Park Dr.; 336-274-6350 or 800-535-9363. 1905 Stick-style house located in the central historic district. Five rooms, fireplaces. Full breakfast. $$$

🕌 Troy-Bumpass Inn. 114 S. Mendenhall St.; 800-370-9070. This restored 1847 home is listed on the National Register of Historic Places. $$-$$$

✗ Anton's Restaurant. 1628 Battleground Ave.; 336-273-1386. Many locals favor Anton's for an inexpensive dining experience. Choose between beef, fish, or chicken dishes—fish may be the best. $-$$

✗ Eastwind Cafe. 119 S. Elm St.; 336-574-0730. Great Vietnamese food; extremely informal. $

✗ Gate City Chop House. 106 S. Holden Rd.; 336-294-9977. Some regulars say they dine here for the elaborate appetizers, but the beef entrees are also top notch. $$-$$$

✗ La Spiedo di Noble. 1720 Battleground Ave.; 336-333-9833. Between the wood-burning oven and the rotisserie, the aromas here are fantastic. The service is efficient and sociable, too, which makes the northern Italian entrees and homemade breads, soups, and desserts taste all that much better. Extensive wine list. $$-$$$

✗ Lucky 32. 1421 Westover Terr.; 336-370-0707. For gourmet pizza or American home-style cooking, place your bets on Lucky 32. Large, open dining rooms create a feeling of casual elegance. $-$$

✗ Spring Garden Brewing Company. 714 Francis King St.; 336-299-3649. Lots of college students endorse the varied

RESTAURANTS & ACCOMMODATIONS

Greensboro *cont'd*

menu and the house-brewed lager. Lunch and dinner. $-$$

X **Stamey's Barbecue,** 2206 High Point Rd.; 336-299-9888. Expect a bustling dining room, fast service, and good food. They cook the barbecue out back: if you get lost, follow your nose. Lunch and dinner, closed Sundays. $

Greenville *map 7-B*

X **B's Barbeque.** Highway 43 and B's Barbeque Rd. One of the few barbecue houses with a road named for it, and one hopping restaurant. The ambiance is rustic, the barbecue great. No phone, but ask anybody for directions: this place has a cult following. $

X **Chico's Mexican Restaurant.** 521 Cotanche St.; 252-757-1666. E. Carolina University students and faculty agree that this is one of the town's best eateries—the chicken soup gets an A+. A wide variety of Mexican dishes, and tastefully decorated dining rooms. $

Hatteras *map 8-B*

X **The Breakwater Restaurant.** Oden's Dock, Hwy 12; 252-986-2733. Soundside restaurant serves its seafood with a northern Italian twist. Dinner. $$

X **Channel Bass Restaurant.** NC 12; 252-986-2250. Seafood dinners year-round. $$

Hendersonville *map 2-B*

⌂ **Apple Inn.** 1005 White Pine Dr.; 828-693-0107 or 800-615-6611. Secluded Romantic Revival inn with gardens, billiards room. Five rooms. Full, home-cooked breakfast. $$

⌂ **The Waverly Inn.** 783 North Main St.; 828-693-9193 or 800-397-0066. This well known 1898 Victorian inn is Hendersonville's oldest. One suite, 13 rooms. Full breakfast. $$-$$$$

THE WAVERLY INN

X **Expressions.** 114 N. Main St.; 828-693-8516. Housed in an old storefront that's been restored with warmth and taste. Sophisticated seasonal cuisine: personable chef Tom Young crafts dishes like grilled swordfish with artichoke relish. An outstanding dining experience. $$-$$$

X **Hannah Flanagan's Pub.** 300 N. Main St.; 828-696-1665. Good sandwiches, soups and salads; the bar is a happening scene at night. Lunch and dinner. $

✗ **Jimmy's Italian Villa.** 1903 Asheville Hwy.; 828-693-0980. A local favorite. Dinner Monday through Saturday. $$

Hertford   *map 8-A*

☂ **1812 On The Perquimans.** One mile east of Hwy 17 on Old Neck Rd.; 919-426-1812. This coastal plantation inn's wharf accommodates canoes, fishermen, and sailboats. Full plantation breakfast. $$

Hickory   *map 3-B*

☂ **The Hickory B&B.** 464 Seventh St. SW; 828-324-0548 or 800-654-2961. 1908 two-story Georgian-style home. Housemade dessert and iced tea served in the afternoon. Four rooms, swimming pool. $$-$$$

✗ **1859 Cafe.** 433 Second Ave. SW; 828-322-1859. Restored homes, especially those of the antebellum period, are ideal for elegant, intimate restaurant settings. This 1859 house is case in point, and you'll enjoy some interesting, if rich and somewhat formal, cuisine in the process. $$-$$$

High Point   *map 4-B*

✗ **Square One Restaurant at Market Square.** 305 W. High St.; 336-889-4464. Located in a furniture showroom complex. Varied menu, reservations.

Lunch Monday through Friday. $$

Hillsborough   *map 5-A*

☂ **Colonial Inn.** 153 W. King St.; 919-732-2461. Built around 1759, this is one of the oldest inns in the nation. Eight rooms furnished with antiques. Full Breakfast. $$

✗ **Colonial Inn.** (See address above) Southern cooking. Lunch and dinner; closed Mondays. $-$$

Jamesville   *map 7-B*

✗ **Cypress Grill.** On the riverfront, this is a true "fish camp": cement floors, pine chairs, fried seafood. If the shad are running, talk with fishermen hawking their catch on the riverbank. Spring only. $

Kill Devils Hill Area   *map 8-A*

✗ **Chili Peppers.** 3001 N. Croatan Hwy.; 252-441-8081. All the menu items here will fire up your tastebuds. $-$$

✗ **Colington Cafe.** One mile west of Hwy. 58, on Colington Rd. 252-480-1123. You need reservations for this popular Outer Banks restaurant, which specializes in French cuisine and seafood. Dinner. Reservations. $$-$$$

✗ **Petrozza Deli and Cafe,** 1712 N. Croatan Hwy.; 252-441-1642. A popular restaurant noted for Italian seafood and pasta dishes. $-$$

✗ **Port O' Call.** Hwy. 12 @ Milepost 8.5; 252-441-7484. This formal, gourmet restaurant serves dinner daily, March to December, but may be best known for its Sunday brunch buffet. Seafood, of course, is its specialty. Homemade desserts, special blend coffees are nice touches in this Victorian-style art gallery. $$-$$$.

Kitty Hawk *map 8-A*

X **Black Pelican Seafood Company.** Milepost 4, US 12; 252-261-3171. This recently restored old standby serves gourmet pizza, fresh seafood, raw bar. Lunch and dinner. $-$$

Kure Beach *map 6-D*

X **Big Daddy's Seafood Restaurant.** Hwy. 421 South @ town stoplight; 910-458-8622. Seafood and steaks restaurant. Dinner, March to November. $$-$$$

Lake Lure *map 2-B*

☶ **The Lodge on Lake Lure.** Charlotte Dr.; 828-625-2789 or 800-733-2785. Mountain views, privacy, canoeing,

THE LODGE ON LAKE LURE

boating. Twelve rooms, full gourmet breakfasts. $$$-$$$

Lake Waccamaw *map 6-D*

☶ **B&B by the Lake.** 404 Lake Shore Dr.; 910-646-4744. Three rooms with shared bath, full southern breakfast. $

☶ **Lake Shore Lodge,** 2014 Lake Shore Dr.; 910-646-3748. Waterfront lodge, continental breakfast. $

Lexington *map 4-B*

Lexington is known for its barbecue, which is made from pork shoulders and dressed in a sweet, tomato-vinegar sauce. You'll find 20 or so restaurants cheek-to-jowl along Main Street. Most slow-roast their barbecue out back. Diners won't be disappointed with any of them, but favorites are **Lexington BBQ #1** (Business I-85S) $ and **Speedy's BBQ** (US 52 North) $.

Linville *map 3-A*

☶ **Eeseola Lodge.** Near the intersection of US 221 and NC 181; 828-733-4311. Rooms in this beautiful old inn have private porches, window boxes, great views. Golf, tennis, horseback riding. Closed October to May. $$$$

X **Eeseola Lodge.** *(See address above.)* Fabulous new American cuisine, which some say is the best in the High Country. Prix-fixe menu, with items like lumpcrab meat with mango slaw and smoked tomato remoulade. Dinner; reservations, coat and tie. $$$-$$$$

EESEOLA LODGE

Long Beach   *map 6-D*

✕ **Jones' Seafood House.** 6404 E. Oak Island Dr.; 910-278-5231. This old favorite specializes in Calabash-style (fried) seafood. Dinner every night, plus lunch on Sundays. $-$$$

Lumberton   *map 5-C*

✕ **Fuller's Old Fashion Bar-B-Q.** 3201 Roberts Ave. (Exit 20 off I-95); 910-738-8694. Weary, hungry travelers on I-95 find this easily accessible restaurant a pleasant respite from the stress of fighting traffic. This all-you-can-eat establishment serves typically Southern fried seafood and chicken, in addition to some outstanding pit-cooked vinegar-and-pepper-based barbecue. Homemade desserts. Very popular in the region. $

✕ **John's Restaurant.** 4880 Kahn Dr.; 910-738-4709. An architecturally bland building hides the fact that some of the most spirited dishes in Lumberton are prepared here. This is where the town's movers and shakers dine, along with those few lucky out-of-towners who stumble in from the interstate. $$-$$$

✕ **Panda Garden Chinese Restaurant.** 1907 N. Pine St.; 910-671-0777. Deep in the heart of Lumbee Indian country, this eatery offers some of the highest quality Chinese food in the region. Soft light and friendly smiles add to the pleasure of dining here. Rated Number 1 in a people's choice newspaper survey. $-$$

Madison   *map 4-A*

✕ **Fuzzy's Bar-B-Q.** Business US 220; 336-427-4130. Western North Carolina–style barbecue: won the annual "U.S. Congressional Barbecue Bowl" as the best-tasting barbecue. Fuzzy's other claim to fame is that it has attempted to market North Carolina barbecue in New York. $

Maggie Valley   *map 2-B*

⌂ **Cataloochee Ranch.** Three miles off US 19 South, near Ghost Town in the Sky; 828-926-1401 or 800-868-1401. This

CATALOOCHEE RANCH

BARBECUE: THE STATE FOOD OF NORTH CAROLINA

Barbecue may not have originated in North Carolina, but try to tell that to a native North Carolinian. From the coast to the mountains, a plate of pig is the food of choice for casual dining. Some say that North Carolinians have had a long-standing love affair with barbecue since the Colonial period, when local Indians showed the colonists how they cooked meat over hot coals. Since then, two distinctive types of North Carolina barbecue have evolved, one on either side of the state, and proponents of each continue to bicker over which is better. In both schools, pork is the required meat, and hush puppies, or fried corn bread, are served alongside. But from there the camps are split, more or less along the Fall Line—the border between the Coastal Plain and the Piedmont.

On the eastern side, the barbecuer uses a vinegar-and-pepper-based sauce to season the whole hog as it cooks slowly over hot coals—traditionally hickory and oak, though today propane gas is more commonly used. (The absence of tomatoes from the eastern sauce may be related to the fact that early colonists along the Eastern Seaboard believed the tomato to be poisonous.) Eastern barbecue, because it consists of the entire hog, tends to be lean and slightly dry, so it is served finely chopped and brought to the table with a bottle of sauce. Eastern barbecue is served with a side of Brunswick stew—a slightly sweet mixture of corn, tomatoes, okra, and meat and/or fish—an ideal complement to the drier, somewhat salty barbecue. Another common side dish is white potatoes, chunks of which are boiled in water seasoned with onions, tomato sauce, sugar, and bacon drippings. In the east, cole slaw is commonly used as a garnish rather than as a major side dish. Eastern cole slaw consists of shredded cabbage and mayonnaise, plus salt and pepper, and sometimes mustard or sweet pickle.

Western, or Piedmont, barbecue is made from pork shoulders, a dark, marbled cut of pork which results in moister meat. While being cooked slowly over a wood fire, the meat is rarely basted. In the west barbecue is normally cut into chunks or slices, although it is occasionally chopped as finely as the eastern variety. Western barbecue comes with a "dip," a sweet and sour sauce with a trace of tomato through the addition of small amounts of catsup or Worcestershire sauce: just enough to add a reddish tint. Otherwise, the ingredients are basically the same for eastern and western sauces. In the west fewer side dishes are served; in most western barbecue houses the only side dish is cole slaw—coarsely chopped cabbage with just the barbecue sauce itself and a little sugar.

NOTE: In North Carolina, the term "barbecue" means the food cooked on a grill over a bed of hot coals; it does not apply to the cooking contraption itself.

Despite the tussle between advocates of eastern and western styles, barbecue is the ethnic food of most native North Carolinians: it is and has always been closely tied to the state's heritage. As Bob Garner writes, "within North Carolina . . . barbecuing was, with a few exceptions, the occupation of farmers and journeymen, white and black, and its arts, methods, and mysteries were endlessly discussed and debated." The hundreds of thousands of newcomers to the state are more than happy to join the natives claiming the tradition.

EASTERN NORTH CAROLINA BARBECUE SAUCE

> 1 quart apple-cider vinegar
> $1/2$ to 1 oz. crushed red pepper (to taste)
> 1 tablespoon salt
> 1 teaspoon ground black pepper

Mix all ingredients and baste pork as it cooks. After meat has cooked, use this sauce to season to taste.

HUSH PUPPIES

> 3 cups yellow cornmeal
> 1 cup all-purpose flour
> 2 tablespoons sugar
> 2 teaspoons baking powder
> 1 teaspoon onion flakes or powder (optional)
> 1 or 2 eggs
> 2 cups lowfat buttermilk
> $1/4$ cup shortening

Mix all dry ingredients, add milk, egg, and shortening. Stir mixture until smooth, about one minute. If mixture is too thick, add more milk. Pour 3 or 4 inches of cooking oil into deep fryer and heat to 375°. Spoon batter into hot oil. As hush puppies float, turn them for even browning. Remove from oil, drain (on paper towels) and eat while hot.

—Thomas Ross

Maggie Valley *cont'd*

ranch's rustic lodge and cabins sit on a mountaintop overlooking Maggie Valley. Horseback riding, moonlight hayrides, hiking, and trout fishing are all popular. So is rocking on the porch. Two rustic lodges, 11 cabins (some with Jacuzzis, most with fireplaces), hearty country-style meals with homemade breads and jams. Rates include breakfast and dinner. $$$$

☵ **The Ketner Inn and Farm.** 190 Jonathan Creek Rd.; 704-926-1511 or 800-714-1397. 1898 inn with antiques, large porches, an outdoor hot tub. Five rooms, hearty country breakfast. $-$$

✕ **J. Arthur's Restaurant.** 2843 Soco Rd.; 704-926-1817. Specialties include prime rib and steaks. Dinner daily during season; Tuesday through Saturday in winter. Children's menu. $$-$$$

✕ **Maggie Valley Resort and Country Club.** Hwy 19, just south of US 276; 704-926-1616. Regional specialties, great view. Jacket and tie, etc. Dinner, reservations. $$-$$$

Manteo *map 8-A*

☵ **Elizabethan Inn.** US 64/264; 252-473-2101. Tudor-style motel with fitness center, racquetball courts. $-$$

✕ **1587.** 405 Queen Elizabeth St.; at the Tranquil House Inn; 252-473-1587. Fine dining. Open for dinner, spring through fall. $$-$$$

✕ **RV's.** Manteo/Nags Head Causeway; 252-441-4963. The lounge of this casual restaurant (seafood, mesquite-grilled fish and beef) is a popular family spot. Lunch and dinner. $$

✕ **The Weeping Radish.** US 64 (by the Christmas shops); 252-473-1157. Authentic German food, in-house Bavarian brewery. Lunch and dinner. $$

☵ **Scarborough House Inn.** 323 Fernando St.; 252-473-3849. Antique furnishings, porch with rockers, bicycles for touring Manteo waterfront, two blocks away. Five rooms, in-room breakfast. $-$$

☵ **The White Doe Inn.** 319 Sir Walter Raleigh St.; 252-473-9851 or 800-473-6091. Queen Anne home two blocks from the waterfront. Tea, fireplaces, full gourmet breakfast. Seven rooms, one suite. $$$-$$$$

THE WHITE DOE INN

Maxton *map 5-C*

✕ **Bill's Place.** 142 N. Patterson St.; 910-844-5137. A slice of Americana and a very good hot dog can be had at Bill's: its small-town, homey atmosphere is right out of a Norman Rockwell painting. Hop up on the swivel stool to eat, but watch out—the homemade chili, from a secret recipe, is spicy, but that's what makes the hot dog so good.

Morehead City *map 7-C*

✕ **Captain Bill's Waterfront.** 701 Evans St.; 252-726-2166. Sanitary Restaurant's rival since the 1940s serves seafood and homemade desserts, including fudge-to-go. Lunch and dinner. Call for winter hours. $$

✕ **Jason's Restaurant and Lounge.** 403 Arendell; 252-240-1040. Formal dining, seafood. Dinner. $$$

✕ **Sanitary Fish Market and Restaurant.** 501 Evans St. (on the waterfront); 252-247-3111. This old favorite has been known for its seafood (most of it fried) since 1938. Grab a seat by the window overlooking the waterway. Closed December and January. $-$$

Mount Airy *map 4-A*

☗ **The Merritt House B&B.** 618 N. Main St.; 910-786-2174 or 800-290-6290. Victorian inn. Four rooms, full gourmet breakfast. $-$$

☗ **Pine Ridge Inn.** 2893 W. Pine St.; 910-789-5034. Grand English-style country mansion on eight acres. Six rooms, one suite. Restaurant. Gourmet breakfast. $$

✕ **Snappy Lunch.** 125 N. Main St.; 910-786-4931. The home of the pork chop sandwich, which was immortalized by Barney on the "Andy Griffith Show."

Lunch every day except Sunday. $

Mount Gilead *map 4-C*

☗ **The Pines Plantation Inn.** Lilly's Bridge Rd.; 336-439-1894 or 800-711-1134. This 1890 plantation house is located on Lake Tillery. Five rooms, full country breakfast. $-$$

Nags Head *map 8-A*

☗ **First Colony Inn.** 6720 S. Virginia Dare Trail; 252-441-2343 or 800-368-9390. A three star B&B with beach access, wrap-around porches, library, and an-

FIRST COLONY INN

tique furnishings in the 26 rooms. Continental breakfast, tea. $$-$$$$

✕ **Sam & Omie's.** Milepost 16.5; 252-441-7366. They've been pouring cold ones and serving seafood and burgers here for more than 40 years. The locals come here to shoot the breeze and shoot some pool. Good food. Breakfast, lunch, and dinner. $-$$.

New Bern *map 7-C*

⊤ **The Aerie.** 509 Pollock St.; 252-636-5553 or 800-849-5553. This Victorian inn, one block from Tryon Palace, offers seven rooms and serves gourmet breakfasts. $$-$$$

⊤ **Harmony House Inn.** 215 Pollock St.; 252-636-3810 or 800-636-3113. An 1850 Greek Revival Inn decorated with antiques and locally made reproductions. Eight rooms, two suites. Full breakfast. $$$-$$$$

✗ **The Harvey Mansion Restaurant & Lounge.** 221 Tryon Palace Dr.; 252-638-3205. Listed on the National Register of Historic Places, this elegant restaurant serves international cuisine. Six formal dining rooms, lounge, and piano bar. Dinner. $$-$$$.

✗ **Henderson House.** 216 Pollock St.; 252-637-4784. Exquisite five-course meals worthy of New Bern's former status as royal capital are served in this award-winning restaurant, housed in a Federal-style home listed on the National Register of Historic Places. Original Robert Weaver paintings hang in the dining rooms, and the formal service creates a mood that enhances the elegance of the delicious food. Dinner, Wednesday through Sunday. $$$-$$$$

Ocracoke *map 8-C*

⊤ **Island Inn.** NC 12; 252-928-4351. This very relaxed inn opened in the 1940s after serving a few decades as a school

and an Odd Fellow's lodge. 35 rooms, pool. (Some parts of the inn are older than others. Ask when you make reservations.) $-$$

⊤ **Oscar's House.** NC 12; 252-928-1311. 1940s house built by the last Ocracoke lighthouse keeper Joseph Burrus, and now owned by author/photogapher Ann Ehringhaus. Four rooms, shared baths. "Hearty, sit-down breakfasts." Therapeutic body work. $-$$.

✗ **The Back Porch Restaurant.** Soundside Rd. just South of NC 12; 252-928-6401. This casual gourmet restaurant serves unique seafood dishes, homemade breads, freshly ground coffees, and homemade desserts. The cicadas and tree frogs in the flower garden provide the background music. Dinner. $$

✗ **Howard's Pub.** NC 12 on the outskirts of town; 252-928-4441. Raw and cooked seafood, plus a wide beer selection. Local musicians perform here at night. $-$$

✗ **The Island Inn Dining Room.** NC 12, 252-928-7821. This well-established restaurant, which serves up dishes made from family recipes, is best known for its crab cakes. Breakfast and dinner. $$-$$$

Oriental *map 7-C*

⊤ **Cartwright House.** 301 Freemason St.; 252-249-1337. Circa 1900 inn with a view of the river. Five rooms. $$-$$$

⊤ **The Tar Heel Inn.** 508 Church St.; 252-249-1078. This century-old home has been restored as an English country inn, with gardens. Eight rooms, gourmet breakfast. $$

Pembroke *map 5-C*

✗ **Linda's Restaurant.** 408 E. Third St.; 910-521-8127. American Indians own and operate this restaurant, which has built up quite a following in the past few years. The fried chicken and Southern-style vegetables draw Indians and non-Indians alike. $

Pilot Mountain *map 4-A*

☂ **Pilot Knob Inn.** New Pilot Knob Ln., Pilot Mountain; 336-325-2502. Six mountainside cabins with whirlpools, stone fireplaces. Pool, sauna, lake. "Continental plus" breakfasts. $$$ - $$$$

Pinebluff *map 5-C*

✗ **Nina's.** US 1, 1.5 miles south of NC 211 and US 1 junction; 910-944-3400. This family-owned and operated establishment draws repeat customers thanks to the good food and the leisurely pace of dining. The owners expect you spend two hours, even though service is efficient as well as friendly. Appetizers, salad, hot rolls, and pasta all precede entrees. $-$$

Pinehurst *map 5-C*

☂ **Holly Inn.** 3200 Cherokee Rd.; 910-295-2300. This beautiful five-story inn

opened in 1895. Antique reproductions, amenity packages, help with golfing arrangements at area courses. Rooms and suites. $$$

☂ **Pine Crest Inn.** Dogwood Rd.; 910-295-6121. This New England–style inn is within walking distance of five Pinehurst County Club golf courses accommodating guest golfers. $$

☂ **Pinehurst Resort and Country Club.** Carolina Vista Dr.; 910-295-6811 or 800-487-4653. This beautiful resort, which opened in 1901, is known for its eight championship golf courses (four by Donald Ross), and gracious style. Golf, tennis, marina on Lake Pinehurst (fishing, canoeing, swimming, etc.) A two-night golf package runs around $650 per person, double occupancy, in high season (spring and fall). $$$$

PINEHURST RESORT AND COUNTRY CLUB

✗ **Carolina Dining Room, Pinehurst Resort.** 910-295-8433. This elegant old jewel overlooks the resort's grounds and meets the dining demands of the resort's affluent visitors as well as well-to-do residents. The dinner menu changes daily. Breakfast, lunch, dinner. $$$

RESTAURANTS & ACCOMMODATIONS

Pinehurst *cont'd*

✕ **Donald Ross Grill.** Pinehurst Country Club; 910-295-8433. Grilled seafood and steaks served in a circa 1895 dining room with arched ceilings and historical architectural aspects. Pinehurst memorabilia are tastefully placed throughout the dining area. An expansive verandah overlooks the croquet court, golf courses, and putting greens. Casual dining: feel free to wear your golf or casual attire, but make reservations. Lunch daily, dinner seasonally. $$-$$$

✕ **The Market Place.** 2160 Midland Rd.; 910-295-1160. The restaurant, which serves lunch only, had its origins as a specialty food store that served sandwiches at three tables. Still small in size, this is a favorite in the Pinehurst–Southern Pines area because of the good sandwiches and the relaxed atmosphere. $

✕ **Sarno's.** Blake Blvd., Pinehurst South; 910-295-3341. Breakfast and lunch only. The food is outstanding, the service amiable and efficient, and the view overlooking a small pond charming. Try the vegetable pita and homemade soup. It will make your day. $-$$

Pittsboro *map 5-B*

🛏 **Fearrington House.** Fearrington Village, on US 15-501; 919-542-2121. Elegant inn surrounded by gardens. Seventeen rooms, 11 suites, full breakfast. $$$$

✕ **Fearrington House.** (*See address preceding*) Highy regarded restaurant serving New Southern cuisine. Reservations.

Dinner Tuesday through Sunday, plus Sunday brunch. $$$

Raleigh *map 6-B*

🛏 **The Oakwood Inn B&B.** 411 N. Bloodworth St.; 919-832-9712 or 800-267-9712. A Victorian-era home in historic Oakwood neighborhood. Six rooms, full gourmet breakfast. $$-$$$

🛏 **The William Thomas House.** 530 N. Blount St.; 919-755-9400 or 800-OLDE-INN. Ca. 1881 house within walking distance of capitol, Governor's Mansion, and museums. Full or light Southern breakfast; wine and cheese. Four rooms. $$$

🛏 **The Velvet Cloak Inn.** 1505 Hillsborough St.; 919-828-0333. This old favorite is best known for its service (i.e., doorman in white gloves and tails). Rooms, suites, pool, atrium. $$

✕ **The Angus Barn.** US 70; 919-787-3505. This extremely popular, award-winning steakhouse is decorated with antiques and Americana. Dinner. No reservations accepted for Saturday. $$$

✕ **Big Ed's City Market Restaurant.** 220 Wolfe St.; 919-836-9909. Downhome cooking using fresh vegetables and other ingredients. Very casual, and very good. Monday through Saturday. $

✕ **42nd St. Oyster Bar and Seafood Grill.** 508 W. Jones St.; 919-831-2811. The name pretty well says it. Lunch Monday through Friday, dinner daily. $$-$$$

✕ **Irregardless Cafe.** 901 W. Morgan St.; 919-833-8898. This casual eatery serves chicken, fish, and vegetarian dishes, and homemade desserts in a simple, friendly setting. Lunch and dinner Monday through Saturday; Sunday brunch. $-$$

✗ **Rathskeller Restaurant and Lounge.** 2412 Hillsborough St.; 919-821-5342. Watching calorie intake or in need of a calorie boost? "The Rat" has something for all tastes, including vegetarian and non-vegetarian appetizers, sandwiches, and entrees. The "un-Southern-un-fried" chicken is a treat. $-$$

✗ **Waraji's.** Duraleigh Corner, 5910-147 Duraleigh Rd.; 919-783-1883. It's not often you can hear a Brandenburg concerto while dining in a Japanese restaurant, but that's just exactly what you could experience at Waraji's. The ambiance is that of a striking Japanese house and garden. Lots of sushi on the menu, plus a wide range of non-sushi items and plenty of appetizers—nega-maki, goma-ae, etc. Good food and outstanding service. $$-$$$$

Red Springs *map 4-B*

✗ **Gore's Seafood.** 221 E. Fourth St.; 910-843-4804. Very rustic, but cozy little seafood house with a personal touch: the owner visits with diners as they eat to make sure the food is right. $

Reidsville *map 5-A*

⌂ **Fairview Farm B&B.** 1891 Harrison Crossroads Rd.; 336-349-6910. A farmhouse complete with rocking chairs and a swing on the wrap-around porch. Near Chinqua-Penn Plantation. $$

Rocky Mount *map 6-A*

✗ **Bob Melton's Barbecue.** 631 East Ridge; 252-446-8513. The original rambling building is gone now, but this site remains the home of the oldest sit-down barbecue restaurant in the state. A terrific view of the Tar River and its tree-covered banks makes for a charming meal. $

Rodanthe *map 8-B*

⌂ **Hatteras Island Resort.** 252-987-2345 or 800-331-6541. Oceanside complex includes 35 cottages, 16 rooms, 16 efficiencies, dog kennel, pool, cafe, etc. on 25 acres. April to December. $$-$$$

St. Pauls *map 5-C*

✗ **Tarpackers Restaurant.** 201 W. Broad St.; 910-865-1560. Carolina sports fans are diehard—it's rare to find North Carolina Tarheels (UNC Chapel Hill) and a North Carolina State Wolfpacker breaking bread together, but Tarpackers (get it?) is that place: housed in a restored department store, the food's so good it brings adversaries together. $-$$

Salisbury *map 4-B*

⌂ **Rowan Oak House.** 208 S. Fulton St.; 704-633-2086 or 800-786-0437. Queen Anne Victorian house in Salisbury's historic district. Four rooms, fireplaces, Jacuzzi. Full breakfast. $$-$$$

RESTAURANTS & ACCOMMODATIONS

Sanford *map 5-B*

✕ **Grace's Little Italy.** 2752 Industrial Dr.; Kendale Shopping Ctr.; 919-774-4623. Family recipes from both northern and southern Italy, including outstanding veal, fettucine primavera, and sauteed chicken. The chef takes great pride in the quality of ingredients here; he uses organically grown vegetables, for instance. House-made desserts include tortoni, tiramisu, cannoli, and a New York–style cheesecake. A friendly staff and music Wednesday through Sunday add to the appeal of this place. $-$$

Shelby *map 3-C*

⏡ **Inn at Webbley.** 403 South Washington St.; 828-481-1403 or 800-852-2346. Spacious lawns and gardens surround this carefully restored 1852 inn furnished with English and French antiques. Ten rooms. Full gourmet breakfast. $$$$

Southern Pines *map 5-C*

⏡ **Knollwood House.** 1495 W. Connecticut Ave.; 910-692-9390. Three acres of long-leaf pines, magnolias, and dogwoods surround this English manor house, furnished with 18th-century antiques. Full breakfast. Golfing, tennis, etc., nearby. Rooms and suites. $$$

⏡ **Mid-Pines Inn and Golf Club Resort.** 1010 Midland Rd.; 910-692-2114 or 800-323-2114. This elegant old hotel (1921), overlooks a Donald Ross golf course. 118 rooms. Packages. $$$-$$$$

⏡ **Pine Needles Resort,** 1005 Midland Rd.; NC 2; 910-692-7111. Rates vary with golf packages. $$$-$$$$

✕ **Lob Steer Inn.** US 1; 910-692-3503. Steak and seafood—plus a salad bar that includes smoked oysters, freshwater mussels, and plenty of greens—attract many locals. Breads are made on the premises. A working fireplace warms the main dining room on chilly nights. Autographed photos of the many famous race-car drivers and golfers who've come here decorate the lobby. $-$$$

✕ **Longleaf Country Club.** 2001 Midland Rd.; 910-692-4411. This club was once a training ground for top thoroughbred horses. Dining room and grillroom. Lunch Tuesday through Sunday, dinner Wednesday through Saturday. $$

✕ **Nature's Own.** 1150 Old US 1 South; 910-692-3811. The freshest ingredients and house-made desserts and breads characterize this Southern Pines favorite. The salmon, served with a roasted red pepper sauce, is fantastic; beef and pork are tasty, too. Classical guitar on certain nights. $$-$$$

✕ **Russell's Seafood House.** Route 22, just north of the downtown area; 910-692-7453. Locally popular seafood house where servings are ample and food is consistently good. Service can be slow because of the crowds. $-$$

✕ **Sleddon's Restaurant.** 275 S. Bennett St.; 910-692-4480. Continental cuisine served in a restored 1920s house, located in a vibrant "small-town" downtown. Each of the dining rooms is unique.

Regular items on the ever-changing menu include lamb and veal. Everything served—including bread—is homemade. Dinner Tuesday through Saturday. Reservations required. $$$

✗ The Squire's Pub. 1720 US 1 South; 910-695-1161. Brit/American menu. Lunch and dinner, Monday through Saturday. $-$$

Southport *map 6-D*

🍴 Lois Jane's Riverview Inn. 106 West Bay St.; 910-457-6701 or 800-457-1152. Beautifully restored 19th-century home with a view of the Cape Fear River. Four rooms, two with private baths. Full gourmet breakfast. $$-$$$

✗ Ship's Chandler. 101 W. Bay St.; 910-457-6595. This well-known seafood restaurant is open for lunch and dinner Tuesday through Saturday. $$

Statesville *map 4-B*

🍴 Cedar Hill Farm B&B. 778 Elmwood Rd.; 828-873-4332 or 800-948-4423. 1840 farmhouse located on a 32-acre sheep farm. Pool, hiking, badminton. Full country breakfast. One room, two cottages with fireplaces. $$-$$$

Sunset Beach *map 6-D*

✗ Italian Fisherman. At Sunset St. Bridge; 910-579-2929. A great view of the Inland Waterway and the last floating bridge in the Carolinas. A marvelous live oak graces the property—perfect for photo opportunities with small children. The food's OK, but the view draws us back. $-$$$

Tarboro *map 7-A*

🍴 Little Warren B&B. 304 East Park Ave.; 252-823-1314 or 800-309-1314. Located a block from Tarboro's historic town common. Full English, American Southern, and Continental plus breakfasts. Corporate rates. Three rooms. $$

Topsail Island *map 7-D*

🍴 Jolly Roger Motel. Topsail Beach; 910-328-4616. Oceanfront motel and pier complex. The older section contains 1940s-style suites; the seaside patio was the launch pad for a now-defunct top secret military operation, Operation Bumblebee. $-$$$

Valle Crusis *map 3-A*

🍴 The Inn at the Taylor House. NC 194; 704-963-5581. "Country elegant" house built in 1910. Five rooms, three suites, cabins. $$$$

🍴 Mast Farm Inn B&B. SR 1112; 704-963-5857 or 888-963-5857. Warm, relaxed inn occupies an 1885 farmhouse. Rooms are furnished with country antiques, quilts, environmentally friendly soaps, etc. Listed on the National Register of Historic Places. Rooms, historic cabins, trails to wander, gardens to meditate in, friendly people. Nine rooms, four cottages. $$$-$$$$

RESTAURANTS & ACCOMMODATIONS

Valle Crusis *map 3-A*

✕ **Mast Farm Inn Restaurant.** *(see address preceding)* 704-963-5857. Outstanding Southern contemporary cuisine served in a peaceful atmosphere. Vegetables grown in the garden down by the river and homemade breads and desserts make this a la carte menu unique. Dinner Monday through Saturday (reservations); lunch Friday, Saturday, and Sunday. $$

Vass *map 5-B*

✕ **Mama's Kitchen.** Union Church Rd.; 910-245-7178. Millionaires and mill-hands come together here for some of the best seafood in the Sandhills. Large portions, friendly waitresses, and a rustic setting make this remote eatery worth the drive. Call for directions. $

Wanchese *map 8-B*

✕ **Queen Anne's Revenge.** Old Wharf Rd.; 252-473-5466. Just-out-of-the-nets seafood. Try the she-crab soup. Dinner. $$

Washington *map 7-B*

⌂ **Acadian House B&B.** 129 Van Norden St.; 252-975-3967. Late Victorian home a block from the Pamlico River. Antiques, bicycles. Four rooms, one suite. Southern gourmet breakfast. $-$$

⌂ **Pamlico House.** 400 E. Main St.; 252-946-7184 or 800-948-8504. Ca. 1900 home in the historic district. Gourmet breakfast. $$

Waynesville *map 2-B*

⌂ **Balsam Mountain Inn.** A half-mile from the intersection of US 23/74 and the Parkway (follow the signs up the mountain); 828-456-9498. A restored 1908 inn with 50 creatively decorated rooms, library, miles of porches, endless views, and silence: no TVs or phones in the rooms. Full country breakfast. $$$

✕ **Balsam Mountain Inn** *(see information above).* 828-456-9498. "The best kitchen in the mountains," one local says. Breakfast, dinner, plus Sunday lunch. Healthy Southern cuisine. Specialty: fresh baked mountain trout. $$

✕ **Lomo Grill.** 121 Church St.; 828-452-5222. Italian-Mediterranean cuisine. Lunch and dinner, Tuesday through Saturday; Sunday dinner. $$-$$$

⌂ **Old Stone Inn.** 109 Dolan Rd.; 828-456-3333. Gourmet homecooking served country-style. Dinner Monday through Saturday, May through October. Reservations only; no credit cards. $$-$$$

Weldon *map 6-A*

✕ **Ralph's Bar-B-Que.** 1402 Woodruff St.; 252-536-2102. Ralph's serves a very good pork barbecue with the typical "eastern" vinegar-based sauce. Unlike many other barbecue houses where the barbecue is chopped, sliced barbecue is available here. Check out the neon pigs marching across the roof. Some good seafood is available, too. $-$$

Whiteville *map 6-D*

✕ **Penn's Grill.** 128 E. Commerce St.; 910-642-2779. The place for real hot dogs and burgers—and oh, those deliciously evil french fries, peeled and sliced here and cooked in 100% vegetable oil. $

Wilmington *map 6-D*

⌂ **Catherine's Inn.** 410 S. Front St.; 910-251-0863 or 800-476-0723. 1883 Classic Italianate home overlooking the Cape Fear River. Wrap-around porches, wrought-iron fences, bedside liqueur. Five rooms, one suite. Hearty full breakfast. $$$

⌂ **Rosehill Inn.** 114 S. Third St.; 910-815-0250 or 800-815-0250. Gardens, antiques. Six rooms, full breakfast in formal dining room, Non-smoking. Six rooms. $$$$

⌂ **Taylor House Inn.** 14 N. Seventh St.; 910-763-7581 or 800-382-9982. Edwardian house in the historic district. Antiques, library. Three rooms, one suite. $$$

⌂ **The Worth House.** 412 South Third St.; 910-762-8562 or 800-340-8559. Queen Anne Victorian house three blocks from shops, restaurants, and night spots. Common rooms, porches. Seven rooms. Full breakfasts. $$-$$$

✕ **Caffe Phoenix.** 9 S. Front St.; 910-343-1395. Extremely sophisticated cuisine: grilled dishes, salads, and desserts are outstanding, but do try the risotto with wild mushrooms and veal. Simply "to die for." Take a table on the two levels inside, or eat on the patio. $-$$

✕ **Elijah's.** Chandler's Wharf, 2 Ann St.; 910-343-1448. A seafood restaurant best known for its chowder and oyster bar. Outdoor dining most of the year. $-$$

✕ **Paleo Sun Cafe.** 35 N. Front St.; 910-762-7700. Innovative menu featuring seafood dishes. In the downtown shopping area. Dinner Tuesday through Saturday, Sunday brunch. $$

✕ **Pilot House.** Chandler's Wharf, 2 Ann St.; 910-343-0200. Enjoy local seafood, special salads, and gourmet desserts, all with a grand view of the Cape Fear River. The chef here is not afraid to experiment with Southern regional dishes. Lunch and dinner, Sunday brunch. Closed Sunday dinner. $$

✕ **Roy's Riverboat Landing.** 2 Market St.; 910-763-7227. Seafood and pasta. Lunch Monday through Saturday; dinner Tuesday through Sunday. $$.

Wilson *map 6-B*

⌂ **Miss Betty's B&B Inn.** 600 West Nash St.; 252-243-4447 or 800-258-2058. Four restored homes make up this "inn," near antique shops, golf, tennis, and pool. Seven rooms, seven suites. Full country breakfast. $$

✕ **Parker's Barbecue.** Hwy. 301 South; 252-237-0972. This eastern style, vinegar-based pork barbecue sets the standard with many locals, and with much of the East Coast, since it's a favorite stop for folks zooming along I-95. Lunch and dinner, cash only. $

RESTAURANTS & ACCOMMODATIONS

Winston-Salem *map 4-A*

☖ **Augustus T. Zevely Inn.** 803 South Main St.; 336-748-9299. The only inn on the grounds of Old Salem. Decorated in authentic Moravian style. Working fireplaces, wine and cheese, breakfast. Rooms and suites. $$$-$$$$

☖ **Brookstown Inn.** 200 Brookstown Ave.; 910-725-1120. This inn occupies part of the revamped 1837 Salem Cotton Company mill. Furnished with Early American reproductions. Wine and cheese, breakfast. 71 rooms. A few blocks from Old Salem. $$$$

☖ **Henry F. Schaffner House.** 150 South Marshall St.; 336-777-0052. Victorian-style mansion, built in 1907. Large rooms, wine and cheese at sunset, home-baked "continental plus" breakfast. Nine rooms, three suites. A few blocks from Old Salem. $$-$$$$

☖ **The Mickle House B&B.** 927 West Fifth St.; 336-722-9045. 1892 Victorian cottage in historic district. Two rooms. Full breakfast. $$

☖ **Tanglewood Manor House B&B Inn.** Tanglewood Park, 10 miles west of Winston-Salem on Hwy. 158; 336-778-6370. This inn is in the 1859 home of R. J. Reynolds's brother, William Neal Reynolds. Reproduction antiques. (Note: overflow guests stay in the no-frills Manor House Motor Lodge so it's best to specifiy.) Breakfast. $$$

✗ **Bistro 900.** 900 S. Marshall St.; 336-721-1336. Italian and American cuisine. Live jazz, Thursday through Saturday. Dinner, Tuesday through Saturday. $$

✗ **The Horse's Mouth Coffeehouse.** 424 W. Fourth St.; 336-773-1311. Sandwiches, salads, desserts, coffees. Breakfast, lunch, and dinner Monday through Saturday, Sunday brunch. $

✗ **Little Richard's Bar-B-Que.** 4885 Country Club Rd.; 336-760-3457. This Q is slow-roasted over wood coals. $

✗ **Old Salem Tavern Dining Room,** 736 South Main St.; 336-748-8585. The most interesting restaurant in Winston-Salem, this 1816 Old Salem tavern serves tasty dishes from historic Moravian recipes: Moravian chicken pie, gingerbread, fresh baked bread, etc. Servers are costumed appropriately, too. Reservations. Lunch Monday through Friday, dinner Monday through Saturday. $$$

✗ **Ryan's Restaurant.** 719 Coliseum Dr.; 336-724-6132. Patrons watch a bubbling brook winding its way through lushly wooded banks while dining in this rustic room. One of the city's favorite fine-dining establishments. $$-$$$

✗ **South by Southwest.** 241 Marshall St.; 336-727-0800. Creative Southwestern dinners Monday through Saturday. $$

Wrightsville Beach *map 6-D*

✗ **Gardenias.** 7105 Wrightsville Ave.; 910-256-2421. Fresh and innovative fare; one of the area's best restaurants. Dinner. Reservations. $$-$$$

✗ **The Middle of the Island Restaurant.** 216 Wrightsville Beach Causeway; 910-256-4277. Locals know "the MOI" for its country-style cooking and easy-going attitude. Three squares Monday through Friday; no dinner on weekends. $

■ FESTIVALS AND EVENTS

In summer and spring, festivals sprout up thicker than kudzu throughout the state.

Small town festivals celebrate everything from herring (Jamesville), to fiddleplaying (Union Grove), to the almost lost art of hollerin' (Spivey's Corner). Some provide kiddie rides, country music, street dancing, clogging, arts and crafts, and carnival fare. The best offer a glimpse into the region's culture.

Spring may be the most popular time for eastern festivals, but October is a big festival month in the mountains. Following is a list of a few of the most fun and interesting festivals in the state. For a complete list of North Carolina festivals, call 1-800-VISIT-NC.

APRIL

Wilmington: Azalea Festival. NC's oldest city festival. The week-long event includes parades, garden tours, horse shows, etc. A celebrity comes in for the event, but the stars of this show are the city's azaleas. Wilmington is most beautiful when millions of azaleas burst into bloom. 800-222-4757.

Wilkesboro: Merle Fest. Four-day acoustic and bluegrass music festival honoring the late Merle Watson, son of festival host "Doc" Watson. Late April. 800-343-7857 or 910-838-6267.

Grifton: Shad Festival. Grifton throws its Shad Festival the first week in April. North Carolina's oldest continually operating small town festival celebrates a small, bony fish that spawns in Contentnea Creek, at the edge of town. *Grifton is between Greenville and Kinston on NC 11; the festival is downtown (there is only one stoplight in this town). 252-524-4934.*

JUNE

Durham: American Dance Festival. One of the most influential dance festivals in North America. This festival includes premieres, performances, and backstage tours. June through July. 800-446-8604

JULY

Grandfather Mountain: Highland Games and Gathering of the Clans. The largest Scottish highland games in the US are held at Grandfather Mountain, near Linville, each July. Dancing, sheepdog herding demonstrations, piping, athletics. 828-733-1333

AUGUST

Asheville: The Mountain Dance and Folk Festival. The region's best mountain musicians and dancers perform at this annual festival, founded in 1927. Held the first weekend in August. 800-257-1300.

FESTIVALS & EVENTS

SEPTEMBER

Benson: Mule Days.

This festival runs from Thursday through Sunday, the fourth full weekend in September. Friday is the day to hoof it into town. Hundreds of mules compete here, leaping tall fences, thundering around a dusty racetrack (or halfway around, depending on their moods). The winner leads Saturday's parade of 2000 mules and horses, floats, and carefully stepping bands. The festival also includes a carnival, rodeo, barbecue cook-off, arts & crafts, street dance, etc. 919-894-3825. *The festival is in Benson, just off I-95.*

Durham: Bull Durham Blues Festival. One of the South's premiere blues events. 800-446-8604.

OCTOBER

October's autumn color brings thousands of visitors to the mountains each year, so October is a big festival month. Among the best mountain festivals:

Asheville: Southern Highlands Crafts Guild Fair. Over 100 members of the prestigious Southern Highland Handicrafts Guild demonstrate and/or sell their work at NC's best highlands crafts show. The fair also includes mountain music and dancing. This outstanding fair is held twice a year, the third weekend in October and the third weekend in July. 800-257-1300 or 828-298-7928. (The guild also has two shops on the Parkway. *See pages 274 and 296.*)

Cherokee: Cherokee Indian Fair. Native American arts and crafts show, Native American foods, agricultural fair, stick ball games, archery contests, blow gun contests, dancing. The five-day fair begins the first Tuesday in October. 800-438-1601.

DECEMBER

Harker's Island: Core Sound Decoy Festival. Once, decoy carving was part of everyday life in coastal North Carolina. Today it's almost a lost art, and a high-dollar art at that. "Nobody's going to throw their decoys in the water anymore," laughs Karen Amspacher, spokesperson for the Core Sound Decoy Festival on Harker's Island. This festival features hundreds of artists plus thousands of visitors who come to buy antique and new decoys, eat some seafood, and check out competitions in decoy carving, retriever showing, and loon calling. Held each December. 252-728-1500.

■ BLUEGRASS AND MOUNTAIN MUSIC FESTIVALS

The mountains are peppered with good music festivals, including those listed above. For instance, the Gospel Singing Jubilee is held the first full weekend in August, in Boone. Ashe County's Fiddlers Convention, held in Jefferson each August, has been a mountain music hot spot for over a quarter of a century.

The best information on musical events in the northern mountains comes through the Boone Convention and Visitors Bureau: 800-852-9506 or High Country Host: 800-438-7500. For the southern mountains, call 800-432-HOST or 800-257-1300. For information on bluegrass events in Eastern NC, call 252-522-1066.

■ CHRISTMAS TRIMMINGS

North Carolina dresses up for the holidays, but some places dress up prettier than others. Try the Christmas tours at Biltmore Estate in Asheville, Tryon Palace in New Bern, "Old Wilmington by Candlelight," Bath, and Old Salem in Winston-Salem.

■ OUTDOOR EXPEDITIONS

You'll find numerous outfitters and expedition directors in the mountains. Two of the best established are:

High Mountain Expeditions. Blowing Rock. Whitewater rafting, kayaking, guided adventures, courses, etc. 800-262-9036 or 828-295-4200.

Nantahala Outdoor Center. Bryson City. Whitewater rafting, mountain biking, kayaking, guided adventures, courses, etc. 888-662-1662 or 828-488-2176.

■ VISITOR INFORMATION

■ VISITORS CENTERS AND CHAMBERS OF COMMERCE

Asheville, 800-257-1300.
Cape Hatteras National Seashore, 252-473-2113.
Cape Fear Coast, 800-222-4757.
Cape Lookout National Seashore, 252-728-2250.
Cherokee Visitors Center, 800-438-1601.
Croatan National Forest, 252-638-5628.
Great Smoky Mountains National Park, 423-436-1200.
Nantahala National Forest, 252-257-4200.
Northern Appalachians, 800-438-7500.

Outer Banks, 800-446-6262.
Pisgah National Forest, 828-877-3265.
Smoky Mountain Host of NC, 800-432-HOST.
Uwharrie National Forest, 910-576-6391.

■ SPECIAL INTERESTS

The NC Department of Transportation publishes information on 3,000 miles of NC roads suitable for **bicyclists.** For information, call 919-733-4171 or 800-VISIT-NC. The NC Department of Travel and Tourism publishes Access North Carolina, a guide for **disabled travelers.** Call 800-VISIT-NC for information.

RECOMMENDED READING

■ JOURNALS AND BIOGRAPHIES

Crabtree, Beth G. and James W. Patton (eds.), *Journal of a Secesh Lady, The Diary of Catherine Anne Devereaux Edmonston 1860–1866.* Division of Archives and History, Raleigh, NC: NC Dept. of Cultural Resources, 1979.

Hakluyt, Richard. *Voyages.* London: J.M. Dent & Sons, Ltd., 1962. (First published in 1589.) The records of England's first explorers to the region.

Jacobs, Harriet A. *Incidents in the Life of a Slave Girl, Written by Herself.* MA & London: Harvard Univ. Press, Cambridge, 1987. (Originally published in 1861.)

Lawson, John. *A New Voyage to Carolina.* Chapel Hill/London: Univ. of NC Press, 1967. Fascinating journal by North Carolina's first literate tourist.

Redford, Dorothy Spruill with Michael D'Orso. *Somerset Homecoming: Recovering a Lost Heritage.* New York: Doubleday, 1988.

■ HISTORY

Barrett, John Gilchrist. *North Carolina as a Civil War Battleground 1861–1865.* Raleigh, NC: Division of Archives and History, NC Dept. of Cultural Resources, 1987.

Ehle, John. *Trail of Tears, the Rise and Fall of the Cherokee Nation.* New York: Anchor Books/Doubleday, 1988.

Jones, H.G. *North Carolina Illustrated, 1524–1984.* Chapel Hill/London: Univ. of NC Press, 1983. More than 1,150 photographs and excellent historical coverage.

Kephart, Horace. *Our Southern Highlanders.* Knoxville, TN: Univ. of TN Press, 1984.

Mooney, James. *History, Myths, and Sacred Formulas of the Cherokees.* Asheville, NC: Historical Images/Bright Mountain Books, 1992. (First published in 1891 and 1900.) A biographical introduction by George Ellison.

Parramore, Thomas C. *Triumph at Kitty Hawk: The Wright Brothers and Powered Flight.* Raleigh: Division of Arch. and Hist., NC Dept. of Cultural Resources, 1993.

Powell, William S. *North Carolina Through Four Centuries.* Chapel Hill/London: Univ. of NC Press, 1989.

Rankin, Hugh F. *The Pirates of Colonial North Carolina.* Raleigh, NC: State Dept of Archives and History, NC Dept of Cultural Resources, 1963.

Stick, David. *Graveyard of the Atlantic.* Chapel Hill, NC: Univ. of NC Press, 1952.

■ FICTION, ETC.

Angelou, Maya. *Even the Stars Look Lonesome.* New York: Random House, 1997. Essays: wit and wisdom.

Edgerton, Clyde. *The Floatplane Notebooks,* Algonquin Chapel Hill, NC: Books of Chapel Hill, 1988. Diary of a fictitious North Carolina family. Also by Edgerton, *Raney* (Chapel Hill: 1985) is the story of a small town Baptist girl who marries an Atlanta liberal, with startling results.

Ehle, John. *The Winter People.* New York: Harper & Row, 1982. A dramatic love affair set in the North Carolina mountains.

Fraizer, Charles. *Cold Mountain.* New York: Random House, 1997. A confederate soldier's odyssey as he walks from Virginia home to North Carolina and the woman he hopes to marry. One of the most highly acclaimed novels of the 1990s.

Gibbons, Kaye. *Ellen Foster.* Chapel Hill, NC: Algonquin Books of Chapel Hill, 1987. The haunting story of an 11-year-old girl's coming of age.

Kenan, Randall. *Let the Dead Bury Their Dead.* Orlando, FL: Harcourt Brace Jovanovich, 1992. Stories about the folks in a small North Carolina town.

O'Leary, Patsy Baker. *With Wings As Eagles.* Boston, MA: Houghton-Mifflin Co., 1997. An Eastern North Carolina farm boy faces his past, and learns the value of friendship. (Ages 13 and up)

Pearson, T. R. *A Short History of a Small Place.* New York: Linden Press/Simon & Schuster, 1985. Actually, a longish history of a strange (but possible) place.

Price, Reynolds. *A Long and Happy Life.* New York: Simon & Schuster, 1987. Love in a small town. First novel by one of North Carolina's best writers. Also by Price, *Kate Vaiden* is narrated by an unconventional 57-year-old woman who looks back on her life in North Carolina. (Boston: 1987)

Wechter, Nell Wise. *Swamp Girl.* Winston-Salem, NC: John F. Blair, 1971. A children's book about a girl who searches for treasure on her family's farm and finds more than she expected.

Wolfe, Thomas. *Look Homeward, Angel.* New York: Charles Scribner's Sons, 1947. Thomas Wolfe's autobiographical first novel, set in Asheville. Wolfe's last novel, *You Can't Go Home Again* (New York: Perennial Library, 1989) tells the story of an American in search of self and home.

■ NATURE AND GUIDES

Biggs, Jr., Walter C. and James F. Parnell. *State Parks of North Carolina.* Winston-Salem, NC: John F. Blair, 1989.

Catlin, David T. *A Naturalist's Blue Ridge Parkway.* Knoxville, TN: Univ of Tennessee Press, 1984.

Fields, Jay and Brad Campbell. *The Craft Heritage Trails of Western North Carolina.* ; Asheville, NC: Handmade in America, Inc., 1996.

Lord, William G. *Blue Ridge Parkway Guide.* Menasha Ridge Press, Birmingham, AL. 1981.

I N D E X

COMPASS AMERICAN GUIDES

Critics, Booksellers, and Travelers All Agree: You're Lost Without a Compass.

Compass American Guides are compelling, full-color portraits of America for travelers who want to understand the soul of their destinations. In each guide, an accomplished local expert recounts history, culture, and useful information in a text rife with personal anecdotes and interesting details. Splendid four-color images by an area photographer bring the region or city to life.

Boston (1st Edition)
1-878-86776-8
$18.95 ($26.50 Can)

Minnesota (1st Edition)
8-86748-2
5 ($26.50 Can)

"This splendid series provides exactly the sort of historical and cultural detail about North American destinations that curious-minded travelers need."
—*Washington Post*

"This is a series that constantly stuns us; our whole past book reviewer experience says no guide with photos this good should have writing this good. But it does."
—*New York Daily News*

"Of the many guidebooks on the market few are as visually stimulating, as thoroughly researched or as lively written as the Compass American Guides series."
—*Chicago Tribune*

Pacific Northwest (1st Edition)

"Good to read ahead of time, then take along so you don't miss anything."
San Diego Magazine

Pacific Northwest (1st Edition)
1-878-86785-7
$19.95 ($27.95 Can)

"Compass has developed a series with beautiful color photos and a descriptive text enlivened by literary excerpts from travel writers past and present."
—*Publishers Weekly*

Alaska (1st Edition)
8-86777-6
5 ($26.50 Can)

Compass American Guides are available in general and travel bookstores, or may be ordered directly by calling (800) 733-3000. Compass American Guides are available at special discounts for bulk purchases for sales promotions or premiums. Special editions, including personalized covers and corporate imprints, can be created in large quantities for special needs. For more information, write to Special Marketing, Fodor's Travel Publications, 201 E. 50th St., New York, NY 10022; or call (800) 800-3246.

COMPASS AMERICAN GUIDES

Critics, Booksellers, and Travelers All Agree You're Lost Without a Compa

Arizona (4th Edition)
0-679-03388-2
$18.95 ($26.50 Can)

Chicago (2nd Edition)
1-878-86780-6
$18.95 ($26.50 Can)

Colorado (4th Edition)
0-679-00027-5
$18.95 ($26.50 Can)

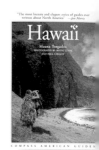

Hawaii (3rd Edition)
1-878-86791-1
$18.95 ($26.50 Can)

Wine Country (2nd Edition)
0-679-00032-1
$18.95 ($26.50 Can)

Montana (3rd Edition)
1-878-86797-0
$18.95 ($26.50 Can)

Oregon (3rd Edition)
0-679-00033-X
$18.95 ($26.50 Can)

New Orleans (3rd Editi
0-679-03597-4
$18.95 ($26.50 Can)

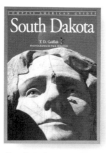

South Dakota (2nd Edition)
1-878-86747-4
$18.95 ($26.50 Can)

Southwest (2nd Edition)
0-679-00035-6
$18.95 ($26.50 Can)

Texas (2nd Edition)
1-878-86798-9
$18.95 ($26.50 Can)

Utah (4th Edition)
0-679-00030-5
$18.95 ($26.50 Can)

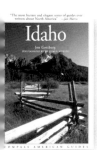

Idaho (1st Edition)
1-878-86778-4
$18.95 ($26.50 Can)

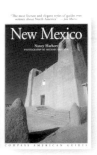

New Mexico (3rd Edition)
0-679-00031-3
$18.95 ($26.50 Can)

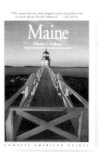

Maine (2nd Edition)
1-878-86796-2
$18.95 ($26.50 Can)

Manhattan (2nd Edition)
1-878-86794-6
$18.95 ($26.50 Can)

Las Vegas (5th Edition)
0-679-00015-1
$18.95 ($26.50 Can)

San Francisco (4th Edition)
1-878-86792-X
$18.95 ($26.50 Can)

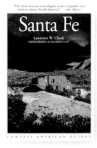

Santa Fe (2nd Edition)
0-679-03389-0
$18.95 ($26.50 Can)

South Carolina (2nd Edition)
0-679-03599-0
$18.95 ($26.50 Can)

Virginia (2nd Edition)
1-878-86795-4
$18.95 ($26.50 Can)

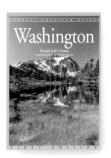

Washington (1st Edition)
1-878-86758-X
$17.95 ($25.00 Can)

Wisconsin (2nd Edition)
1-878-86749-0
$18.95 ($26.50 Can)

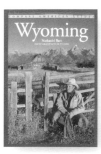

Wyoming (3rd Edition)
0-679-00034-8
$18.95 ($26.50 Can)

R. L. BEASLEY

■ ABOUT THE AUTHOR

Sheila Turnage, a native North Carolinian, lives on a tobacco farm near Farmville, NC, with her husband R. L. Beasley, and a throng of friendly beasts. Her work has been published by the *Atlanta Journal & Constitution, AP, Reuters, American Legacy, Early American Life, Mid-Atlantic Country, Outdoor Traveler Mid-Atlantic, Destinations, Our State,* Penguin Press, and the *International Poetry Review,* among others. She is also the author of a children's book, *Trout the Magnificent* (Harcourt Brace Jovanovich), and a contributing editor for *Carolina Gardener Magazine.*

■ ABOUT THE PHOTOGRAPHER

Jim Hargan started his career as a photographer with both a bachelor's and master's degrees in geography. After a 17-year stint in Florida as a specialist in urban planning, his interests increasingly turned towards geographic photography, which seemed a natural way for blending observation of surroundings with his academic background in geography. Jim now practices freelance photography full time from his home in the mountains of North Carolina, where he lives with his wife in the community of Possum Trot. His work has appeared in numerous magazines, calendars, postcards, and books. His signed and numbered art prints are purchased by businesses and private collectors and are represented by agencies worldwide.

Comments, suggestions, or updated information?
Please write:
Compass American Guides
5332 College Ave., Suite 201
Oakland, CA 94618

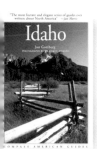

Idaho (1st Edition)
1-878-86778-4
$18.95 ($26.50 Can)

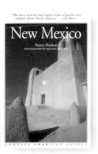

New Mexico (3rd Edition)
0-679-00031-3
$18.95 ($26.50 Can)

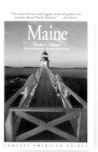

Maine (2nd Edition)
1-878-86796-2
$18.95 ($26.50 Can)

Manhattan (2nd Edition)
1-878-86794-6
$18.95 ($26.50 Can)

Las Vegas (5th Edition)
0-679-00015-1
$18.95 ($26.50 Can)

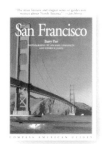

San Francisco (4th Edition)
1-878-86792-X
$18.95 ($26.50 Can)

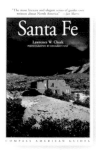

Santa Fe (2nd Edition)
0-679-03389-0
$18.95 ($26.50 Can)

South Carolina (2nd Edition)
0-679-03599-0
$18.95 ($26.50 Can)

Virginia (2nd Edition)
1-878-86795-4
$18.95 ($26.50 Can)

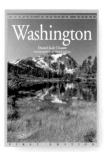

Washington (1st Edition)
1-878-86758-X
$17.95 ($25.00 Can)

Wisconsin (2nd Edition)
1-878-86749-0
$18.95 ($26.50 Can)

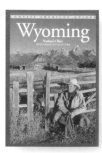

Wyoming (3rd Edition)
0-679-00034-8
$18.95 ($26.50 Can)

R. L. BEASLEY

■ ABOUT THE AUTHOR

Sheila Turnage, a native North Carolinian, lives on a tobacco farm near Farmville, NC, with her husband R. L. Beasley, and a throng of friendly beasts. Her work has been published by the *Atlanta Journal & Constitution, AP, Reuters, American Legacy, Early American Life, Mid-Atlantic Country, Outdoor Traveler Mid-Atlantic, Destinations, Our State,* Penguin Press, and the *International Poetry Review,* among others. She is also the author of a children's book, *Trout the Magnificent* (Harcourt Brace Jovanovich), and a contributing editor for *Carolina Gardener Magazine.*

■ ABOUT THE PHOTOGRAPHER

Jim Hargan started his career as a photographer with both a bachelor's and master's degrees in geography. After a 17-year stint in Florida as a specialist in urban planning, his interests increasingly turned towards geographic photography, which seemed a natural way for blending observation of surroundings with his academic background in geography. Jim now practices freelance photography full time from his home in the mountains of North Carolina, where he lives with his wife in the community of Possum Trot. His work has appeared in numerous magazines, calendars, postcards, and books. His signed and numbered art prints are purchased by businesses and private collectors and are represented by agencies worldwide.

Comments, suggestions, or updated information?
Please write:
Compass American Guides
5332 College Ave., Suite 201
Oakland, CA 94618